T0302576

Slave States

The Practice of Kafala in the Gulf Arab Region

Yasin Kakande

zero books

Winchester, UK
Washington, USA

First published by Zero Books, 2015
Zero Books is an imprint of John Hunt Publishing Ltd., Laurel House, Station Approach,
Alresford, Hants, SO24 9JH, UK
office1@jhpbooks.net
www.johnhuntpublishing.com
www.zero-books.net

For distributor details and how to order please visit the 'Ordering' section on our website.

ISBN: 978 1 78535 100 6
Library of Congress Control Number: 2015935798

A CIP catalogue record for this book is available from the British Library.

Design: Stuart Davies

Printed in the USA by Edwards Brothers Malloy

CONTENTS

Preface 1

1. Kafala: The Greatest Insult to Islam 5

2. Segregation and Desperation 47

3. Enslavement: Losing Human Dignity 159

4. Bureaucracy: "Eating People's Money with Greed" 197

5. Sexual Starvation 225

Epilogue 280

Notes 287

Dedication

To Sauda, Latifa, Taqiu and Hadijja. I feel blessed having you all in my life.

Preface

I arrived in Doha, Qatar on 19 June 2014. It had been two months since I was terminated from *The National* newspaper and expelled from the United Arab Emirates (UAE) for publishing my autobiographical book *The Ambitious Struggle*. The whole of Doha currently is like a construction site and workers can be seen busy on construction sites even well after midnight, as I discovered when I arrived in the city and a taxi driver transported me to my hotel. The driver told me the city's biggest problem is rent prices rising every day and more people from everywhere coming to work in Doha. He told me he already had taken five clients that night, four of whom (including myself) had arrived in Doha for work. Although I was coming to look for a job, my mind was already set that I was not going to stay in any GCC country for much longer. I was trying to set moderate targets and this time was mainly needed to complete this book.

My expulsion had come when I was about to complete this book's first draft, but still a lot of work needed to be done including the editing, proofreading, designing and even publishing, all of which required money that I could not raise easily in my native country of Uganda. I set my sights on completing the book, paying all the necessary expenses, and then quitting the Gulf Arab countries.

My Doha visa proved to be an expensive one. While Qatar Airways has direct flights to Uganda and an office in Kampala, the tickets sales assistants insisted they could not issue any visa without confirmation of proper employment and an endorsement from my employer that I would be returning. I went to Mombasa again where a friend conferred with his contacts at the Nairobi Qatar offices, who eventually approved my visa with conditions of a US $1,000 deposit, a hotel booking of at least three paid days (US $400), a return air ticket of $1,100 and finally a tourist visa of US $110. If one is a European or an American who is given a visa on arrival at the airport, that individual could never imagine what a hassle it is for countless millions to visit these GCC countries.

Therefore, as I present this book, I am quite sure there will be many other books about the plight of migrant workers in the GCC countries, but very few will be written from the perspective of a poor migrant worker who lived and shared these squalid accommodations with other workers. No, an expatriate journalist from Africa cannot make a comfortable, stable livelihood, especially for a family with young children, in the GCC, given the current rules that impose many restrictions upon immigrants especially from the poorest subcontinental regions of Africa and Asia.

The book comprises five sections. The first section offers a brief history of Kafala and the power of the sponsors' lobby which has worked aggressively to sustain the system even as serious moral challenges to its continuing existence are raised. The introductory section also focuses on the perils that immigrants face as they seek work in Qatar and neighboring GCC countries, and the troubles of those who remain in the shadows because of their undocumented status.

The second section goes into extensive detail about the second-class status of immigrants who labor under Kafala sponsorship and the effects and impact of societal discrimination that borders on humiliation and indecency. It explores how societal exclusion is enforced through punitive threats and strict controls that prevent migrant workers from traveling freely and safely at their own will. The extent of abuses under Kafala covers a disturbing range in which fraud and wage exploitation are rampant, and workers dissatisfied with their employers or employment conditions soon discover they have virtually no recourse for remedying their circumstances. They are forced to live in cramped accommodations and often have little hope of securing long-term financial stability. Even if a few immigrants are fortunate enough to have their disputes adjudicated, many of those challenges reach a dead end where sponsors and employers – who knowingly abuse the legal requirements of Kafala – often are beyond legal reproach.

The third section focuses on the manifestations of modern-day slavery in which racism plays an unfortunately significant role. Hate propaganda, stigmatization and subjugation are rarely challenged with any rigor or clarity by the local or national media, which dutifully respects the ruling elite's objective of maintaining the status quo without any threat of disruption or change. Even cases involving violence and murder are persistently framed in a way that demonizes immigrants, especially when the evidence would suggest that employers and sponsors were irresponsible about their own legal obligations. Few manage to escape with any hope of having their own human dignity and respect fully and rightfully restored.

The fourth section chronicles the immense hurdles of bureaucracy that immigrants encounter, where the economic self-interests of Kafala sponsors and employers always trump the concerns or expectations of workers – and even the well-being of members of immigrant families.

The fifth section includes accounts about how the most basic emotional, sexual, and personal rights of immigrants are controlled and ignored. One's own right to intimate and sexual dignity is denied, as one essentially loses control over the right to one's body. The most unsettling accounts of sexual abuse and exploitation are consistent with all other forms of abuse that are witnessed within the practice of Kafala sponsorship. To dramatic effect, one's soul is starved in ways that permanently damage one's emotional capacity for true and sincere intimacy. Prostitution and human trafficking occur with a level of frequency that should upend the most popularly conceived notions about moral decency and strictness in the Gulf Arab region.

The concluding portion of the book is an epilogue about my own experience as an immigrant employee (journalist). In it I discuss how rigorously sustained press censorship thwarts even the capacity to ask simple questions about the propriety of a sponsorship system undermining the most basic principles and tenets of a faith and culture that have defined the long and incredible history of the Gulf Arab region.

Section 1

Kafala: The Greatest Insult to Islam

1.1 Understanding Kafala

After winning the bid to host the 2022 FIFA World Cup, Qatar, a small Gulf Cooperation Council (GCC) state, promised to prepare the most extravagant and expensive World Cup ever.

A massive infrastructural project of $100 billion was announced to incorporate building: nine stadiums equipped with the most advanced cooling technology to beat the intense summer temperatures which can rise easily to 120 degrees F and higher; a new airport with a sail-shaped terminal; public transport infrastructure including $20 billion worth of new roads, a bridge to neighboring Bahrain, and a rail system; luxury hotels; and 54 team camps.[1]

The small emirate emerged into the global spotlight for several reasons – for the bribery related to attaining the bid, for its hostile climate, and for the extraordinary costs of the projects associated with the world's largest sporting event after the Olympic Games. Though the world knows they are rich, questions of how they are able to meet the requirements of these undertakings continue to arise with little in terms of freshly revealing information.

Suddenly, and surprisingly to some, the treatment of foreign workers came to light and was revealed to be as hostile as the hot regional climate. The plight of workers who have long toiled at the front of the Gulf Region's construction boom is coming into sharp criticism ahead of some of the world's most lavish building activity. What few really know is just how tiny Qatar has perfected the practice of worker exploitation in ways that would have inspired the Europeans during their colonization of the New World and the arrival of the Industrial Revolution. For those skeptical about where Qatar could meet the demands of building an infrastructure that in magnitude and scope would even trip up larger, more experienced nation-states, the questions would be swiftly answered by observing Qatar's disturbing capacity to draw countless thousands of poor, vulnerable people from East and West Asian countries who desperately want a modicum of the global economic pie. As global wealth imbalances continue to widen inexorably to the point where increasing numbers of families find it difficult even to provide basic food needs to their families, the migration of the poor citizens of East Asia and Africa will accelerate. Yet these migrants will go not to Europe or America where financial crises have rendered even local citizens jobless, but instead to the rich GCC countries, regardless of the probable yet significant human costs of exploitation and abuses.

Qatar has learned all too well how to leverage the misery and desperation of workers to a point rivaling the economic impact of petrol dollars.

The New York Times predicted in 2013 that perhaps a million foreign workers are expected to arrive in the next few years to build the Qatar projects.[2]

Even before Qatar won the honors to host the World Cup, some had begun to scrutinize the country's immigration system, which has relied on the provisions of Kafala 'sponsorship' that has enslaved millions of workers in the whole GCC region.

The UK's *Guardian* newspaper laid out the initial groundwork in December 2010 in a piece asking that "Qatar 2022 not be built on brutality," in which the writer discussed the "systematic exploitation of the country's migrant workforce and the possible enslavement of thousands, if not hundreds of thousands, of impoverished south Asian migrant workers, who will be imported to meet the demands of a construction sector." The article branded Qatar's treatment of foreign workers as "crude and brutal" and urged the country to use the World Cup hosting opportunity to clean and abolish the Kafala system.[3]

Four years later, as construction began, another *Guardian* journalist revealed how exploitation and abuse of the impoverished workers in the rich emirate had taken a priceless toll: "This summer, Nepalese workers died at a rate of almost one a day in

Qatar, many of them young men who had sudden heart attacks," the report said. The report found workers not being paid their wages, as well as without access to free drinking water in the desert heat with temperatures rising above 50 C (122 F).[4]

In October 2013 Amnesty International published a report, "The Dark Side of Migration: Spotlight on Qatar's Construction Sector Ahead of World Cup," also revealing widespread and routine abuse of migrant workers that was likened to forced labor. "It is simply inexcusable in one of the richest countries in the world, that so many migrant workers are being ruthlessly exploited, deprived of their pay and left struggling to survive," Salil Shetty, Amnesty International's secretary general, commented on the research. "FIFA has a duty to send a strong public message that it will not tolerate human rights abuses on construction projects related to the World Cup."[5]

As Qatar was troubled with explaining its Kafala system to critics who demanded the World Cup be an opportunity for them to change and respect other human beings, nearby Dubai won its bid to host another massive global event: Expo 2020. In my *Al Ittihad* office as we celebrated the Dubai victory with a big feast of local Yemeni food known as Mandi, my colleagues debated whether Qatar or Dubai had won a bigger bid. One Emirati female reporter declared Dubai's Expo 2020 to be bigger, justifying her claim by explaining that the World Cup was childish entertainment while the Expo would be about business, productivity, and maturity. I cut in, arguing that if the World Cup was for children, her husband would always be a child, even at 70 years, but no one heard or seconded my sentiments. I decided to keep my critical comments to myself and stay peacefully in the office.

There were, of course, forthcoming reports criticizing Dubai's 'sponsorship' system in the international media, while the local media ran tributes about the country's great achievements.

All of the reports came to the same conclusion: dismantle

Kafala. It is pure slavery, not sponsorship, and soon many came to realize that even high-profile events could not force changes in the practice. Another GCC nation, Saudi Arabia, plays host regularly to the largest religious ritual gathering in the world (Hajj) but its appalling mistreatment of poor foreign workers has never abated and the Kafala system remains securely in place. With the sonorous texts of Islam calling for justice and equality of all human beings, regardless of their race or country of origin, the continued implementation of Kafala in the holy lands is the gravest insult to Islam.

1.2 So what is Kafala?

The words and phrases "Kafala sponsorship" and "Kafeel" (representing the sponsor) come from the Arabic root "Ka Fa La" meaning "guardian," "vouch for," or "take responsibility for" someone.

The term comes from the Bedouin customs of temporarily granting strangers shelter, food, protection, and even tribal affiliation for specific purposes.[6]

There are a few verses in the Quran that also have some references to Kafala and in each of these verses the translations have referred to the word as "in care of"; for example, in one verse God places Maryam (Mary) *in the care of* Zakariya.[7] In another reference when two disputants come in front of the prophet Daudi (David) seeking his counsel, one complains that his brother has 99 ewes while he possesses only one. The brother demands that he put even that one he has *in his care*.[8] If one draws similarities between what is written in the Quran and the Kafala in the GCC countries today, one quickly encounters problems. Today the term "care" has been replaced with exploitation and abuse in the relationship between the GCC citizen sponsors and their sponsored immigrants.

The term Kafala has traditionally been applied in the canon of

Islamic literature to refer to "security" in financial terms or "guarantor" in legal court language. When the Islamic court, like other courts, asks for a Kafeel (a sponsor), it requires an individual to stand in for the person requesting sponsorship as a guarantor, to guarantee the court to which your request for Kafala will be heard.[9] It is this connotation that one scholar from the Sharjah Awqaf Mosque explained in relating to Kafala as an immigration system. He added that by instituting Kafala the GCC governments wanted a local who would guarantee the visiting person stays within the designated limits of visit or work time and would promise to turn the individual over to authorities if he (or she) went missing.

However, the scholar said the system could not be defended on identifiable merited ties to Islam and that the topic demanded further research by Islamic scholars, especially concerning its modern-day applicability in all GCC countries.[10] The Kafala system was adopted as an immigration protocol for the GCC countries in the late 1950s when oil revenue started flowing in the region. The GCC nations needed more foreigners to work in their oil fields and to do most of their domestic work that they no longer could (nor wanted to) do, given the raise in status and flow of oil money.[11]

Today the system prevails in all GCC countries of the UAE, including Kuwait, Qatar, Saudi Arabia, Oman, and Bahrain as well as other Arab states such as Jordan and Lebanon.

The Kafala system gave every citizen in a GCC state the right to sponsor a certain number of people for the purposes of coming to their respective countries as employees or domestic workers. Foreigners from European or American countries are exempted from having a Kafala if they are on visit or tour in some of these countries. Saudi Arabia is the exception here. But if they want to work in any of these countries they need a Kafala as well, and generally that sponsor would be their employer.[12]

The employment relationship in the Kafala system is the only legal basis by which a worker can remain in the country, as overseas nationals are largely ineligible for permanent residency status or citizenship.[13] In business, employers in all categories had been assumed to be the sponsors of their employees. But foreign business persons or investors also needed to have a local citizen sponsor before they could turn around and sponsor their employees.

Children of expatriates are only sponsored by their fathers and their ability to stay in the UAE is contingent upon this sponsorship. Boys must seek alternative sponsors when they become employees after their 18th birthday, or, in some countries like Saudi Arabia, it is illegal to have a young male of 21 on parental sponsorship while young women would be eligible for their husband's sponsorship at marriage.[14]

Kafala regulates foreign labor through citizen sponsorships. This functions as a built-in enforcement mechanism for temporary residency by holding citizens directly responsible for the residency violations of non-citizens. This process of vouching for someone is unlike the enforcement mechanism often used by banks or bail-bond agencies when they require a third party to co-sign a loan or bond with the borrower being potentially held responsible in the case of defection. This sponsorship arrangement effectively privatizes some of the costs of migration and enforcement by directly holding individual citizens financially and legally accountable for each and every non-citizen. Through Kafala the states delegate to private citizens the surveillance of migration."[15]

Under the Kafala system the GCC countries were able to abdicate their responsibilities of protecting the rights of migrant workers and having them delegated entirely to the purview of sponsors.[16]

This is not an open system that allows foreign workers to have residency visas to legally enter the country and then compete in the labor market for jobs. Rather, each non-citizen worker enters the country already tied to a particular job that is sponsored by a national citizen or company (Kafeel).

The system is centrally administered and regulated through the Ministries of Interior of each GCC country.[17]

The worker is not free to choose his or her sponsor, as the recruitment agents do this and even when the sponsor is abusive the worker is also not permitted to transfer or change the sponsor lest he or she will be deported.

Kafala also does not place the worker and his/her employer on equal levels with regard to the salaries or benefits allowable to take home, and once a worker is in the GCC and discovers the employment arrangement either to be poor or deceptive, that worker has little choice and cannot back out and find another sponsor.

There is no other currently operating system that is as widely criticized as Kafala. It ranks as badly as apartheid in South Africa. Kafala is ruthless system devoid of any compassion which embeds insensitivity among local citizens concerning the suffering of immigrant workers. The researcher Pardis Mahdavi compared the Kafala system to structural violence favoring the sponsors. The rules operate in only one direction with regard to whom they protect.[18]

The Migration Forum in Asia called Kafala a costly, bureaucratically flawed restrictive immigration system.

It is appalling to consider that so many people enter a labor migration system that carries such significant detrimental risk to their long-term physical and psychological well-being. Despite their numbers, migrant workers have limited options for protection or influence under the sponsorship system.[19]

1.3 The Kafala Lobby

The calls for abolishing Kafala continue to grow, as stories of inhumane treatment continue to spread in the press and through social and digital media channels. Still few, even of those directly involved in Kafala arrangements, grasp the negative impacts. There is still wide confusion about Kafala, given its roots in the 1950s when it was adopted as a hospitable gesture of Bedouin Arabs toward foreign travelers. Others say that claims about the inhumane nature of Kafala are heavily exaggerated and do not rise to a level sufficient to warrant abolition. There are also the benefactors of this exploitative system. Local citizens enjoy the power the system puts into their hands and Kafala has emerged to help locals assert their socioeconomic status in their communities, especially if they can publicize how many immigrants they sponsor through Kafala.

The GCC countries lack the bold political will to replace the Kafala system with a fairer immigration system and this is exacerbated by the perception that the poor countries in East Asia and Africa, which are responsible for funneling the largest numbers of migrant workers into the Emirates, lack bargaining power given their economic dependence on remittances sent home by these migrant workers.[20]

Of course, the strongest opponents against reforming the Kafala system and replacing it with more fair immigration reforms are the ruling elites. As architects of this inhumane system, they can profit and leverage the fruits of exploitation with locals. Thus, citizens can safely abuse housekeeping employees or default on their payments but they would still not be blacklisted or denied more victims. The ruling elites have consolidated a unilateral laissez-faire arrangement that has virtually shut out locals from any potential form of relief or redress for abuses. So entrenched is the system that even those who find it disturbing would have no choice as it is being fostered by the governments or rulers as a normal way of doing business. In effect, the GCC has shut off any pragmatic channel for addressing the real and urgent concerns of worker abuses and exploitations.

The local citizens also fear that abolishing Kafala would wipe away all the wealth they have accumulated as individuals from the work of these immigrants. Everything has been so intricately interwoven that a single strand could unravel the system in total and cause widespread economic damage.

An economically strong local business community is expected to oppose any systematic reform even if its members are not within or closely allied to members of the ruling families because many also have enjoyed the halo effect of surpluses, courtesy of Kafala. A recent survey from Qatar University's social and economic survey research institute found that 88 percent of Qataris sampled did not want the Kafala system reformed, and, in fact, 30 percent wanted it strengthened.[21] Other locals also have become so accustomed to accept any policy the ruling elites throw their way, mainly because they risk losing economic stability if they challenge the status quo. Such citizens deem Kafala as a prescription, not choice, but once they are sensitized toward viable fair and just alternatives, they can articulate arguments to ban Kafala and to replace it with a system that is universally based on economic justice and common welfare for all workers.

The Kafala lobby group has regrettably persuaded many citizens that things would be worse for many of the immigrants in their countries without the system, and that whatever oppression and abuse they might experience in the GCC could never be harder than the economic uncertainty. Trying to sell the merits of the argument on the glass-half-full philosophy is as intellectually dishonest as it is unethical, especially when the glass unfortunately is empty from the vantage point of the Kafala worker. The Kafala lobbyists know that their arguments are precarious, because once stripped naked of these mildly socially appreciative virtues, many would understand just how cruelly unjust the system has become. There is historic precedent, as we see in the United States, which even to this day still struggles with the aftermath of the Civil War and the absolute moral wrongness of slavery. To wit: "a slave on board a Guineman, in respect of Food and Attention, is as well, perhaps better, situated than many kings and princes in their country. The slaves here will sleep better than Gentlemen do on shore ... they are comfortably lodged in Rooms fitted up for them ... They lie on the bare boards, but the greatest princes in their own country lie on their mats, with a log of wood for their Pillow."[22]

In fairness, it should be noted that there are many GCC citizens who believe the Kafala system must be dismantled and new immigration protocols put in place. Khawla Al Mattar expressed openly a sentiment that is shared by conscientious GCC citizens: "Any real solution will need to abolish the sponsorship system and combat the trade in work permits, which in itself represents a form of forced labor and human trafficking. Both these issues are covered in the eight agreements of ILO [International Labor Organisation]."[23]

Unfortunately, there are too few citizens free and confident enough to voice their dissatisfaction with anything that the ruling families desire because they know to challenge them is to run serious risk. These citizens are bound into a system where virtually all ideas are beyond discussion. Giving voice and visibility to Kafala will be essential if the feelings of human compassion and Islamic morality can be stirred to raise the appropriate debate about the Kafala system.

Kafala is not a concept unique to the GCC region. Prior to 1998, Italy had its own version of citizen sponsorship for migrant workers but the Italian framework operated with more flexibility even if the principle was the same. By 2002, the system was reformed and replaced with a "stay permit for employment purposes" that allows foreigners to enter and stay in Italy as long as they have a job.[24]

Bahrain is the only GCC country that has attempted to change the Kafala system, as its ruling elites claimed to be like everyone else in seeing the system's flaws and injustices.

In a public statement repealing the Kafala system in Bahrain the Labor Minister Majed Al Alawi also likened Kafala to slavery.[25] The government was the first in the GCC to abolish the Kafala system shifting the responsibility of local sponsors to a government authority – the Labour Market Regulation Authority (LMRA).

In the aftermath, there have been several lapses in the new system and a lack of willingness on the government's part to enforce the new rules. Some analysts have found nothing really changed from the past rules of sponsorship. While the government agency acted as the sponsor, workers still required an individual or company to guarantee their legal stay in Bahrain.[26]

The other GCC countries have played games of syntax, playing around with the terminology. Workers are considered to be temporary contract labor and the official use dictates "guest workers or expatriate manpower." Therefore the restrictive immigration policies of the Kafala system have acted in theory to limit the stay of overseas workers to the duration of their contract.[27]

While the Ministries of Interior in various governments have effectively foreclosed non-citizen access to citizenship, they have not successfully prevented temporary workers from increasingly becoming permanent residents.[28]

1.4 Kafala: The Ownership of People

The legislators in these countries and initiators of the Kafala system have given the local sponsors absolute power over the sponsored foreigners in almost the same way old edicts gave masters power over their slaves. Kafala laws bring about metaphors of chains that tied slaves in the previous generations. The laws tie immigrants from doing anything without the approval and consent of their sponsors. Immigrants must seek permission from their sponsors for tasks many of us consider routine: getting a phone card, obtaining a driver's license, buying a car, changing jobs, going back to school, traveling outside the country and even making arrangements to get married or bring family into the country.

Everything, minor or major, requires a sponsor's approval. Some even joke half-heartedly that they should just keep praying that one day the sponsors don't require their sponsored immigrants to seek their permission to sleep with their women every night. Kafala chains people completely. Even when an immigrant dies, the body remains chained by these Kafala laws and it cannot be moved anywhere, buried, repatriated or cremated without the sponsor's explicit consent. One anecdote from Saudi Arabia told of a local sponsor who refused to consent to the repatriation and burying of his Indian worker's body, claiming that he owed him 170,000 Saudi riyals and that he had stolen from him.[29]

The Indian had worked for the sponsor for about 20 years and though the sponsor claimed he had stolen his money on his road to death, the deceased's family claimed instead it was the sponsor who had not paid the deceased's wages. In such instances where the deceased cannot be consulted, the Indian family could not easily win that battle and the body of their loved one remained unburied in the mortuary for months.

A sponsor also does not need to explain any reasons for canceling the immigrant's visa and any disagreement however minor could lead to the sponsor taking such drastic action. Many sponsored immigrants endure absolute submission and obedience to their sponsors as the only hope for staying in the country and earning a living that will help their families back in their home countries. However, there are no guarantees. Even a sponsor's casual dislike can lead to termination of a Kafala arrangement. In Abu Dhabi an Emirati woman terminated her maid because she thought she was more beautiful and likely to attract her husband.[30]

The threat of deportation is extremely stressful for any immigrant or foreign worker anywhere in the world. It's even more challenging if the virtues of being good, obedient and law-abiding cannot save a foreigner or immigrant from deportation, especially when the jealous and ill-advised emotions of a sponsor cannot be re-examined. But such instances of jealously are not uncommon among GCC Arab sponsors. Feelings of jealousy could arise from virtually anything, from one's good looks to genius and merit at work. And once any of these spiked bad emotions are inflamed in a sponsor's heart, the unassuming worker has just earned a one-way ticket out of the Arab land.

The Emiratis have themselves tasted this kind of deportation from Saudi Arabia. Three Emiratis were deported from a Saudi festival because they were considered too handsome and some feared that Saudi women could fall for them. The April 28, 2013 story became a sensation online and in the Emirati media which carried a few pictures of one of the "handsome men," along with comments from women about him being irresistible and others overlooking it because he was Arab who believed that women should wear burkhas.[31] Despite all the sensationalism behind the account of the trio being deported, the stories of many other workers who have been deported from the UAE or Saudi Arabia for petty reasons are rarely if ever covered or highlighted. Not one worker among those deported could even afford a single press interview, as for them doom had already descended on their livelihood along with deportation.

And it was not only due to the whims of individual sponsors that some foreigners found themselves unable to renew their visas or even get new ones. The government also often black-listed some nationalities.

Kenyans, for example, had trouble getting UAE visas after immigration officials interrogated four members of the UAE royal families in Kenya as terror suspects and deported them. The men were reportedly on a holiday in Mombasa during Easter of 2010. As a response the UAE authorities stopped issuing visas to Kenyans and announced that it would only accept Kenyan graduates.[32]

The Kenyan foreign minister traveled to Abu Dhabi to defuse the row, but still Kenyans complain of trouble getting visas especially those for residency. Four years later poor Kenyan workers are still being affected by the actions of their security men against the ruling family's members. Two Kenyan nationals working for Emarat in Sharjah told me they were unable to get Abu Dhabi visas when the Abu Dhabi-based Adnoc took over the operations and staffs of Emarat in a fuel-related crisis that had long gripped the Northern Emirates. The two workers – a man and woman – were both told by Adnoc human resources administrators that they had tried everything but there were no security clearances coming from the Abu Dhabi government.

The security clearance required to work in Abu Dhabi is the most difficult one to obtain in the region. Many colleagues who were recruited had to wait for four months to get these clearances. A journalist colleague had to shave his long beard completely before undergoing the clearance procedure because it was widely believed that a suspected Islamist could not be cleared when the government was striking Islamists in countries such as Egypt and Mali as well as in its own backyard. The fortunate thing for these Kenyans was only that the Dubai-based Emarat accepted them back and they were allowed to relocate to Dubai. In interviews, both workers said they missed out on a higher salary that Adnoc was offering just because of their Kenyan nationality.

The Bangladeshi community has experienced some of the most severe visa problems with the UAE, as there was a time when a no visa announcement for Bangladeshis was given.[33] And then it would be followed by an official denial of a visa ban to

Bangladeshis by the same sources.[34] A Pakistan journalist friend of mine in the UAE (who asked not to be named) told me most Pakistanis worried about getting UAE visas or renewing them after a local UAE English-language newspaper ran an editorial demanding answers from Pakistan about why it did not vote for Dubai in the Expo 2020 bid campaign.[35]

The editorial criticized Pakistan and Afghanistan for betraying the UAE, which is a key financial supporter and investor for both nations and for their large communities in the UAE.[36] The Pakistani foreign minister called the allegations baseless and malicious, insisting that his government had voted for Dubai in the later stages of the Expo 2020 vote. The minister also explained that Turkey, which was bidding against Dubai for the event, had contacted them first long before Dubai entered the bid process. Pakistan had sustained its support up until the time Turkey withdrew from the process and then Pakistan voted for Dubai in subsequent rounds.[37]

Afghanistan did not even respond with a general indication or explanation, but most Pakistanis and Afghanis thought the anger of their governments' actions could well be turned on them.

"They can't cut any relations with the government because all our deposed leaders get shelter in Dubai and bring with them a lot of money that promote businesses here even though the opinion did not mention this," one of my journalist colleagues told me. "All they can do is to punish us, the poor people who have nothing to do with their Expo bids voting by stopping to issue us visas or renewing them."[38]

The practice has a fairly long precedent. After the Gulf War in 1990, work permits were issued in relation to nationality. For example, many Palestinians, Jordanians, Yemenis and Iraqis had their visas cancelled or not renewed and were thus forced to leave the country following the war.[39]

A government system that completely subjects its immigrant workers to the whims of its locals cannot be distinguished from slavery. It was only during the times of slavery that people were considered to be like a commodity. These people had no rights whatsoever although they were burdened with enormous duties. What difference is there between slavery and Kafala, a system that subjugates and makes other people completely dependent on their GCC sponsors? The only difference would be the presence of people in impoverished countries willing to surrender their freedom and honor and accept servitude of GCC sponsors in order to earn a living. Slavery has always been forced upon innocent victims. However even this understanding can be drained by the fact that the deceptions behind today's recruitment of GCC workers is tantamount to forced labor. It is therefore only disturbing to learn that the anti-slavery activists have yet to take up the cause against Kafala, which is engendering racism in the Gulf Arab states precisely in the manner in which it flourished in the United States. Simply, if you give someone complete power over whether someone else can live in a country – a favor suggesting one-sided superiority – then how can you convince people they are equal to their dependent workers and not above them in rights and privileges.

The understanding of ownership of a worker in the Kafala system is standard knowledge. At *The National* we had a local news desk editor who punctuated most of his emails to the group with the "ifs of firing":

> If anyone receiving this e-mail does not want their job or they are prepared to resign today, then please fucking do so.
> If you are not happy find another place to work.
> If anyone wants to have a conversation with me, then do so.
> If I can do without you for a month then I can do without you for good.
> If you want to resign, then fucking do so.[40]

One reporter friend told me that even though the editor sounded like he would fire any reporter or sub editor without any consultation, the fact was he would not and that he needed to convince his superiors that a certain reporter was useless and should be fired. But if one knows the realities of having been fired once and surviving without a job in a GCC country, that individual would never try to test the possibility of being fired again. I think most of the reporters who were fired in the first months of the editor taking on the local desk all had these delusions that firing is not as simple as he made it sound, and some realized quite dramatically how wrong that perception was.

And one time after such an email was sent, we received more correspondence with the "ifs of apology," saying that the earlier email had been "unprofessional, unkind, and wholly inappropriate. I am sorry! If anyone would like me to apologise in person, please give me a call and we can talk." A new female Arab reporter, not used to the use of the word "fuck," had found the emails offensive and reported so to the management.

Then a day later a fellow reporter wrote a long email entitled "petition to keep" and said that the boss's job was up for review in two days because of one of his recent emails. She wanted all reporters and sub editors, former victims of these rude emails, to sign a petition she had set up in Google documents to save the local editor. And she indicated she had received approval from the executive editor to do so and submit the petition to the human resources office on Sunday before their meeting. When I opened the petition in Google documents, of course just to see but not sign, I found that only 14 members of his local desk team of more than 40 members had signed. Those who didn't sign like me were also voting on the other side and no matter whether our voice was heard as we were the majority, at least he would learn something. Most of his juniors did not want to be motivated with obscene language, as this was work, not a casual setting of friends teasing each other. And it was not his job alone in the balance but also his stay in the UAE, as the two go hand in hand, so the man who always used obscenities to threaten the jobs of his juniors was now desperate for the same juniors to come up with kind words describing him and save his own job. This was the Kafala system at its best, as no expatriate would grow so big as to be immune from the potential tremors of being fired and thrown out of the country even by way of an act that might normally be seen to be inconsequential.

Kafala created a permanent culture of dependency that not only affected unskilled workers or those working in the tourist and hospitality industries but also in the professional working classes.

Kafala also made it difficult to discern just how much worth or value truly lay in the hands of the worker or employee. Many sponsors – even those working in the media – believe they own our thinking and ideas as well as part of their Kafala package to employ us. Thus, many must endure this kind of servitude to obtain permission when we are talking to other people or interacting with friends on social media. In one instance, I replied to a tweet of a story about Abu Dhabi in the western media. The writer had praised the development of the capital and dismissed critics of the rulers' crackdown on opposition voices. A colleague in the paper had first commented on the story as the best ever to highlight the capital's positive elements. I responded on her tweet and said, "You must pocket generously to write such a piece."

A day later the editor in chief, who was an American Iraqi, called me, the first phone call he had made to me in five years, and asked why I had written such an insensitive tweet. It was a Thursday evening prior to the weekend and he wanted me to come to his office first thing on Sunday, making it sound like there was too much at stake. He followed up his demand with a formal email copying the news editor and my cluster editor.

It was a long weekend full of worries and panic, wondering how the editors who were supposed to stand by and protect me were themselves turning up to taunt me for anything I wrote even on social networks. It was hard to believe that a tweet that was just nine words had without any notice compromised all the countless thousands of good words and praises I had written in newspapers about the country and its rulers, and was now threatening my job and stay in the UAE. And even though all tweets were supposed to go through editors, so that if those words were damaging they would have been 'held' and not published. That was the purpose of editors like the one that was summoning me. They helped to filter what came from our minds to go to the public and by doing so, some of us with critical minds were still employed and allowed to remain as legal residents.

Simel Esim of the International Labour Organisation did express it accurately. "With the Kafala system you are creating a total dependency of the worker on the employer for her food, sleeping, health, everything ... Total dependency creates total vulnerability and opens the door wide open for exploitation."[41]

1.5 Kafala in Moral Perspective

Morals are conceived and perceived differently in every society, even as there are common values of moral import shared across the globe. What is morally acceptable in one society might be considered even abominable in another and vice versa. In GCC society Islam serves as the main yardstick of what is perceived to be morally acceptable. The region is home to the birth place of Prophet Mohammed and is host to the two holy mosques of Mecca and Madina. To most of the world, it seems that any act in this region would be adjudicated according to Islamic standards and protocol. Contrary to that general perception, there are still several practices and policies not supported in the teachings of Islam which prevail in this region and would never be challenged by even the most pious modern-day scholars of Islam.

The government policy of the exploitative, abusive and

discriminatory Kafala system without any doubt would fall into the category of non-Islamic practices flourishing in the region. There would be some disagreements – I am not a crowned Islamic scholar so cannot issue what is right and wrong, but I have asked and found several scholars who agree with this view. The major problem is that they cannot openly declare their stance on the government systems because they fear oppression from their respective governments. Still there is room to disagree with my understanding of Islam, especially for the scholars paid by the system and directly benefiting from its exploitation and abuses of the poor workers. Yet supporting clerics would still find it hard to explain why the Kafala would be acceptable under Islamic law. Why God would favor a certain few human beings and discriminate against the majority others, simply on the basis of nationality and race. Why?

There are already many scholars today who find the Kafala system disturbing at least and wonder who devised it and how it was implemented and tolerated for so long by its victim immigrants. To some GCC citizens this amounts to nothing so long as the critics are not GCC nationals. As many Emiratis have responded to any criticism: "*This is our country, and our rulers and their people know what is best for their country, so those who cannot cope can leave.*"

One popular Emirati blogger posted on his Twitter that he didn't care what non-Emiratis said about the 94 political prisoners, echoing the contention that in the UAE only the Emirati voice mattered. The same blogger simply bought his popularity by posting blogs on the Egyptian revolution and he never cared whether Egypt also had its citizens called Egyptians. The thing is when people point at something being wrong it is not always intended to transmit negative sentiments. This is a common misconception of criticism in most of the GCC that prevents improvements or change. In fact more often than not they care so much to tell persons what is wrong other than others who simply back bite an individual in question. Emiratis or Saudis could insist that whoever finds fault with their Kafala or any other abuses perpetuated in their country should simply leave, but regarding these immigrants they also are justifying an injustice, too, simply because their countries of origin have partnered and contributed to the development of the counties in question. Becoming arrogant and oppressive to other people because of the wealth one has recently accumulated is synonymous to the stories told in the holy Quran of people like Qarun (Korah):

> Verily, Qarun was of Musa (Moses)'s people, but he behaved arrogantly towards them. And we gave him of the treasures, that of which the keys would have been a burden to a body of strong men. Remember when his people said to him "Do not exult (with riches, being ungrateful to Allah). Verily Allah likes not those who exult."[42] But seek, with that (wealth) which Allah has bestowed on you, the home of the hereafter, and forget not your portion of lawful enjoyment in this world; and do good as Allah has been good to you, and seek not mischief in the land. Verily Allah likes not the Mufsidun (those who commit great crimes and sins, oppressors, tyrants, mischief makers, corrupters.)[43]
>
> And the faithful slaves of the Most Gracious (Allah) are those who walk on the earth in humility and sedateness, and when the foolish address them (with bad words) they reply back with mild words of gentleness.[44]

Islam itself has honored human beings regardless of their colour, creed or citizenship. God has indicated in the holy Quran that they had favored the genealogy of Adam referring to all human beings. Laws that chain and degrade human beings on the basis of their migrant status are a result of sheer arrogance. As Ahmad ibn Hanbal said: "These genealogies of yours are not a reason to revile anyone. You are all children of Adam. No one has any superiority over another except in religion and *taqwa*."[45]

However, migration is not new in Islamic history or the region. The history of Islam is full of anecdotes of early Muslim converts who migrated to other lands. Most of the early migrants were running away from oppression and looking for freedom to worship God. They were received hospitably in the Lands of Abyssinia (present-day Ethiopia) and Yathirb, which is present-day Medina. Among the early migrants were the beloved prophet of Islam Mohammed and his companions. When they arrived in Yathrib, the people of city gave up the name of their city and called it Medinatul Al Nabbi – "the city of the prophet." They also ceded many possessions, giving them to the migrants, and with this generous gesture they came to be called the "Ansars" or helpers. Although the reasons for migration were different for those early counterparts, they all nevertheless are related to survival.

The early migrants wanted to escape the oppressors and thrive independently, and todays' migrants want to escape their home poverty and earn a living on their own merits and skills. This is a justification for migration even in Islamic texts. I recited a particular verse of the holy Quran to a senior immigration officer in Dubai during my earliest days in the emirate when my visa was about to expire and I learned that I was not entitled to a renewal, which I needed badly.[46] Fortunately, he understood and extended my visa, taking heed of the recitation from the Quran I offered.

Besides the early migrations, there were many other anecdotes that foreign workers wanted the local GCC nationals to reflect upon in the hope they would change their hostile attitudes towards foreigners. One Egyptian worker I met in Saudi Arabia told me his grandfather had a good tale of the state of affairs in Saudi Arabia 70 years back. Whenever they came for Hajj they brought with them food and clothing for Saudi people who were very poor at the time. It was free to enter Saudi Arabia at that time, something that changed with the oil boom. They had introduced the Kafala system to restrict the movement and freedom of Egyptians who had helped them build their infrastructure. Only the Europeans and Americans who did not need to have a sponsor to enter these GCC countries were rewarded handsomely.

The ironic, funny if not tragic, story of this oppressive Kafala system is that most victims are fellow Muslims. They are deluded to think that the teachings of brotherhood and justice in the Quran will always be practiced and followed. Many East Asian Muslim workers who come to the GCC countries think they are coming to their spiritual home, and that they will find the citizens of the Holy Land to be like Ansars and will be treated like the earlier generations of migrants.

To find themselves rejected and abused by the inhabitants of the Holy Land – their religious brothers and sisters – is incomprehensible. More than one billion Muslims prostrate daily in worship facing these Lands and everywhere many wish to one day make the Hajj pilgrimage or the lesser Umrah pilgrimage. They envision these lands to be inhabited by God-abiding people who practice justice and treat every person well according to the instructions in the texts of Islam. To the contrary, the experiences of the few Muslims who have made it to these areas to earn a living betray the great image. And it is not only those who have turned up at airports of Saudi Arabia or Qatar to find these abuses. The question no one can answer is why can there be no justice in Saudi Arabia.

1.6 The Kafala's Visa Mafias

It was in the days when my mother was struggling with cancer and the whole family was in a panic trying to find the best way to save her life. I wrote to my human resources office asking for help to obtain a visa on her behalf, with me as the sponsor. Unfortunately, the reply from the compliance officer was "Sorry, Yasin, the Abu Dhabi media policy only permits employees of your grade to sponsor their wife and children but not mother." The restrictions disturbed me, but there was no time for grievances which would not make a difference. Feeling the weight of urgency, I checked into the visa black market to get my mother a visa. All the visa mafias could offer was a two-year residence permit at 10,000 dirhams – the equivalent of US $2,717. It was not feasible for me to spend such a large sum on the visa considering I had yet to make arrangements for my mother's air travel and for her care and medications. I scaled the request back to a three-month visit visa and the offer was in the value of US $900. The visa would cover two months with a third month extension, but the mafia required – as customary – one to pay for the extension 1,000 dirhams (US $270) even though the official extension is 500 dirhams (US $135). I settled for this offer but my mother passed away before the deal could be sealed.

Four months later I tried to arrange for a visa for my younger brother, Wahab, who was hoping to land a job after graduating with a degree in radiography. Again, my employer could not help me make the arrangements. I went to the immigration office directly with all my documents but the policy was not just an office interpretation but an immigration one, and they did not approve sponsoring a brother even on a short visit. One employee at the immigration office advised that the rules had changed recently, and suggested that I wait for a few months in the hopes that the officials would again reverse course on their policy. It all happened like this. Their rules were like a prison. They serve as sponsors but the workers are not allowed to have visitors even if that visitor is a family member. I went back to the visa mafia guy, who had offered to help with my mother. At first he had trouble with the student status of my brother's passport, advising that we change it to business but after some wrangling he could only manage to secure a two-month non-renewable visa, further advising that students could not get a renewal visa.

The visa mafia dictated arbitrary prices for visas, far different from the fees officially levied by the government. Visit and residency visas were among the most affected and the visa mafia applied discriminatory pricing depending upon one's gender or country of origin. Women, for example, would be charged higher fees than male counterparts while some nationalities would also be charged higher fees depending on the intensity of need that country's resident had for a visa to stay in the GCC. A residency visa for three years was often tendered out for about 10,000 dirhams for most countries but for one that was engaged in civil war such as Syria in 2013, the residency visa for the UAE was being tendered out by the Kafalas at 50,000 dirhams. One Syrian national who had secured a visa for his mother at that excessive price directed me to visit the Al Qasba mosque in the evening where groups of old Syrian women met to discuss their complaints about visas for the GCC countries.[47]

Whether one obtains this visit visa from a tourist company or another individual, it always links to an Emirati sponsor. And all categories are quite expensive; more so than the official fee schedules and the secret is one cannot obtain a visa directly without the intercession of a Kafala sponsor. The government has given citizens a chance to make money from the desperate expatriates struggling to come to their country. This source of income has also helped to diffuse the tension between ordinary citizens and the rich ruling families. One Emirati sponsor whom I had asked for help once put it to me this way: "The government says we gave you the money from visas and now leave for us the money from the oil contracts."

However, this was not to suggest that all the money in immigration is an exclusive purview of the citizens minus their government. The government is, in fact, taking as much as the citizens collect. In the GCC, everybody technically is in the visa business.

John Willoughby, a scholar who has studied the flow of Indian immigration to the Gulf, argued that the officially declared total amount of money extracted from Indian workers entering Gulf countries in 1998 for visas, airfare, agent commission and even cheating – $1.7 billion annually –was heavily underestimated. Noting that it likely is more than $4 billion yearly, he adds, "Facilitating the entry and maintenance of Asian workers to the gulf is more than a billion dollar industry."[48]

Human Rights Watch (HRW) quoting a World Bank study on Immigration from Nepal to Qatar also found that recruitment agents in Qatar received between US $17 million and $34 million in commissions from Nepal each year.[49]

Because the system is broadly lucrative, the magnitude of the opportunity tempts frequent abuses of the system, especially by the local citizens themselves. Ibrahim Ahmed Ibrahim Ali has pointed out some locals would apply for visas on behalf of some workers and then arrange with them the same workers just to have them abscond at a certain fee and brings others on board. Ali called it "free visa trading."[50]

There are also other local researchers who have chronicled the chronic abuses in the Kafala visa system. One notes that large numbers of visas are issued not to domestic servants but instead sold to foreign skilled workers who enter the country as menials. These workers can then secure jobs in the actual field of their expertise.[51]

GCC nationals with business licenses have also been given work visas for a specified number of immigrants. They may sell these visas to others, leaving the migrant workers undocumented.

As a result, visa trading is now a multimillion – if not billion – dollar industry. There are high fees for the initial sponsorship, followed by two year renewal fees. In the UAE, a two-year work visa for an Indian worker sells for around US $2,000 and for an Iranian worker for US $4,000. It remains extremely easy for GCC citizens to make a good income simply by visa trading; despite the fact that this is unlawful, there has been no known prosecution to date of GCC nationals for these activities, and the migrants and occasionally employers are held to account.[52]

In Saudi Arabia, Abid Khazandar, writing for a local paper, called the work visas the biggest gift a Saudi could get because of the profitability of the visa trades in the black market.[53]

"People who sell work visas have made millions of riyals. [T]hey recruit a foreigner on a work visa then free him to work in the market in exchange for a monthly fee. They can also sell visas to other brokers or merchants," he wrote. "The safest and most stable profit, however, comes from Tasatur [where foreigners run and control a business in exchange for a monthly fee paid to the registered Saudi owner] especially in the contracting sector."

He recalls a foreign carpenter who had five million Saudi riyals in his bank accounts because he ran several business names under an assumed Saudi name.[54]

Problems of visa mafias have also cropped up in Kuwait. In July 2013 nearly 700 companies in the country were charged with allegations of trafficking in visas.[55]

The report mentioned that about 1,000 employers had been blocked from being issued new visas after officials found that workers on their sponsored visas were actually working elsewhere. The system that exploited all the loopholes in Kafala operated like this, where traffickers would create employment visas for fake companies or nonexistent jobs and then sell them to unskilled workers in Asian countries. Once the workers arrived in Kuwait they found no job and had to resort to hard labor just to earn a living without a valid visa.

In Qatar, the visa mafia sells so-called "free visas" to victims of their fraud. The companies who are authorized to sponsor workers would sell their work visas to poor immigrants without necessarily offering them jobs. Once the workers arrive in the country they are on their own and become quick prey for other traffickers who would exploit their desperation and make them work for almost free. In one event I covered, the Qatar authorities from the Ministry of Interior called this kind of visa trading the main facilitator of human trafficking.[56] The Ministry reported to have collected 4.27 million Qatari riyals in fines (nearly US $1.2 million) in 2013 alone. The Ministry found that 1,043 workers were illegally transferred to new sponsors, while 165 complaints of illegal visa trading were filed at the Ministry and 128 were referred to court while 51 firms were prosecuted for trading in visas. There were 43 verdicts leading to the arrest of violators who were imprisoned for up to three years, as I reported. Brigadier Nasser Al Sayed, director of the search and follow-up department at the Ministry of Interior, said the government was committed to stopping the flow of illegal visa trading activity but that he and the others were flummoxed about how to resolve the situation so that visa applications would be securely coordinated through a standardized procedure at all diplomatic missions and embassies of the countries involved.

But it is not the local Emiratis or Saudis alone who exploit the Kafala visa system to abuse workers; some workers are abused also by their own countrymen who take on the roles of middle men and recruiters, as documented by several researchers.

The Ugandan government, as one case, had established and licensed a number of recruitment companies that would hire workers to go to the UAE or other Gulf countries. When the recruitment flows grew and Ugandan workers were being admired for their fluency in English, the government became tough in the guise of protecting these workers. It was difficult for anyone with an employment visa to go through airport immigration if he or she was not being offered a deal from the government-established companies.

One friend had been in the UAE on a visit visa, got a job and returned to Uganda in order to change the visa status to employment. He was stopped at the airport and asked who was taking him or who had secured him a job. When he mentioned how he had obtained his new job he was told bluntly that such independent offers were now banned by the government. One had to go through the right channels established by the government to get an offer from Dubai or Doha. The immigrant officer wanted a bribe of $250 to let him pass and with all alternatives closed he paid the bribe and came to the UAE.

There were many similar stories and many workers started changing routes if they had obtained Dubai jobs independently without the Ugandan government middlemen. They would go to neighboring Nairobi or Kigali instead and board a Dubai flight from there. The Yoweri Kaguta government also became strict on those coming to Dubai with visit visas, as it presumed once they came on these visas they would easily get employment, thereby bypassing their own recruiting companies. If an individual asked any officer from the Ministry of Labor or Immigration why they were stopping people from getting jobs on their own in the Gulf countries, the official answer was always the same: There have been several reports of work abuses in these countries and the government is coming in to regulate the flow of workers and to ensure their rights are well stipulated and observed.[57]

Only if an individual had established a good rapport with the officer, assuring him of anonymity, would he then admit that, of course, all workers going through these companies are paying a lot of money; the government takes some from these recruiters. In addition, most of the recruiting companies are owned by well-connected people in the government. But it was these same recruiting companies that abused and cheated the workers. They were taking air tickets and visa fees from the employing or sponsoring companies and again asking the workers for each to pay for his or her air ticket and visa, thereby cheating in doubles.

They charged these workers excessively and lied unashamedly to them about their salary being quoted in dollars, not dirhams. They ambled freely through deceptions, recruiting university graduates as cleaners and housemaids because all they needed was the number of workers indicated in their contract and these people had to be able to pay their dubious fees and tickets.

1.7 The World of Undocumented Workers

There was one day when I nearly ran into trouble with the Dubai police who were chasing illegal residents in Deira. A dozen black people were running on the streets behind the Naif market area and each of them urged me to join in and run without even understanding why they were running. Instead I just stood in place knowing something was not right. Then three police officers appeared and hurriedly sought my arm, asking me for my name. I replied: "Are you chasing all those black people to know their names?" First they laughed and then turned serious, requesting my Bittaqa or documents. As soon as one of the officers noticed my Emirates ID he laughed and said to his colleagues in Arabic: "ho ho ho, a Zoro Sahafiiii," meaning "the man is a journalist." (Zoro is a Sudanese word referring to a man. The GCC people used the word in reference to every black person, perhaps because they thought most black people were Sudanese. The same word in my native Luganda tongue translates to "mad," and this is why I hated the term as a personal reference.) Each officer closely inspected my ID as if it needed to be confirmed, especially because a black man happens to be a national journalist.

Bittaqa IDs or *Jawwaz* passports represent the only protection an immigrant has to walk on the streets in a GCC state. Being found without any of these papers could prove fatal and explanations of forgotten or lost documents simply won't help. The police always look to raid enclaves of undocumented immigrants and check to see if documents were legitimate and verifiable. Still the number of illegal immigrants living in these countries has multiplied quickly and once a person becomes an illegal the person had to learn basic survival tactics to evade police searches. The illegal immigrant is one of the disturbing outcomes the Kafala system has inflicted on the GCC governments.

The system turns many immigrants into innocent illegal residents.

GCC governments have had to give multiple amnesty provisions every few years to allow undocumented immigrants to leave their countries. The amnesty provisions have always followed raids on streets and worker dormitories to find the illegals still staying in the country. In December 2013 three Ethiopian migrants to Saudi Arabia died as a police raid turned into a full-blown riot. More than 150,000 Ethiopians were expected to be repatriated after the seven-month period of Saudi government amnesty for all illegals living in the country to leave peacefully expired. Agence France Press called the operation the largest human airlift operation in recent history.[58]

Sharon Dimanche of the International Organisation for Migration (IOM), which assisted the Ethiopian government in repatriation, called the incident an emergency that needed to be resolved in a short period so that people's lives were no longer endangered. She said they needed about $13.1 million to support the returnees.[59] This makes those who left in 2012 look like miniscule drops of water in a sea of undocumented individuals supposedly because the amnesties had become so familiar and disrespected.

One report in the UK's *Guardian* predicted that about 2 million migrants would be deported annually from the country.[60]

1.8 The Most Dangerous Route into Saudi Arabia

The BBC's Yalda Hakim called the migrants' journey from Ethiopia to Saudi Arabia the most dangerous trek on Earth.[61] She traced the paths of 80,000 Ethiopians who attempt to reach Saudi Arabia every year with prospects of a better economically sustainable life. The men and women have to cross the Red Sea, trek 500 kilometers through the desert and then evade Saudi border guards.[62]

Other researchers from the Danish Refugee Council (DRC) and Regional Mixed Migration Secretariat (RMMS) have offered similar damning reports of this desperate trip. The most dangerous route is entering Saudi Arabia through Yemen where kidnap, torture, sexual violence, abduction and extortion have become widespread for Ethiopian migrants. The ongoing instability in Yemen has attracted many illegal (undocumented) migrants because it is considered easier to enter and transit the country.[63]

The journey from Ethiopia to Yemen is physically demanding and migrants are vulnerable to the physical rigors of the trip, facing abuse from crews controlling the sea-crossing and violent attacks from criminal gangs. The migrants typically walk for days or weeks to reach the coast to Djibouti or Puntland with little access to food, water or shelter. Other migrants are smuggled in container trucks to the coast, potential death traps because of heat and lack of fresh air. Some numbers collected in February 2012 indicate that a container truck was stopped in Ethiopia near the Djibouti border with 75 migrants and 11 had suffocated to death. In June an accident resulted in the deaths of 27 Ethiopians and injuries to 54 others. Researchers noted that most people died overland more than they did on the seas.[64]

"There were so many dead bodies and skeletons en route from my home in Wollo to the coast of Djibouti that if you had to make the journey on your own, you would not get lost because you would follow the remains of all those people who failed to complete their journey," an Ethiopian immigrant told the DRC and RMMS.[65]

Still once they embarked on the boat migrants faced death due to drowning or the brutality of the crews throwing some people overboard to control others. Female migrants were assaulted and raped. Some passengers died of exposure, dehydration and suffocation as they were stowed below the deck in toxic conditions among petrol fumes and with fuel mixed with water, along with feces and urine from their fellow passengers around and above them. Dead bodies were thrown into the sea.

On arrival at the Yemeni coast migrants still reported ordeals of being taken by hostages, and then beaten and forced to hand over any money or valuables such as mobile phones and watches. They would be forced to call their families to demand ransom for their release. Some hostages are shot dead, either because they protest or try to escape or because the hostage takers want to make an example in order to quieten other hostages.

In about six years at least 230,000 Ethiopians have entered Yemen as illegal maritime migrants. However, because Yemen also has similarly poor economic prospects, many migrants treat Yemen as merely a transit stop. From Yemen migrants attempt to cross into Oman or Saudi Arabia. Some travel independently, others with the help of smugglers. Most illegal migrants attempt the flight from Yemen to Saudi Arabia during Ramadan because the patrol guards are thought to be less alert and effective during the times of fasting. Staff members working for the Yemeni and Saudi Arabian borders are often complicit in illegal immigration and accept bribes. There also are highly organized smugglers with contacts who allow certain vehicles and individuals to pass unhindered into countries. One Yemeni border guard claimed to be earning $20,000 a month for facilitating this wave of illegal migration.[66]

The problem of undocumented migrants is more prevalent in

Saudi Arabia than other GCC countries. The country has about half of an estimated eight million expatriates working in the country without valid papers.[67]

Besides the Ethiopians, those among the beneficiaries of the amnesty have mostly been Yemeni Arabs. There have been reports of about 2,000 undocumented Yemeni migrants leaving Saudi Arabia each day by buses, making this the largest group to leave.[68]

The violators of immigration rules in the Saudi kingdom face hefty penalties including imprisonment of up to two years, and fines of up to 100,000 riyals (US $27,000).[69]

Saudi officials have also been blamed for violating the deportation rules by dropping Ethiopian migrants in the desert several kilometers from the border with Yemen, so that they have to travel the remaining distance without food or water. Immigrants forced out of Saudi Arabia in this fashion also report having passed dead bodies of hundreds of immigrants who didn't make it. At the Yemen border the immigrants have to bribe their way into Yemen – usually about the equivalent of US $25, whilst those without money hand over their valuables such as watches or jewelry – and it was common for women to be allowed across the border in exchange for sex.[70]

Even in the UAE several immigrants unable to find a sponsor choose to enter the country through illegal and dangerous means. There have been several reports of immigrants caught trying to cross the Oman–UAE border, walking long distances in the desert when the temperatures were 50 degrees C or higher (120 degrees F). Few of these immigrants make it to the UAE as many run short of food and water in the middle of the desert and die there. The Ras Al Khaimah deserts are primarily targeted for the desperate undocumented infiltrators entering the country this way.[71]

Undocumented migrants also have risked the same routes to go out of the country, with some trying to dodge the airport's iris scan.[72] I also did quite a number of stories chronicling police rescuing stranded and dehydrated undocumented migrants in both Sharjah and Ras Al Khaimah as well as stories of finding dead bodies. Yet, these paperless immigrants are coming into the country not only through deserts but also via sea and air.

The UAE government has been giving illegal immigrants amnesties almost every five years to help bring down the number of workers staying in the country without valid papers or those who have run away from their sponsors or who outstayed their sponsor visas. In the previous amnesty that lasted from December 2012 to February 2013 the UAE Ministry of Interior announced that a total of 61,826 illegal immigrants had taken the amnesty opportunity and left the country.[73]

The Ministry, as in most of the country's PR department's releases, does not stipulate how many illegal residents actually live in the UAE in order to ascertain who left and who stayed. But if one were to make comparisons, a total of 341,958 undocumented workers had left the country during the 2007 amnesty.[74]

The UAE also has been strict on companies that have hired undocumented migrants, or workers they did not sponsor themselves. The Ministry of Interior also announced that it would be levying a 50,000-dirham fine to any companies or individuals whom they found employing illegal workers without sponsorship.[75] Raids for illegal workers are common on Dubai streets, worker dormitories and even workplaces, especially whenever the given amnesty period has expired.

Other GCC countries such as Kuwait, Qatar and Bahrain are less willing to offer similar amnesties but they as well have suffered from chronic problems of workers not being able to renew their visas because of the strict Kafala laws. Or, they have experienced a falling-out with their sponsors while others choose to enter the country illegally because they cannot find a sponsor.

In Kuwait official statistics of the Ministry of Interior indicate that more than 95,000 violators of residency law are far from the grip of security operatives.[76] In all GCC countries the undocumented migrants have to go through the prisons to exit these countries. It is only in prisons the governments will compensate them for their contributions toward building the country. Only in prisons will the government make the expenditures to give them food. No wonder they insist that everyone has to be incarcerated first, not like other countries where an undocumented migrants who turns up at the airport willing to leave the country is deported immediately.

The undocumented immigrant amnesty provisions also work as collective deportations across the GCC countries. There are always large queues of migrants in all immigration departments, with many being housed in tents that are temporarily set up to manage the traffic. These tent scenes crowding the airports are common especially during amnesty periods. In one scene I witnessed at Sharjah International Airport, police officials screamed at their loudest to keep the poor immigrants away from wealthy visitors coming into the country. Raids against undocumented migrants intensified whenever an amnesty period expired. Other immigrants, especially the Yemenis from Saudi Arabia, were repatriated in bus loads.

The show became tense once the amnesties expired and the police started their crackdown raids on undocumented immigrant havens. The melee had resulted in scuffles between police and the immigrants in Saudi Arabia claiming lives of the poor immigrants as well as injuring many others.[77] One video that went viral on social networks during Saudi Arabia's crackdown on Ethiopian immigrants showed a Saudi man dragging an Ethiopian man out of his house and beating him in the streets. The result was a large riot among the immigrants with the security personnel resulting in one Ethiopian death as well as the death of a Saudi national.[78]

Workers who did not leave the country during the amnesties would face multiple penalties including fines, prison terms, deportation and a lifetime ban from the country. And even though the deporting country was required to meet the repatriation costs, all GCC countries required undocumented immigrants to pay for their one-way return tickets to their respective countries. There were many immigrants stranded in prisons because they could not afford a return ticket back to their homeland. In the case of our Ugandan communities we always mobilized and collected money among ourselves to buy the air tickets of our arrested colleagues awaiting deportation in the jails.

1.9 The Oldest Illegal

From December 2012 to February 4, 2013 the UAE had given two months amnesty for all those staying in the country illegally to leave the country without paying fines. One of the residents supposed to leave was Mohammed Jamua Yousuf, who was 74 and ailing. He had left his native Somalia and started working in the UAE during the 1950s and for the last 20 years he had been living without a sponsor and therefore was considered an illegal in the UAE terminology. A colleague in office gave me the telephone number of one of the Somali community members who was trying to help Yousuf find a sponsor so he could remain in the UAE.

Yousuf stayed in a small dwelling among the dilapidated homes that had been targeted by municipal authorities for demolition in the Karama area of Ajman so that new construction projects could begin. Most of Yousuf's neighbors had already vacated the premises either for their safety or because of a municipality notice to leave, but the old man had more pressing worries than a dilapidated home. He had been staying in the country without a sponsor and it was fine when he was healthy but now his body had started failing him and he needed regular medical attention and check-ups. To get these check-ups he needed to have documents including a visa, which required a sponsor.

After we had taken our seats in his room, me sitting with him on his bed and my contact who brought me sitting on a small stool, the old man started by apologizing that he could not afford to offer us anything to eat or drink. We quickly reassured him that this was fine for us.

He then launched into his problems about how he wished he should go back to Somalia with this amnesty opportunity but was afraid there was no one there to take care of him. Yousuf, who was childless, said all his compatriots had earlier succumbed to the war or age and he doubted he knew of any living relative there to receive him.

Yousuf had been in the UAE for more than 50 years. When he came during the 1950s, he had worked in the British Army, which had responsibility to protect the states that were party to the truce. He was briefly posted to Yemen for two years together with some notable Emirati men of that time and then reposted back to the UAE. He was relieved of the UAE army responsibilities in 1974 and from then he worked in a transport company of one of his former military colleagues (Ahmed Mohammed Al Midfa) for some time. In 1992 he was unemployed and had to arrange his own residency visa, which started by finding a sponsor. He was conned by an Arab man out of 3,600 dirhams (about US $1000) to obtain a sponsor and visa which were never delivered. From that year he became an undocumented man, and he took his case to court but the conman outsmarted him and disappeared.

Yousuf's home was given to him by an Emirati friend, who also took care of his feeding by sending his maid to bring him food every day. I asked him if this man could be his sponsor and give him a visa. He answered that indeed he would be willing to help in any way but the fines he accumulated over the years were too much of a financial burden for his sponsor. Yousuf contemplated taking this amnesty and returning to Somalia for good. I asked him about how I could help and he replied that I should make requests from the sheikhs. "Because if a sheikh says I can stay, I will stay well and get papers to be able to go to the hospital and get treated," he explained.

Yousuf's request at first sounded unrealistic, considering that I likely did not have sheikhs among my friends. However, he was right. Some sheikhs read newspapers and listen to the radio, and they help so many – especially local people whose troubles are brought to the media. *The National*, an English-language and less popular paper, was however not the best media outlet to deliver on his hopes to reach the sheikhs, I told him. I decided to ask my Arabic-paper colleagues if they could help. He relied on the local Somali community members to buy him medications but the members had already exhausted their contacts to have treated twice in Ajman's Sheikh Khalifa hospital where he had been diagnosed with diabetes and high blood pressure. I published his story in the newspaper I was working for then.[79] Most of my Arabic-newspaper colleagues wanted him to go to the amnesty offices and present himself there for them to pick up the story, but his Somali friends advised him not to take the risk, in case they threw him out of the country.

It is so disparagingly easy to become an undocumented migrant in the GCC. Even migrant workers deciding to leave their workplaces without the consent of their sponsors or employers are considered absconders and become illegal at the drop of a hat. It is a criminal offence to abscond in these states. This is the case even if the worker leaves because of a genuine reason like escaping an abusive sponsor. That person is still a criminal.

And local GCC laws are also strict on anyone employing a runaway worker. In Qatar the employer is liable for imprisonment and payment of a sum ranging from 20,000 Qatari riyals (US $5,490) to 100,000 Qatari riyals (US $27,450) as fines.[80]

The UAE government also announced plans to financially

compensate sponsors of absconding domestic workers. The amount would be taken from the fine of 50,000 dirhams levied against the new "illegal sponsor" who hires the worker, after both have been arrested.[81]

The Kafala system is responsible for making many workers undocumented or absconders, especially in cases where a worker comes into conflict with the sponsor and all legal recourse ends with deportation. Likely, many workers simply seek to abscond and become illegal without valid papers.

Human Rights Watch has also found many illegal workers in Qatar whose sponsors have failed to secure or renew their work permits due to their unwillingness to pay related fees; and still these workers are at risk of being arrested and deported from the country as illegal residents.[82]

And illegal migrants usually find work among the GCC citizens themselves who want to avoid the costs and strictures of the Kafala system of hiring a worker. Unfortunately, undocumented workers are especially vulnerable to sexual and physical abuse and coercion to submit to poor living and working conditions as employers threaten to report them to the police. Additionally, although not officially confirmed, migrant workers can be blacklisted by the authorities and they could have trouble even going to any other GCC country after being blacklisted in one.[83]

Even children are identified as undocumented and illegal within the UAE Kafala system. Most of those borne by undocumented immigrant parents carry on the status of their parents. Some children have their visas expire and their parents cannot afford to renew them thus rendering them illegal. In other instances both parents' and childrens' visas expire together. The Ajman police commander-in-chief Brigadier Ali Alwan told us in a press conference that the presence of undocumented families is increasing and that police have launched a crackdown campaign including knocking on family's doors to make them show their papers.[84]

Other children are simply smuggled into the country by parents living legally in the country but their sponsors do not allow them to live with their families. Most expatriates labor especially in low-paid jobs and they are the majority who cannot bring in their families in the UAE. So those whose visas do not allow them to bring in families resort to desperate illegal measures to bring their children into the country. There was a story I worked on in Sharjah in which a five-month-old baby boy showed up on the airport baggage scan. His parents of Egyptian descent were trying to smuggle him into the country as they could not afford to sponsor him on their visa.[85]

Section 2

Segregation and Desperation

2.1 Desperate Voices from GCC Work Sites

Harriet was an aircraft cleaner with a large private security company. She had worked with one of my school friends in Kampala before coming to Dubai.

The friend had given her my number when she was struggling to raise the funds for a return ticket back to Uganda after losing hope on her Dubai dream.

He advised her that instead of soliciting from old friends for a return air ticket she could contact me, an established journalist, and I could get her a job as a photographer. This was a pervasive myth my Ugandan friend believed about me being able to get everyone a job. She had worked as a manager of a studio back in Uganda before she was tricked to come to Dubai and now she was trapped. However, in her call, she did not ask me for a job but told me she wanted to meet me in order to pass over some things for my friend. She told me later she had feared that if she revealed exactly what she wanted, I would not have turned up. We met at Al Khail Mall in the Al Qouz Industrial Area 4, just a few meters' walking distance from her accommodations – a room she shared with three other women, one from Uganda and two Filipinos. She started by showing me a few pictures of functions, mostly weddings, she had taken earlier on while in Uganda along with her resume including details of her previous experience and skills. I noticed she had a higher degree diploma in Social Sciences from one of Uganda's largest institutions of learning.

She was now earning a monthly salary of just 800 dirhams (US $215) from a security company as an aircraft cleaner at the Dubai International Airport. She showed me a rash on her arms and part of her face and said she had contracted it from a detergent called Bacoban used to clean the aircrafts. She had complained to her supervisors, who took her to a hospital where she received some treatment. Things were fine until the last month when her salary had been slashed by 75 percent.

She received just 200 dirhams (US $54) that month and they told her the remaining had gone to cover the cost of her treatment. She was by then planning to go back for treatment as the rash had persisted and the constant itching made her sick all of the time. With these salary cuts she had to cancel the plans of returning for further treatment, as she could not afford another similar cut the next month. Most companies in the GCC countries did not simply require their poor workers to pay for their treatments but also issued penalties for taking a day off work because he or she was sick. Amnesty International's report on Qatar found that a penalty of missing a day's work due to sickness in Qatar varied from one day's salary to as much as four days in pay.[86]

Harriet complained repeatedly about working more than the stipulated hours in a day without a single break to even take water or any other refreshment. She told me that a colleague from Kenya had fainted inside the plane because the air conditioning was not working and she had not eaten or drank anything since early in the morning. There were some women who lifted food or water from the plane's cabin but this was at the risk of serious consequences. The arrangement in her accommodations was disturbed and offended her, as her two Filipino roommates were lesbians and brought other women into the space without checking with her. There were all sorts of activities forbidden from the shared accommodations, including cooking, and their supervisors required them to buy food from restaurants with the meager salaries they offered. Residents were banned from washing clothes inside accommodations and the management had instead installed a coin-operated washing machine. It cost four dirhams (US $1.20) just to launder work uniforms. She said violating these rules was the only way for them to survive but they had to be especially creative to evade being noticed and this came with its own stress. They prepared meals using cooking utensils that were cached away from sight and they did their laundry in bathtubs and sinks.

Her work supervisor, an Indian man who hardly spoke a single English word correctly and seemed to lack even the common sense of a high school graduate, regularly harassed her verbally and physically. He would inspect her cleaning the plane's cabin, occasionally leaning down to grope her. When she asked what he was doing, he would tell her, "Sorry, banana standing. This banana big problem."

Every one of her colleagues complained about his conduct but no one dared report his actions to superiors, as in the past someone had been dismissed from work after she reported a similar incident of sexual harassment. "They would twist everything and turn it around accusing you of being a prostitute and dismiss you from work," she recalled.

The only thing she thought was good in her department was the day off every week, a privilege considering that few other employees – such as security guards – enjoyed the privilege. She said on her off day she would stay in her bed and cry. And it felt good that she had this chance to cry in private because she could then avoid breaking down in public. Crying was the only way she could reduce the burden of her problems that her head alone could not fix.

She also felt unsafe about leaving her room and going around their accommodations. Although the residence quarters were reserved for women, groups of tense aggressive men swarmed around the complex, begging and baiting any women to come out. The situation was worst at night. When I dropped her home around 7:30 in the evening, premises were very busy. It was also hard to discern the space as exclusively for women, since most of the people in the compound were men. Cars from the latest models of Land Cruisers to older makes of Toyota Corolla constantly streamed in to pick up or drop off women.

Harriet told me most women complemented their meager earnings with prostitution and these cars were all in the service of transporting escorts, not true dating acquaintances or friends. Other women were dropped off at Al Khail Mall and they would walk the short distance simply to disguise their activities. The men who crowded the accommodation compound were there only to look at those being picked up and dropped off but it seemed that none of them could afford a woman who had just been transported by a driver in a Land Cruiser. However, Harriet said I was wrong, as it was a matter of price discrimination.

She challenged me to walk around in those dark corridors of the neighboring buildings that acted as short-term lodges with scenes of poor couples in compromised scenes. She told me of reports of some angry groups of men raping some young women at night who happened to pass by and said this is one thing that stops most women from going out, especially once night has fallen. Instead, they would rather sleep hungry without eating anything than attempt walking those roads to go to neighborhood restaurants or the mall.

Al Qouz Industrial area is a well-known residential hub for most low-wage construction workers in Dubai. Unlike Sonapur, where the accommodations are mostly for men, there are a lot of female accommodations in Al Quoz. In fact, in the neighborhood of Al Khail Mall there are plenty of mixed accommodations, where men can stay in one room and women occupy the next. Harriet's accommodation, however, was only for women who worked at a widely known private security group which supplied all categories of workers at the airport.

On my way back to Sharjah after dropping her off, I drove down Al Khail Road and then Business Bay Road. On both roads the fruits of the poor workers from the emirates are visible. From the roads one has a good view of Burj Dubai, now renamed Burj Khalifa Tower, the tallest structure in the world. Looking at these icons one easily offers eulogies to the ruling elites and less often a thought of the misery of workers who made these fantastic structures possible. I knew the images of women's misery, such as Harriet's, which would catch up with me even when I boarded their fine aircrafts, and perhaps sat in a seat she had cleaned herself. I thought about their insecure accommodations and remembered how bachelors had been evicted in all areas designated for local Emirati families in Sharjah. The concept of family was always a euphemism for women, of course, in the UAE, but not these poor women of Al Qouz. They were neither family nor Emiratis.

In the ensuing weeks, Harriet checked out jobs in the classifieds and sent emails as per my advice. She received a few responses but whenever she turned up for interviews, she was asked if her sponsor was willing to give a No Objection Consent (NOC) letter to facilitate a change in jobs and sponsors in the UAE. She had no idea about such a document and when she queried her current employer's human resources office, she learned they did not give such a letter and added that she would be banned from working in the UAE if she tried to change jobs. Once again she was at the mercy of her sponsor to allow her to go for another job befitting her qualifications, but this was a gesture of mercy her sponsor was not willing to extend. NOC requirements are only made to limit the mobility of workers and they are enacted at the pleasure of lawmakers who also happen to benefit from the business of Kafala. They essentially bind the workers to their servitude and they cannot conceive of a situation when a worker would be free to move from his exploitation, because they know no one would stay.

I say this from experience, as I was once banned after leaving my first journalist job, because the media company refused to give me a NOC letter. I still remember the substantial price I paid for disengaging from my exploitative employer.[87]

Harriet was an evangelical Christian and often would say she thought Muslims were decent people but her experience in a Muslim country had evaporated all feelings of good will. While she knew I was a Muslim, I felt her agony and I tried to reassure her that not all Muslims acted like this. I was uncomfortable with anyone trying to make such a sweeping generalization.

Certainly there were many other Muslims workers in her company with problems like her. However, I did not believe the kind of exploitation and abuses at her company were the product of Islamic teachings.

2.2 The Societal Segregation

Not all worker problems in the GCC are perpetuated by governments. The society also has inflicted its own wounds on both unskilled laborers and professional workers such as journalists like me. Social differences in race or religion divide people in penetrating ways. It is common to find most Christians feeling alienated and segregated on the basis of their religion in the GCC. At times I also believed that my being a Sunni Muslim had been an advantage helping me to stay in the *Al Ittihad* office on amicable terms. I recall a Shia colleague in the same office being discriminated against by his fellow Arabs. He was always backbitten, teased about his manner of talking and spoken of derogatorily, even in his presence. He was far more segregated than me and often counted me as his lone friend and neighbor in the office.

He never attended our congregation prayers and regularly quarreled with the office manager. He would tell me things about the Shia I didn't know and always emphasized that his differences with the office manager were religious, not professional. One of the things he always emphasized in our private talks was that there was no tangible differences between Shia and Sunni. And all the differences were politically motivated by various group clerics for their own political and financial benefits, but not spiritually for a larger, ecumenical community.

"Now, me and you, Yasin, what do we have to gain from these differences, we are both hard earning our living so why should we be enemies," he told me one time. "This is what most of these people in office don't understand. I don't pray with them because I am told a different way of folding or not folding hands in prayer; it doesn't make us enemies."

He would always relate myths that clerics had perpetuated to fracture the Shia–Sunni unity. One was the widely known Shia secret among Sunni circles of religious group sex, which fell in the category Sunni scholars called *taqqia* (secrets). Many preachers including my Islamic teacher in school stressed that no Shia would confess this to a non-Shia, as it is their most significant secret. My colleague started me by deconstructing this, asking me how in this era of information revolution people would not find images of such group sex on YouTube or Facebook sites anywhere. Then he argued that if such practices were actually being propagated by Shias with religious blessings, "all Sunnis would be Shias, and everyone among the people of this world would be willing to convert to Shia because these are the things all people want." I tried to explain not all people were looking for sex in religion or life. In Uganda, my country, there was a religious group that conducted night prayers and rumor held that they were engaging in group sex during these prayers. Many Ugandans believed this rumor but not all Ugandans joined this particular religion.

Perhaps the most convincing explanation would have been that most Sunnis including myself have heard about this doctrine and have always believed our clerics who wrote it into syllabuses and curricula but we have not joined the Shia sect. But I knew it would be rude putting myself among the people who have always believed bad things about my friend and his religious sect.

Instead I told him about a female Saudi national reporter of another Arabic paper who mentioned that Shia men did not enjoy virgins, as during their wedding night they had to take their virgin brides to the Shia cleric to enjoy and take away their virginity. He stopped me in the middle of the details, as he was familiar with the story and of the reporter who had relayed the story to me. He suggested I ask the colleague questions such as, "How many people get married in a day? Does she know the number? If a cleric was going to start breaking virginities of all brides in a night, would he cope? Even if he took all the Viagra from the manufacturer and cancelled all other work including religious sermonizing to do only this, he would not be able to accomplish this."

I always preferred having our religious chats in secret because I never wanted my other colleagues, most of whom I led in prayers, to learn that I was listening to him.

He almost landed me in trouble when one colleague came into the office in the middle of our conversation and he didn't stopped talking. It was during the time when the Syrian conflict had escalated rapidly, and the Lebanese Shia led by Hassan Nasrallah had joined the war to fight on the side of Bashar Al Assad's Shia government. My friend said the Shias had fought alongside the Sunnis in all their battles with Israel, especially in Palestine, and that he had offered the Sunni Hamas leaders sanctuary in their country. But when the Israelites with America joining them invaded the Shias in Syria the same Sunni brothers abandoned them and joined the Israelis. The man who had ventured into our conversation immediately asked him to stop, asking when he started saying these things in the office. My friend was deported a few weeks later and when he left he never dared to say his farewells to any of us in office including me, his best friend.

Tolerance is not simply lacking for Christians in the GCC, it also is a fundamental deficiency spanning all spheres of belief and it rejects anyone different from the predominant faith. One important awareness in these countries that sadly falls short of the ideal is one of universal humanity: that a person is a human being whether he or she likes you or not, whether a Shia or

Sunni, a Christian, Pentecostal, Hindu or anything else, or whether light-skinned or dark-skinned, black or white. It is even more disturbing when we, as Muslims, cannot live in peace and harmony with our fellow Muslims just because of a few differences in the interpretation of the holy texts.

2.3 Fostering Exclusion with Impunity

The Gulf countries argue that if migrant workers become naturalized citizens, they will eventually dominate and erase their Arab Gulf identity, leading to the gradual subordination of the Gulf countries to other nations.[88]

A sentence from a study nearly twenty years ago clarified the point for me: "Social Exclusion matters because it denies some people the same rights and opportunities that are afforded to others in their society. Simply because of who they are, certain groups cannot fulfill their potential, nor can they participate equally in society."[89]

There are plenty of notable instances in various reports and studies. Author and researcher Khawla Mattar explains the new GCC efforts to distance the countries from any responsibility to the poor migrant workers building their countries. He notes how categories have been reengineered to move away from terms and phrases such as "migrant labor force" to "temporary labor force" or "contractual labor force." This consequently avoids being subjected to international agreements associated with migrant laborers.[90]

Nasser Al Shamsi, the permanent representative of the UAE to the UN, wrote in a September 29, 2006 letter to Human Rights Watch that "Workers hosted by the UAE and other GCC countries cannot be considered migrant workers, as they work on temporary basis and according to fixed-term employment contracts. Upon expiration of these contracts, they return to their home countries. Therefore the immigration laws applicable in western countries cannot be applied to these workers ... the internationally accepted concept of migration does not apply to them."[91]

However thinking that workers were coming into the GCC and then leaving was a delusion, as Noori Lori explained. "There is nothing more permanent than temporary foreign workers."[92] The rich ruling elites of these countries knew that people were not coming temporarily but instead were settling into the country and branding expatriates as the word "temporary" was simply a semantic manipulation to enhance their exploitation without taking responsibilities. "We asked for workers and we got people."[93]

Evidence has shown that about 15 percent of non-citizens in the UAE are children younger than 15, which suggests they were born in the UAE. Another focusing on the aging population showed that about 8 percent are over 60 years and have resided in the UAE for more than 30 years, which would account for most of their working lives. The group approaching retirement age would either have to go back to their countries, or find a new country that accepts them in old age, as they can no longer stay in the UAE where residency is appended to the conditions for an employment visa.[94]

Reality suggests otherwise, as many such as the old Somali man I mentioned earlier rather would stay in the country illegally in their old age and forgo medical care or other benefits that require one to have a residency visa.

Also employers prefer to limit worker turnover, so most workers stay. The employers always aim to minimize employee training costs but not even the GCC citizens are sure their governments' efforts to distance or keep away foreigners in their countries are working. Al Sharyani shared a cartoon that appeared in the *Al Ittihad* newspaper on January 19, 2002 illustrating the cynicism with which the citizens view the government's effort to stop immigration. It connects the expansion of high-rise buildings to the same government officials who claim to push hard for the country to close its borders to a certain class of expatriates while welcoming others. In the cartoon, the man on the right asks, "All these high rises – I wonder who is going to occupy them?" The other man, presumably a policy maker, assures him: "Don't worry. We'll import people to live in them."[95]

Despite all the fruits of economic progress foreign expatriates have brought to the UAE, one finds the integration of foreign communities into local communities not to be a worthy topic for discussion on any table. Most Emiratis still regard the foreigners as one of the 'problems' their country must overcome. The sentiment is shared not just on the street or among conservatives in the mass public but by even the most seemingly progressive liberals, pundits, and intellectuals.

One of those lamenting intellectuals was Ibrahim Ahmed Ibrahim Al Ali who two decades ago in his doctoral dissertation cited political threats behind the reluctance of Emiratis to integrate with foreigners.[96] He recounts numerous incidents in which immigrants have played crucial political roles in the Gulf's political future especially when they comprised the majority. Among them were Iranian immigrants of Kuwait demanding their rights in 1935. According to Al Ali, it started with the establishment of private schools and immigrants then moved on to demand representation in the league council. He also attributes the takeover by Iran of UAE's three islands, the greater and lesser *tunbs*, to the Emiratis' former mistake of integrating with foreigners. Iran announced the takeover in 1971, a few days before the unification of the UAE.

More than 20 years after Al Ali's thesis was published, this thinking has not evolved among Emiratis. And his thesis did not blame exclusively the Gulf Arabs for making the mistakes of integration with larger foreign communities who it was feared might take hold of power. He also cites the Singapore case on a global scale where Chinese immigrants managed to rule Singapore after becoming the majority and the original population becoming the minority.

For the UAE he argues that foreign laborers could be used as a political weapon against the host country, as threats of withdrawing the qualified labor pool could damage the country's economy. These threats are not unprecedented, as some countries threatened to pull the immigrant pool of domestic workers — maids, for example – to most of the GCC countries, but these threats were framed not as political but rather as social, resulting from the inhumane mistreatment of poor vulnerable workers.

Another fear for foreigners is that few officials in the GCC countries openly discuss the issue of intermarriage.

It is nearly as significant as in Western countries, with fears that foreigners would be taking their jobs. And this fear is not a monopoly of only men but it also is symmetrical, as the men fear for their women and the women who by cultural norms cannot marry outside of their upbringing also fear for their men.

An Ajman Radio talk show *Al Rabea Wa Nassi* is popular for receiving calls by mostly poor Emirati women and men first eulogizing the greatness of their rulers and then narrating their financial problems and urging any kind listeners to bail them out. Its popular presenter Abu Rashid listens to most complaints and sympathizes or promises the callers that if someone contacts the station, he or a staffer will ensure the offer is relayed to the caller. However, his sympathies do not lie with every caller, at least not for Emirati women in relationships with foreigners.

Whenever an Emirati woman calls with a problem related to foreign marriage, he will publicly chastise her. In one such incident, an Emirati woman who had a foreign Arabic husband called and as soon as she mentioned her marriage to the Iraqi man the host pounced upon her. He switched off the call and then criticized her, asking how many times people needed to learn not to get married to foreigners.[97]

When I was working on a follow-up story for *The National* about the Sharjah ruler offering equal pay to children of Emirati mothers born to foreign fathers,[98] I asked the source in human resources why more funds needed to be disbursed in these cases to children when the president Sheikh Khalifa already had declared them to be nationalized once they turned 18.[99] The source told me I didn't understand the politics surrounding the children of Emirati mothers and asked that I did not report what he was about to tell me. He said the government generally asked the embassies and consulates representing the fathers of these children to give them passports of their nationality instead of Emirati documents. He also told me that most foreigners who fathered children with Emirati women fled the country fearing reprisals from the woman's family. This left the woman with the children, almost as though they were orphans, and the state also went ahead and disowned them, not giving them any documents and denying them any chance to travel or go to school. They were similar to the bidoons or stateless citizens and even their maternal uncles could simply (and legally) discriminate against them.

Intermarriage is not the only reason why people fear foreigners, and does not of course downplay other reasons such as the fact that some Gulf nationals, as with their counterparts in Western countries, worry that they will jobs to foreigners. However, these are not serious threats, as Arabs in these countries are fully aware that foreigners and nationals do not perform identical jobs. Not even a single Emirati or Qatari can be found in jobs such as maids, construction labor, taxi driving, or cleaning, which are so widely occupied by foreigners. The only competition is found in white-collar jobs but still foreigners and Emiratis are not deemed as equally qualified for these positions. The education system struggles to train locals in specific fields that don't match their interests or skill levels. The Sharjah

Education Zone in June 2012 announced that it was launching a study to determine why there were no male Emirati teachers in schools.[100] Even fields such as nursing were still dominated by foreigners, despite several attempts by authorities to encourage more Emiratis to join the profession.[101]

Some local GCC scholars, however, have blamed foreign immigrants for fostering the climate of exclusion and non-integration. Ibrahim Ahmed says foreigners themselves segregate from the local population and prefer to live in their own enclaves of same nationalities. He gives as an example the Patan city in Al Ain with a population of 40,000 immigrants from the mountainous areas of Pakistan and Afghanistan who stay together as tribes. Each home displays a flag representing its tribe and each tribe has a leader available to consult during a crisis. The tribes often quarrel and street fights are common. One night in 1981 police raided the area closing all roads into and out of the city, and arrested the illegals staying in the city.[102]

Kuwait has taken a more radical step with its parliament submitting a proposal to reduce the number of expatriates in the country by more than 1.3 million in five years, starting from 2014.[103] Already the tiny GCC country leads in discrimination of foreigners with laws regulating the times foreigners can go to hospitals so as not to interfere with services being available to local citizens,[104] a law that would be deemed incomprehensible in any other part of the world. Foreigners are not permitted to visit public hospitals in the morning hours, in order to leave them available for local citizens who have complained repeatedly about overcrowding in these facilities.

Other laws permit foreigners to drive on public roads only if they hold a university degree, earn 400 dinars (US $1,386) a month and have lived in the country for at least two years.[105]

It would be understandable for the GCC countries to be forceful with foreign workers and deny them citizenship, but what's gravely troubling is how this mean-spirited nature extends to their own people. People born into the country, speaking the same language and dialect, of the same religion, same color and same culture are consistently denied citizenship and referred to as "bidoon" or stateless.

The bidoons are prominent in rich GCC homes, serving tea and coffee while dressed in Emirati attire. They also serve at key local functions performing local dances and other entertainment. A few are employed in police and municipality jobs, especially as those tasked with collecting parking fines. A Zayed University study found that average male Emiratis receive benefits in free education, health care and free land worth 204,000 dirhams (US $55,500) a year.[106] This is the single most frequently cited reason why GCC governments are reluctant to accept more people, even their own, as citizens.

But as the Arab spring began to sweep the region and governments were sensing pressure to be more accountable to their people, the best thing the GCC countries managed to do was to keep the number of those people they would have responsibility over low and manageable. The UAE had raised salaries by about 120 percent while freezing those of expatriates in an effort to demonstrate its responsibilities but this had to be controlled. No wonder several stateless individuals in the UAE had sought passports for Comoros Island, a country they had never been to, had no ties to and often could not even locate on a map.[107]

The stateless is only one word that can describe such heartless greed. Even the poor countries like my own Uganda accept their people while rich GCC countries worry that if they allow their people to have papers, the oil wealth will not be enough to distribute. It is like a big sister starving all her siblings while sitting with a big round plate of food, that she ironically will not even finish eating.

However, it is not only the foreigners who would benefit from a fair immigration system in the GCC states. The GCC citizens as well as their respective economies would do well to replace the abusive Kafala system with one that is fair and respects the principles of economic justice. For example, Dubai slipped into a financial crisis in 2008 (as did many countries around the world) and several companies abruptly canceled their workers' contracts and visas. Workers had only one option: leave the country.

There were also no end-of-service or contract benefits. The UAE labor law specifies some categories that protect companies from paying their workers end-of-service benefits, especially when a worker was dismissed by the employer for any reason, including misconduct. Companies leveraged these laws as they looked to dismiss their workers and that meant many of them received nothing in severance when they were fired. Of course, the deepening recession left these workers without a lifeline and they became the immediate and first victims of a devastating economic event.

Workers ended up being stuck on all sides, as they had to leave the country and they had nothing to take home. Anybody who has ever worked abroad can only imagine such a dire situation. At the same time if they opted to stay in the UAE to look for other jobs, their employing companies or sponsors had already cancelled their visas. The laws unfortunately do not accommodate the privilege for one to find a new sponsor while still in the country.

And hiring was almost at a nil during the recession which affected every industry. The response among middle-class workers and unskilled construction workers differed. Most middle-grade workers chose to simply flee the country by abandoning their bank loan cars at the airport, as several reports told. *The National* newspaper in Abu Dhabi, the only local paper bold enough to then expose the problems of Dubai, put the number of cars being abandoned at airports in the thousands.[108] Banks recovered and repossessed the cars and then went to monthly auctions at the Al Aweer motor market under the supervision of the public prosecution and Ministry of Economy to help recover the outstanding balance of the loan.[109] Unfortunately, the sole option for low-skilled and unskilled workers was to risk becoming illegal residents.

Things would have been different if the UAE had fair labor and immigration laws, instead of the abusive system that Kafala had evolved into as the country's economy expanded. It was not helping the economy at all for the expatriates to leave the country in the crisis as their visas expired and their sponsoring employers could no longer afford to keep them. As more left the country, more houses became empty and the real-estate market that had been a major source of Dubai's growth collapsed.

2.4 Possession and Control of Passports

Passports are and should be honored as representing an individual's natural rights. Governments in the GCC have claimed the practice of local sponsors withholding expatriate passports is illegal and all those doing it are guilty. The UAE court of first cassation once issued a ruling that banned such a practice. The ruling, quoted and highlighted by Human Rights Watch, indicated: "It is not permitted for any employer to confiscate the passport of an employee and prevent him from his natural right to travel and move whatever the nature of the relationship that ties them together."[110]

The ruling came in 2001 and in the following year (2002), the UAE Ministry of Interior issued a decree that banned passport confiscation by employees or sponsors. The country was immediately praised by all local media (as usual) for implementing the decision to ban acts that the International Labor Organization had long considered bad practice. However, all of the media reports missed that actually the previous practice was allowed to continue unabated in the country with no willingness among the authorities to crackdown on violators so long as they were companies owned by Emiratis.

And if one had a word with an Emirati or Saudi about why he insisted on keeping a person's passport, the response would still be: "It is our country; you can go back to your country if you don't like it." With that, the person can claim the passport is kept by consent not coercion, as the sponsored employee has an option of going back to his country and keeping his passport. What these free-thinking people have not realized is how they are violating their own laws – the laws of the country they claim to love with full heart and devotion. The laws in each Gulf Arab country which state a passport is the legal property of the beholder, and that it should remain in the person's rightful hands and it should never be confiscated by anyone.

These laws were made by them and they own them like their own children, but they change them to suit their own ego for subjugation. These laws also are made for the international community, and for the purposes of placating advocacy groups such as Human Rights Watch (HRW); they are made to earn a good reputation for the country, not to account for workers' rights, and certainly not for the benefit of the foreign workforce. The laws are paper tigers. It is not worthwhile for the authorities spending the country's vast wealth to implement laws protecting foreigners from locals, as the country belongs to the Emiratis and only Emiratis are worthy of protection.

Authorities will always claim the immigration sponsorship system is illegal and an employee has a right to ask for his passport back. Okay, but if he asks for it and it's not returned accordingly, what avenues are guaranteed to provide relief to the employee? Report the incident to police or open up a legal case in court? We are talking about workers earning less than 1,000 dirhams (US $280) and the question is who amongst them can foot legal expenses ten times their monthly expenses just to regain a passport. A government that leaves workers in any country to rely almost solely upon opening up legal cases as the road to relief is hardly satisfactory solace. Even for white-collar employees (such as myself), when I worked at *The Gulf Today* our passports were retained by our employer and we did not see any personal security being preserved in opening a court case to retrieve our passports. It was not because we believed that supervisory colleagues were mean-spirited or petty but to pay a lawyer for the purposes of igniting a potential conflict with one's employer is something that would only be feasible if the employee already has lined up work elsewhere. There is no evidence whatsoever even among the advocates of taking the case to court authorities that an employee anywhere has successfully reported the case to court, regained the passport and stayed at work. There is a wide gap between the rules and actual practices in the GCC countries. And even with numerous reports of rules violations and abuses, the authorities do not realize (or deliberately ignore) that having a set of rules on paper is nothing if these rules cannot be implemented as they were intended.

In two research surveys cited by Amnesty International in Qatar, the results showed most workers in the country had their passports confiscated by their sponsors/employers. In one study conducted in 2012 by Qatar University's Social and Economic Survey Research Institute, of 721 migrant workers surveyed only 11 percent had possession of their passports. In other research by the Qatar National Research Fund in the same year, 90 per cent of 1,189 surveyed workers reported having their passports confiscated by their sponsors.

The withholding of passports is also used by sponsors to blackmail workers, reminding them forcefully not to ask for redress of their rights, and this tactic is most popular in cases of nonpayment. In some cases sponsors exchange the passport for a declaration that the worker has received all wages due, prior to changing employment or exiting the country.[111]

There also have been reports of employers who confiscated their workers' passports abusing such privilege of authority.

Employers, especially in the difficult economic times that swept Dubai during the Great Recession, often sold their workers to other sponsors or companies without even the affected employee's knowledge. The transaction was easy, as an employer who was holding the passport would cancel the visa and let the new sponsor make another visa. Once the deal was done the worker would be notified of the change in sponsor and employment. "While formally illegal, it is clear that a trade in passports has emerged in the Gulf, which allows employers to sell their employees' labor services to another company," John Willoughby wrote in a 2005 paper entitled "Ambivalent Anxieties of the South Asian-Gulf Arab Labor Exchange." He adds, "This arbitrary tying of a worker to an employer not of her choosing leaves him or her with little recourse. For many the only realistic fall-back position is a return to an impoverished home country with even poorer job prospects."

After I resigned from *The Gulf Today* the human resources director instructed me to give my flight ticket details to the department so that my passport would be handed back to me at the airport check-in time. *The Gulf Today* owner, like other Emirati employers, kept our passports and only gave them to us if we went on an approved vacation or holiday and the employee who failed to return the passport to his employer a day after the holiday could face a stiff financial penalty that would accrue for each additional day past the time when the passport was to be returned to the sponsor. The government had on several occasions distanced itself from employers keeping employee passports, stating that it classified the act as an illegal practice but it also surprised me how powerful employers, especially those well connected with the government, often turned a deaf ear to their respective country's legislation. Rare was it to hear from a government official criticizing the practice of confiscated passports only to be released as necessary for pre-approved travel. We lived and worked in their country at their pleasure and they owned the right to throw us out any time, even if applied capriciously or arbitrarily.

The driver who brought my passport to the Sharjah International Airport instructed me to be at the airport two hours before my check-in just because he also was scheduled to deliver a passport to another employee who was flying out of Dubai International Airport at almost the same time. The human resources office driver maintained a busy schedule with this practice, and I was somewhat sympathetic to his schedule demands so I arrived on time.

I had few queries at the time on why we were being treated that way or questions about how my resignation almost meant my deportation. Only in deportation cases would one receive his or her passport at the airport. I was just excited about a new job in Bahrain that offered a few thousand dirhams more than my *Gulf Today* position. A year later, when I returned to Dubai, I boarded another flight to Entebbe through Addis Ababa and an Ethiopian maid was sobbing and being pulled by her employer to sign her out through airport immigration. It was not a deportation or due to any kind of misconduct on her behalf, as she told us in our departure waiting room. She had just been in the country for three months and the employer's wife despised her to the extent that she instructed the husband to cancel her visa and return her to Ethiopia and cancel all her three months' salary, and she had just been told that she would have to purchase the airfare with her own money, which she did not have. She had nothing and was poorer than when she came, and no one was waiting to pick her at the airport because her family had been mobilized and sold most of their possessions in order for her to go to Dubai; they were not expecting her. One Ugandan woman who heard the story cursed the Arabs for their callous discrimination and gave the maid 500 dirhams (US $135). Two others joined us to help round out the contributions of money.

The Ajman free zone was among the major companies that

betrayed their use of the free zone and chained their workers with passport confiscations. As I sat in the office of one of my friends who worked for a foreign company that had offices in the free zone, he recalled numerous stories of similarly abrupt betrayal.[112] Fred [a pseudonym] told me they were obligated to keep their passports with the free-zone authority and monetary fines of 100 dirhams could be assessed for each month the passport was missing. They could allow only a month of vacation time and any other extra time off would be punished with these fines. Only the investors or owners of the companies were saved from this rule of handing over passports to the authorities.

At the time, Fred worked for another company's station in another country and had to return every six months in order for his visa not to be cancelled because he would have been treated as a sponsored worker who had gone AWOL for six months. Whenever Fred returned to refresh his visa eligibility he also had to deposit his passport to the authorities for about a week and pay the fines. His office agreed to pay these fines but it still troubled him why such a major government authority that referred to itself as a free zone openly chained the employees of their investors and openly violated the country's passport confiscation laws. And it was not only this policy of passport confiscation that disturbed Fred, as he mentioned that the free zone acted as their local sponsor and had to charge them for everything a sponsor in another free zone was asked to do on behalf of an employee. They would charge them for a letter to open up a bank account, a letter to get a driving license, a salary certificate letter and everything that people in ordinary companies would normally be able to obtain for free from their sponsors. All of these routine miscellaneous items were charged to the worker by the free-zone authority.

There also have been reports of local government authorities that are tasked with implementing these rulings of not confiscating worker passports but actually see no problem in appearing as officially supportive of the illegal practice. A Human Rights Watch (HRW) report quoted Lt. Col Rashid Bakhit Al Jumairi, the assistant director of follow-up and investigation at the Dubai Naturalisation and Residency Administration, who said, "they [the employers] should not hold passports ... [b]ut sometimes workers lose their passports so the safest place to keep it is at the company's offices." Another government official, also quoted by HRW, was Major Aref Mohammed Baqer, who justified the practice as customary for business culture and as a requirement for the employers to prevent workers "from stealing money or trade secrets and information from the company."[113]

If the people deputized to enforce the rules find loopholes in the law and instead of amending them promptly simply encourage the breaking of the law, then, of course, one is going to expect the situation to be disturbing. And why would employers in the UAE, Saudi Arabia and Qatar insist on keeping their employees' passports? Certainly, it is not about preventing employees stealing the company's money as the Dubai senior police officials have alleged earlier and it is not even about identifying employees, as originals of these passports could be copied and maintained in secure data repositories for identification, as needed. Such tiresome methods of keeping large volumes of passport books would be an outdated means given modern-day technology.

However, the Emiratis and Saudis have another reason for keeping their employees' passports – to control their lives from every movement to every job transfer. They are accustomed to controlling anything not Saudi or Emirati that happens to be on Saudi land. They would control human beings by tying them to a single job with no alternatives not unlike the herder who has tied his goat to a tree to eat in one place. That the employer should know each and every reason someone wants to go outside the country. That the sponsor should know the whereabouts of his worker at all times the same way a slave master knew the whereabouts of his slaves in older times.

And despite all the government rhetoric of the practice being illegal, there are still no known prosecutions of their citizens who have withheld passports from the poor workers.

There was one time when a young Ugandan woman working for a local petrol station called to ask me how to replace her lost passport. She told me the human resources department that was supposed to keep all employee passports had lost hers and the staff wanted her to take up the process for obtaining a replacement. This was just one repercussion of confiscating passports that was widely accepted even by major corporations such as her employer. As I advised her to contact the embassy in Abu Dhabi, she explained that she considered suing the company for mishandling her passport since it was technically illegal for her employer to withhold passports.

I laughed at the suggestion but she was serious and it was here that she told me she was actually a lawyer having studied at Makerere University in Uganda. She apparently had told the Filipino human resources office that she was suing the company. The staff member was afraid upon hearing the threat of civil action, as she knew a lawyer must know her rights even when she has worked as a sales assistant. "Okay, this is what I think," I told her. "Your Filipino HR lost your passport and she is afraid of her bosses but not your legal knowledge or case. She is a worker like you and since she is your senior, be careful because she may take her revenge once all this passport crisis is over."

2.5 Exit Stamps

Unlike during times of slavery when the victims were dragged to foreign lands in chains, today most immigrants going to the GCC countries are doing so because of free will, even with the few exceptions of those being recruited through deception and false promises. The road going to the GCC region is full of thorns, as many must sell all their property in their homelands and suffer through ordeals fraught with risks of being cheated. As difficult as it is to enter Doha or Dubai, getting out is always much harder. One of the funny things about the Kafala system is the requirement of an "entry visa" for any worker coming into the country and an "exit visa" for any worker leaving the country, as both items come from the local citizen sponsor or employer, of course. The exit visa is a requirement in Saudi Arabia, Kuwait and Qatar.

In Qatar, workers as well as professionals have been trapped in the country because their sponsors would not permit them to leave the country or approve an exit visa. Among the victims of this exit stamp policy was French footballer Zahir Belounis who was trapped in Qatar for two years as his football club Al Jaish refused to sign his exit visa unless he dropped a claim against the club for two years of unpaid wages. Belounis' two daughters were also trapped with their mother in the country, and the athlete threatened hunger strike at times when human rights activist were demanding that FIFA cancel Qatar's 2022 World Cup bid, as the country did not respect human rights.

Another footballer Abdelsalam Ouaddou, playing for Qatar Stars League, also came into conflict with his football club and had barely received his exit stamp after threatening to report authorities to international human rights activists .

Nasser Beydoun, a former CEO of the Wataniya Restaurants group who was also once trapped and struggled to get an exit visa, summed it up best: "You cannot leave without your sponsor's OK. You can't rent a house. You can't open a checking account. You can't get a driver's license. ... and if you get into a legal issue with them, they have the home field advantage."

Amnesty International also documented several cases of construction workers stranded in Qatar even after they resigned from their positions in the required manner but the Qatari sponsors/employers did not return the employee passports or even issue the required exit visa/stamp. "The employers' power to restrict workers' freedom of movement has a profound psychological effect on workers, who throughout their working career in Qatar are always aware that their employers have the ability to prevent them from going home," the organization's report noted.

The researchers also interviewed employers who restricted workers' rights regarding a return to their home country, finding that the reasons were best described as exploitative and economically based. Some employers prevented workers from leaving Qatar because their companies had fallen into financial problems and wanted these workers to stay and work on new projects and raise new capital. Other companies had been blacklisted by the Ministries of Labor and Interior for violating labor laws so they could not recruit new workers and they sought to stop the existing workers from leaving the company, thanks to the power entrusted to them by their government of having the final word about whether a worker leaves or stays in the country.

Authorities in Qatar also seem to realize the true impact in the bondage of exit stamps. Sheikh Hamad bin Jassim Al Thani, the former prime minister, is reported to have remarked in 2007, "It is difficult to retain the exit permit system in its existing form … It is being likened to slavery. It can't remain like this."

Qatar has endured significant pains to promise repeatedly its intent to reform the Kafala system because of the criticism that has come with winning the bid to host the World Cup. Unfortunately, several years after winning the bid these reformations remain merely insincere words spoken by Qatar's leaders on international television.[114] The Qatar media have carried a few articles about what will change indicating that expatriates likely will be allowed to change a sponsor after serving their original sponsor for five years. It is disturbing that leaders cannot acknowledge that the system needs to be scrapped immediately, not reformed in dubious increments stretched out over long periods. How could one realistically expect someone to whom an immigrant has been enslaved for five years to be willing to allow that individual to change jobs?

I had my own troubles with the exit permit when I applied for two weeks' unpaid leave at the newspaper I worked for in Doha. It was supposed to be unpaid because paid leave is approved only for those who have been at work for six months and an airline ticket is allotted for those at work for nine months, according to company policies. The purpose for the leave was to renew my passport which was due to expire in a few days. I also anticipated the leave to break the enormous boredom and stress that was burdening me in Doha and I needed the chance to recharge my batteries. The approval process was slow, with my managers insistently querying why I was going home after a few months, but it was mostly the exit permit that represented the true test in the matter. The exit permit would be valid for only seven days and therefore it is advised the application be made within three to five days of the scheduled departure. I followed the advice putting in my application on Thursday but the human resources coordinator said the system, for some reason, would not accept my application, so we tried four days later (Sunday) yet the system still would not accept it. Two days later, there still was no progress and I was scheduled to leave that evening. Despite the pressure, I had to remain calm, knowing the delay was not the fault of the human resources coordinator and was likely a technical or software glitch in the system. Likewise, he also was classified as an employee who would have to go through the same process to obtain an exit permit. Abruptly, he discovered the reason why the permit was being denied, the company's online permit system privileges had expired and required renewal from the Ministry of Interior. It was around midday when my colleague went to the Ministry to renew the permit, and four hours later my exit permit had been approved.

Exit permits made for many anecdotes. A roommate, who worked for Qatar Airways, needed an expedited permit so he could fly home to attend arrangements for his mother who had died suddenly on a Thursday, the last day of the work week. No permits would be issued on the weekend (Friday and Saturday) and I stayed with him on that Friday as he watched his mother's funeral on a free Internet call service (Viber) that was coordinated via a phone connection with his sister back home. I listened to the services and to the eulogies in which each speaker expressed concern and dismay that the eldest son had been trapped in Qatar, a Muslim country that knew the Islamic practices for immediate burials. My friend, at least, was able to participate even at this long distance. There were six of us who witnessed this virtual funeral being broadcast from Uganda. I knew the pain my friend endured by not being able to lay his own mother in her grave – a pain no Muslim son would wish to undergo. I had laid my mother into her grave with my own hands, realizing properly the satisfaction and acceptance of death I had received from this act. Because of an unfair, inconvenient bureaucratic process, my friend would never be able to find comparable solace or reconciliation. He finally obtained the exit permit on Sunday, the first day of the new week, and went back to Uganda the following day for his duties as a family mourner.

The exit permit represents one of the most painful legislations in Qatar that needs reform, but like all other Kafala-related sanctions, the country's promises of removing this legislation have remained in thin air. In February, when the Qatar emir announced that he had implemented pay reforms, mandating all firms to pay their workers' salaries in banknotes, a major Malayalam TV channel in the country broadcasted the news as ending the restrictive exit permit and Kafala systems. The community rejoiced briefly only to learn that the most oppressive practices were still intact.[115] The Qatari rulers were eager to show off prominently as making significant labor reforms that would silence especially the most vocal critics of Qatar's World Cup bid. Unfortunately, the effort was symbolic and non-serious, as Amnesty International once again criticized the emirate for dragging its feet on reforms.[116]

2.6 The Delayed, Low or No Pay Jobs

In almost every labor strike that I have covered in Dubai, Sharjah and Ajman during the decade of my work as a reporter in the UAE, the event was related to either low wages or no payments at all. From the taxi driver strikes in Sharjah to worker protests and sit-downs in Dubai, there were stories of heartless rich people subjugating workers without even paying for their sweat in this economically fertile region. There was plenty of evidence that small companies working on minor projects regularly fled the country without paying the workers, especially during the financial crisis years of 2009 to 2011. There had also been many large strikes in which companies delivering on the Emirates' best-known icons, such as the Burj Khalifa, went on strike for low pay.

One such incident occurred on March 21, 2006, when almost 2,500 workers on the world's tallest tower Burj Khalifa (Burj Dubai then) rioted, protesting their low pay of 28 dirhams (US $7) a day and the poor working conditions. On May 16, 2006, another 8,000 workers of the Besix Company also laid down their tools, demanding an increase to about $163 a month from the $106 they were being paid.

The wages workers are supposed to get from their GCC employers are persistently too low to allow decent living conditions but many still considered their low pay a modest blessing. The sponsoring employers have no reservations about retrieving profits off the workers' sweat, or to drive the latest 4x4s and have the older models parked on their spacious multi-storeyed villas they call homes. They believe that workers at construction sites or in their homes do not count as human beings whose demands merit satisfaction; that they are entitled to a very few dirhams, just barely enough to buy some food and eat but still only when the sponsor wishes to pay. Paying the workers their full due is not deemed as a worker's right.

There also are indications that GCC citizens routinely exploit worker ignorance of the law by not paying them or by paying them just half of their wages. Complaining could lead to conspiratorial action by the sponsor, resulting in the worker being deported or imprisoned upon fabricated charges. The domestic workers, with their little knowledge of any legal recourse to recover their salaries, suffer the most. One day I was reporting in Sharjah court and an Indonesian maid had appeared with her boss on a case of non-payment of six months' salary. After the case hearing I happened to see the local Emirati employer entering his Land Cruiser a few vehicle away from mine in the parking lot. I rushed over to talk to him, first by complimenting him on the beauty of his car and then asking him how with that gift from God he could fail to pay a maid her meager due of 600 dirhams (US $180). He first recited verses from the holy Quran and then swore with God's name about how they treated the maid well like a sister giving her food and whatever she wanted. There was no mention about her salary even after I had reminded him three times about his obligations to make good on the previously agreed rate.

In their focus on migration in Qatar, Amnesty International researchers witnessed eleven men signing papers in front of government officials, falsely attesting they had received their wages in order to get their passports and leave Qatar. "It should go without saying that no worker should be asked to sign away their rights to unpaid salaries and other benefits in order to merely leave the country," the report indicated.

In correspondence with the victims of non-paid employees for Kraft Engineering, Amnesty International excerpted a worker's email as representative of the problem: "[b]ut they have taken my signature for all pending salary slips and two blank letterheads. Without paying a single penny. These people are totally crazy, they don't have human quality to understand the people situation they torture beyond limits…"

In one of the Islamic prophecies, it is said that a worker should be paid before the sweat of his work even dries. It is saddening given the wealth of GCC countries to see some workers who helped build these magnificent structures scavenging for food through charity or begging. And the police are always busy arresting the beggars but if someone is not paid how does one logically believe they are going to sustain themselves? In poor countries like Uganda it is different because those people who do not have food or other basic items have no jobs and have not worked for anything. In the GCC region, however, there are plenty of jobs and people work at exhaustive levels but still receive little or no pay. The incredibly rich owners of these projects have no moral qualms about sucking out the blood of poor workers in order to become richer, or to have the tallest and largest complexes, all for the purposes of fulfilling their egos with the pride of being number one in the world. They do not realize once they cheat one worker, it is like cheating dozens of others who rely upon that particular employee for their well-being and for whom he has taken on the enormously momentous decision to come and work in a foreign land.

The no-pay cases as well exert tremendous pressure upon GCC workers with some ending tragically in suicides. Some continue to repay the loans they incurred in the recruitment process which allowed them to come to the GCC region, and the banks definitely do not hesitate to confiscate whatever land or collateral property they had put up as security. Others still pay rent to their houses, and their families are always at the brink of being evicted for non-payment and the other usual basics which include school fees for their children.

The race for unparalleled excellence in Dubai and its sister emirates has exacted an irrecoverable cost affecting the most vulnerable. In most instances the local investors do not establish initially where construction project funds will be coming from even as they rush to bring workers onto the site. There is no consideration of what should be done if the project stalls out because of financial troubles and workers are left unexpectedly without even the slightest safety net.

The predicament is not eased because of rife discrimination in the region, for despite reports of the shortages of funds to pay worker salaries, one readily finds that most of these same projects did not report shortages in construction materials as much as they did on worker salaries. Not paying workers is never considered a violation or an unjust act. So when the workers deliver the tallest buildings in the world, they are destined to live in poverty and deprivation, never having the chance to recoup even a modicum of wage fairness, much less pay equality.

Sometimes the situation arises because of higher expectations of returns from investments the rich GCC companies undertake with substantial risks that tempt them to cheat workers on salaries or benefits such as airfares. If their return on investment begins to lag, the first order is to delay worker salaries for a month, and then another before it accumulates to a level where the chance of reconciliation becomes hopeless. Taking advantage of a legal system that allows them the discretion of impunity; few employers hesitate before throwing workers out of the country without paying them.

Also, most employers would withhold one and a half or two months' wages as "security" to prevent workers from running away to better jobs. This custom is normal and whenever workers complain of withheld wages, the affected amount has already accrued to six months' salary.

Sometimes it was not the employers who perpetuated abuses related to salary discriminations but employees assigned to supervisory positions. There is a pervasive sense of insecurity in the GCC region that anyone working today is not assured of being at work the next day. This insecurity engenders Darwinian struggles for survival. Employers allocate a budget for every department, leaving it to the unit head to divide the funds accordingly to work groups. Employees in decision-making positions – such as editors at newspapers – see no qualms in rewarding themselves with fat salary contracts, taking their share first and leaving the small leftovers to be divided among others on a basis dictated by favoritism, not merit.

2.7 Taking Much More Than They Are Giving Out

Most research on exploitation in the GCC countries has centered on the defaults and low pay of construction workers and other unskilled laborers. However, in a system developed and bred in exploitation like Kafala, such practices are manifested even among skilled and professional workers.

I did occasional freelance assignments in the UAE that were never paid. Going freelance is always a hard, risky choice but as the cost of living has increased and responsibilities have multiplied and the newspaper freezes the salaries of expatriates, the only alternative is to find extra work. Mostly, I translated content from Arabic to English for three public relations firms and a magazine. They all had the same routine: first two or three assignments would be paid, a fourth paid in half and then they would default on the others until one quit in desperation. Then one Emirati colleague in office linked me to a friend who wanted me to help him with his MBA thesis research. The friend told me his lecturer had expected him to find someone to help with the research, as he was busy with works for His Highness, a title intended for all royal family members in the UAE. Whenever I brought up the question of how much he was offering he would tell me, "Money, no problem; you just do the work very good and you will be surprised what I will give you."

I checked with the office colleague and he assured me the client was a rich man working for His Highness, so there was no reason to worry. When the research was completed and his lecturer accepted it to be bound, he asked me for a good typing center where we could bind the work. I waited two hours for him at the center where I had bounded my research two years earlier, and I hesitated to pay from my pocket for the binding. We talked by phone and he agreed that he would reimburse the cost of binding when we met that evening. That was the last time I saw or heard from him. My phone calls also went unanswered the same way conmen do after taking their bait's money.

My office colleague also told me he was shocked that the man could get away with that. I again found another Emirati man who was writing profiles of the UAE's best companies and needed a freelance writer and researcher. When he showed me a sample of a previous edition he had published, the work was promising but still he did not want to discuss money. "It will not be so big, but I will give you something handsome," he would say, eager to dismiss my reservations. Every week we wrote about eight companies, researching them on the Internet, and he would also send along some information given by the companies that paid him to be listed. After a month we had finished nearly thirty companies and he still gave no hint about paying. I quit after that. It was so hard to understand why they all wanted people to work for them for free, even when they were going to be paid for by a client.

Exploitative games with salaries and benefits prevailed just as broadly with professional employees at perfectly legal workplaces as they did with unskilled laborers and domestic workers. In professional jobs the companies would cheat their workers on airfare or other benefits. Most companies would never give a pay rise to their staff even when the cost of living skyrocketed. In late 2013, when I worked at *The National*, rumors were rife of a pay increase. My colleagues at *Al Ittihad* newspaper, the Arabic language publication which with *The National* belonged to Abu Dhabi Media, claimed they had concrete evidence about new contracts being prepared for signatures and they would carry increments. For *Al Ittihad* staff members this would be their second signing of a new contract in less than three years, and since the last time they signed the contracts they had a pay rise, it would be understandable if they accepted the rumors as verifiable. Then an email arrived from *The National*'s executive editor, a Canadian woman, calling for reporters to collect their new contracts to be signed. The correspondence opened with a statement that there would be no salary changes. I passed it along to my *Al Ittihad* colleagues with whom I shared office space and I translated for those who did not read English. The response was mixed, as some thought *The National*, an English-language newspaper that had failed to earn profit in any given period, deserved not to have increments, but some reporters also were skeptical whether their (*Al Ittihad*) contracts specified the same terms. Most called the human resources office to verify, as they were anxious about not having a raise for three years, or five years in the case of *The National*. After the calls, a colleague said the Emiratis were getting increases but the expatriates were not, a statement that further infuriated the other Arab reporters who genuinely did most of the work for their lazy Emirati colleagues.

However, it was not only the news about no salary increments that disturbed the staff, but the fact that the new contracts had reduced previous benefits by excising annual air tickets, recreation fees and furniture allowances. The contract stipulated that instead of giving these allowances in one lump sum as previously, they would be paid on a pro-rata basis each month. One photographer in the office said, "This means I am now supposed to save for my family's air tickets instead of collecting it in kind or at once as we used to do. It's going to be tough."

There was no clear explanation for this, as with most policies, so we all kept on speculating about a giant company trying to save on staffing costs by paying our air tickets or recreation allowances in installments, which junior staff members never had nor had ever known their existence. The next day we received another email announcing that the CEO from another Arab country, who had been here for only seven months, had resigned and the chief operating officer was now the acting CEO. In three years the company had seen three CEOs, each introducing new rules aimed at cost savings and preserving what surely was a lucrative position. Surely the GCC Arabs treated these CEOs as cheap disposables, as they did with the unskilled laborers. This is why CEOs who did not have job security often paid themselves huge sums of money to compensate themselves before a layoff they inevitable knew was coming. There was one CEO who had managed to infuriate even the Emiratis in the office after they learned about the size of his monthly salary from internal sources.

My Emirati neighbor who told me the news was especially annoyed. He complained ceaselessly about how someone could take all that money simply because, as he put it, he "was British." I didn't understand his problem, mainly because he also was getting at least double what I was, simply for the reason he was Emirati and this fact he knew was not justifiable. However, once he mentioned the CEO's salary figure, my head was spinning. "It is 80 times my monthly salary," I said. If I had all along begrudged those who served in the same role as me and did less work but received double my salary because they were from a finer country than mine, I didn't know what to do with this particular CEO. I understood that his role – monitoring all departments to ensure an acceptable level of profits while at the same time protecting the UAE's intricately cultivated image and its rulers – was admittedly a more demanding task than just running up for stories in different emirates, but still I thought that was, well, a lot of money. Finally, I told my neighbor, "Thank God he is gone, and hopefully we shall all get a pay rise with the new CEO." Of course, it didn't happen. This worsened with salary discrimination once one considered how it varied on a country-to-country basis, but we were all losers, and there certainly were no winners. The Emiratis frowned at the British who came into their country and received several times more than them. Other Arabs, such as Egyptians and Syrians, frowned at Emiratis, Asians did likewise with Indians, Filipinos shared similar sentiments against Arabs, and Africans carried these perceptions against all of the groups.

Returning to the story about office salary increments, my colleagues called the Abu Dhabi office to find out who was getting a pay rise and who was not after years of waiting. One Emirati female reporter broke the news as soon as she learned what was intended. Emiratis were getting a 100 percent increase and all the expatriates were getting nothing. There were no usual exchanges of *mabrooks* – or, congratulations – as is always the custom when one or a group of colleagues achieves something. This time the whole office just went silent. Things had been uncomfortably sensitized, as it always seems when one group is being favored over another by those with power. The Emiratis soon left the office, well before their usual 3 p.m. checkout, and the only ones remaining were us expatriates. The air lightened up considerably and an Egyptian resumed the conversation, asking, "Why are you all still here working and working when those getting pay rises have all left. Can't you understand that the logic to pay rises is becoming Emiratis not working hard?" As our laughter mixed with our anger, another colleague replied, "That's why they are denying thousands of their people passports and calling them *bidoons* (stateless); they want to have a small group of Emiratis to give benefits to like pay rises."

These increments were merely facades to underscore the fact that the ruling class cared exclusively for citizens of the same national birthright. Emiratis knew this well, as their rulers favored British and American expatriates with huge salaries compared to theirs for many years. The delusion was also obvious, even with this huge increment, as Emiratis, especially in managerial positions, would still be paid less than British expatriates serving in the same role. These confusing offers of care are always a tested and failed ploy of all dictators on fire for taking more than their share from citizens. Libyan dictator Muammar Gadhafi tried it earlier when he offered massive cash handouts to all citizens before the revolution led to his removal and death. GCC countries including the UAE loathed Gadhafi and even participated in his overthrow, but this did not stop them from taking lessons from his failed policies of trying to bribe the citizens into keeping the status quo.

The Arab expatriates, my colleagues, sympathized with me. When I first came to their office they all thought I was overpaid and wanted to know my salary. They had heard many reports about their company being especially generous with the English-language newspaper and giving its British staff substantial salaries. When I told them my take they were shocked, and nonetheless the reports they heard were true and they all understood mine was the exception. They often asked sympathetically how I managed to live with a family on that salary. And now with the salary freeze for expatriates they said their plight seemed to be at least better than mine. One recommended that I confront the editor. "Those British editors only listen to strong language, Yasin. You should be like an African and talk to them emphatically. Tell them you just want to be treated and paid like everyone else in your role."

The new contracts were coming at the time when my first book, *The Ambitious Struggle*, was rolling out and some colleagues had already read either its introduction or the whole book. Many mentioned how impressed they were with a bold book that could (and did) cost me my job. With a photographer on assignment, I found an injured laborer walking with a plastered leg, and we chatted for a few minutes about how his injury happened and how he was recuperating. The photographer was getting ready to snap shots of the worker and I interrupted, indicating that I would not be filing a story and that we would not show his image. The photographer asked if I was taking notes for *The Ambitious Struggle II*, adding jokingly that the company then would have a good excuse to let me go without another contract. So when I asked the HR woman for my contract, she said that it had slipped her mind and that I would have to wait for a few months to process my contract. I was divided into wondering whether it was because of my being "insignificant" to the company's expenses because they were trying to cut expatriates' expenses to boost the pay for Emiratis. However, she added that in the interim I still would have to abide by the new policy rules in the new contract that I had not yet received or signed. What bothered me most in the new contract was the stripping away of the airfare benefit. My family was yet to return to Uganda at the end of January and was planning to make use of the office-provided airfares. This was important because the family wanted to stay for two months during the children's holiday and the office airfare had been helpful to facilitate this remaining contact, especially amid the tight budget I had been working on with the recent spate of inflationary spirals in the cost of living.

When I called the HR rep to ask for at least a one-way ticket to return my family home for good, she responded with the tone of a saleswoman handling family visa cancellations. "We shall give them an additional 20 kilograms on their one-way return tickets if you cancel their visas." It was quite painful to cancel the visa, not because of the several journeys I had to make to Abu Dhabi to fulfill the office and immigration bureaucracies of canceling, but also because my wife was openly against it. She thought I was just trying to get rid of my family and find another woman, and every day and night we had long debates about this.

Then once the visa was cancelled and I gave everything to the HR woman, the same one replied that a senior had told her they could not give me the family tickets as it was against the company's new policy. She advised I could pay the tickets myself and claim a refund once I was leaving the company. I remember forwarding it to my cluster editor first and writing things that could only be said in severe distress. That after six years of my working at *The National* my salary remained the lowest of all the staff with whom I had served in the same category. Even the fresh graduates who had joined the company would still get several thousand higher than me. And when they take away these benefits they expect me to afford the same things others afford with their good pay. I told him that I felt deeply discriminated against and equally as disappointed. This was as strongly worded an email as I had ever written and though the cluster editor was the only superior with whom I had forged a close relationship, I could not think (nor expect) he would keep it confidential and I didn't care whomever he shared it with in the office. He replied in a few minutes saying everything was messed up but he would try to talk to the local editor and reconcile the matter, adding that he could not promise anything. In the end, I lost and had to be forced to take an advance loan and return my family home. And when I was fired three months later, the HR administrator again broke the promise to refund my previously paid family airline tickets. After I queried her, the Canadian executive editor responded that, indeed, she had guaranteed me a refund on exit but she also said the company's policy had changed since then, as they no longer would cash in any refunds.

A female Arab colleague once told me there were only two ways of getting pay rises at the office: a promotion or a strong recommendation from the local supervisor. It was also too simplistic to think that Emiratis were being favored with the 100 percent increments and would be happy to celebrate while their expatriate colleagues despaired. The most intellectually curious individuals would still question the timing of the selective increments when governments of other Arab countries were collapsing amid the anger of their citizens.

Another Emirati colleague in *Al Ittihad* office told me he had worked with the company for 15 years and had always been paid "peanuts." That foreigners from Syria and Egyptians always led the editorials and favored only journalists from their countries, and they gave them promotions and increments while he simply looked on patiently. Unlike my Emirati neighbor who blamed the low salaries on the British CEOs taking all the money, this second Emirati colleague frowned at fellow Arabs from other Arab countries who comprised most of the paper's editorial team. He said that coming from an inferior emirate also always worked against him; that even though Emiratis from Dubai and Abu Dhabi could be highly respected in the paper's editorials, those from other emirates had never been considered equals. And, now this increment was coming in big bundles for the benefit of Emiratis from the most powerful emirates as well as those from smaller ones as if to compensate for all the years he had been exploited. Their wealthy governments had all along had the potential, thanks to the country's oil resources, to pay them as much as they were now increasing salaries. The question was why did this not happen sooner. So if more governments would fall or face the risk of being removed via popular revolt they would assuage the angry by raising their wages to two, three or four times their original levels. The ruling family elites still would not feel the economic impact of such large-scale wage increases, as their wealth is unquestionably enormous. The real sting comes in cheating on the benefits and salaries of expatriates in order to increase those for Emiratis. This was perfecting the method of taking from the vulnerable. Taking from the expatriates could be silenced with a "go back to your country" response.

In Sharjah the ruler had formed a new division called the Districts and Villages Department to look into the living conditions of village people. I covered a story when the officials of this new department came to the Sharjah consultative council to account for their policies and progress a year after their founding. They said they were reaching out to poor families with financial assistance and even soliciting more help from local charities such as the Sheikh Khalifa bin Zayed Foundation. More than ever the ruling elites did not want to alienate any categories of people from the fruits of the country's oil. However, the frustrations of local citizens could not be bribed away by these petty increases. In fact most Emiratis – even those who received pay rises when we didn't – shared the workers' frustration, especially of expatriates like myself who were being short-changed by a discriminatory, exploitative system.

One Emirati mentioned that he preferred being an expatriate because he could be married and build his own house without begging the government for loans. He said the loans could only be given to those who learned the art of obedience and loyalty. "Even the money they advertise themselves to have given us is not enough to do anything anymore in this country and they give us in one hand and take it back in the other hand through their bank interest loans and other avenues; but raising such issues is to run a serious risk," he said. I understood his frustration, as the young Emirati people were all under pressure to have a big villa and 4x4 car like some of their family or friends. A culture of taking loans with high interest rates was common among Emiratis, in order to live a fictitious life of success. This is the same culture that already has ruined many young families, whose marriages start in debt and end inevitably in divorce. How could they be happy with debt, high divorce rates and others who struggle hopelessly in trying to obtain this ideal life of stability? When they end up begging, these few families that own the government always bail them out in return for a worshipping demeanor of endless loyalty.

As my friend chatted about the local Emirati problems, we agreed that frustrations in this country applied equally to locals and expatriates. So when they increased the Emiratis' salaries and didn't increase those of expatriates after the Arab Spring, that became a bargaining card of "see, we care about you the most, not foreigners." This new ploy of playing up care and turning it into a divisive card between Emiratis and their expatriate colleagues could work only for a short time at most. Educated Emiratis, in general, do not want to earn more than their colleagues, as they do not match themselves with expatriates as much as with a few Emirati families who reaped the greatest largesse from this exploitation and subjugation of workers. These were the families embodying the roles of rulers, legislators and business persons. The families that gave them loans also bailed them out accordingly because they owned the government and its cabinet, judiciary, banks and the companies that employed and exploited the millions of workers. It is clear that such families would also only make laws that safeguard their interests and strengthen their grip on people. Even with the laws they have enacted, it is at their discretion to see which one to implement and which one to neglect. After all, laws are now like clothing fashion styles. If most of the world has a certain law they will also have it, but not implement it.

And not all Emiratis were being given this increment, as some were being played by their respective departments. Emirati public school teachers uncovered this tomfoolery when the Abu Dhabi Education Council (ADEC) claimed to have increased their salaries when, in fact, they only added the housing allowance to the given salary. Some 28 teachers organized and signed a petition to the director general of ADEC and, with great boldness, one female Emirati victim discussed this official fooling to the media, something unprecedented considering how local citizens, especially women, are subjugated readily by a governmental department. Every detail was clear that the waves of change sweeping the region were not as isolated as some of the international media had characterized them, but had affected the local citizens and were slowly empowering them to find their voice in matters that once were so easily taken for granted.

2.8 The Outbursts of Anger

A common perception in the GCC among anybody who is dissatisfied with his or her employment is to quit and look for another job or go back to the homeland. However, not all job-related grievances are settled by quitting. Expatriate workers in these countries have invested most of their lives in building the economies and large towers in the GCC region. Many have lost all contact or working knowledge that would be applicable in their homelands. They cannot just quit and go essentially nowhere. Instead many expatriates consider trying to change the conditions of their work and gain the respect they deserve.

The Islamic Prophet encouraged people to confront injustices with three weapons: actions, words or dislike. In a popular tradition, as reported by Abu Said Al Khudri. The prophet said, "Whosoever of you sees an evil action, he must change it with his hand. If he is not able to do so, [then he must change it] with his tongue. If he is not able to do so then [he must change it] with his heart and this is the weakest [manifestation] of faith."

Among the many ways immigrants in the GCC have tried to change the evil of exploitation and abuses is through the right to strike. Covering labor strikes as a reporter at *The National*, I could always empathize with this tradition, where workers simultaneously sought to establish their rights while fulfilling a popular prophecy. I could echo their courage but only do so within myself because while their grievances paralleled mine, I could not myself go on strike or recruit fellow journalists to seek collective action similarly. Sometimes I pondered if my hesitation arose because of a personal, yet unarticulated, fear that should they succeed, I would suffer the burden of the sacrifice in order to provide their economic relief. This theory seemed to work, especially with my editors being keener to use their power to kill stories I believe merited publication. The editors potentially would lose several times more than what I would lose, once we were both fired and deported. However, writing about worker protests as well as highlighting their nightmares with their oppressive sponsors and employers were activities that filled me with the right humility and self-awareness. Whether it was in my book manuscripts or in the news articles I wrote during my time as a reporter, I wanted to convince myself that this writing constituted the second category of "words" which the prophet had also encouraged and that I was not, after all, in the third category of the weakest.

As Dubai's economy was poised to recover after the Great Recession, construction workers sent a message to their rich employers: that they would not get away with past exploitations that once financed their lavish projects. So the key players in the new building boom recovery in Dubai were shocked when workers of their leading construction company Arabtec, the company responsible for the magnificent and world's tallest building Burj Khalifa, refused to turn up for work, as part of their strategy for demanding wage increases. The workers earning $160–$190 monthly in the scorching heat of up to 45 degrees C found they would lose nothing when they didn't turn up for work. Their message was unmistakably transmitted to the governments and contractors, who have always viewed Asian workers as cheap disposables that could easily be replaced. But such calculations already were running dry and every worker that was dismissed for demanding a fair pay would be replaced with even more radical and demanding workers.

The local media downplayed the effects of the strikes,

splashing about headlines such as, "Arabtec says projects unaffected by strikes," or more threatening ones like "Striking Dubai workers face massive deportations."

My newspaper (*The National*) was more polite in covering the deportations, telegraphing the headline "Strike instigators will be held accountable under the UAE law." In another article it positively portrayed the strike response as helpful action for the worker's benefit: "Striking Arabtec workers in the UAE helped to return home." And, when the remaining workers finally returned to work there were no mentions of a pay rise or anything that the four day strike had achieved. Thus, the headline read, "Strike over as Arabtec builders in the UAE go back to work."

And despite all the attention this strike garnered in the press, it was not the first such labor stoppage affecting the UAE's leading construction company (Arabtec). The company had plenty of history about workers going on strike and demanding pay rises. In 2007 when the Emirates still were making economic miracles, about 30,000 Arabtec workers went on a 10-day strike. In 2011, there were reports of 70 workers from the company being arrested on charges of instigating a protest for higher wages among 3,000 workers.

Strikes were not among construction workers alone. Taxi drivers have persistently staged similar strikes in all emirates. In 2007 there was a spate of taxi strikes I covered in Dubai and Sharjah, all because of pay demands. In 2010, about 2000 Sharjah cabbies also went on strike demanding the reversal of a Sharjah Transport Corporation rule that had called upon drivers to be responsible for paying petrol costs for their taxis. About 600 drivers left the country after the strike, either as part of their resignation or deportation.

"No one listens to taxi drivers; all authorities here believe taxi drivers are desperate poor people on favors to be working in the UAE," one taxi driver told me, when I was working on the story.

"When we had taxi strikes for fuel increases we moved to all offices, from the Labor Ministry to the Sharjah Transport Corporation and then police," he said. "No one listened to us; they told us to go away and if we want we could resign and they will bring other drivers from Pakistan."

Security guards also went on strike, and one of the most visible, popular stoppages was not reported in the media. Ugandans in the Sonapur labor camps were responsible for this stoppage, which happened when one of their own died at the hands of the company's administration. A Ugandan security guard had been sick but always went to work because sick days were not excusable and always incurred a stiff garnishment from wages. For each day of absence, a worker could see 100 dirhams garnished from his salary, which was no more than 800 dirhams a month. And, as noted earlier, the costs of any medical treatment were deducted from your salary.

The ailing security guard had returned home from work and collapsed. His panicked colleagues carried him to the reception desk in their accommodations and they demanded administrators summon an ambulance for the hospital. They were told to leave him on the stretcher, as administrators would deal with the emergency. Feeling restless, they returned to their rooms and after about half an hour they returned to the reception desk to seek any new information. Instead, they found their friend still on the stretcher. He had died.

The men went on strike, not looking to seek pay increases but instead as a measure to remind their superiors that they deserved to be treated with the dignity that should be accorded every human being, regardless of country of origin. They contacted me to help spread the news but because Dubai was not part of my normal beat, I could not work on the story without editorial approval. I tipped my editors who said they would handle this, and, of course, nothing appeared in the press. The only thing this strike achieved was the company agreeing to return the body of the deceased, which was no small concession in the men's minds. More often than not, the body would never be returned to loved ones of the deceased. Community members frequently have to mobilize and make arrangements, otherwise the body would be buried in an unmarked tomb in an Emirati cemetery. Some tombs would be marked with gravestones while others would not, depending upon the deceased individual's culture or religion.

There always seem to be disturbing tales about employer negligence and policies forced upon workers, especially those who not only are sick but also have been seriously injured during work. In Dubai, as in most GCC countries, the governmental agencies do not publish data on work-related injuries or fatalities and if they do the data are suspect for inaccuracy. For example, Human Rights Watch noted it had been informed by the Ministry of Labor that only six workers died in work-related incidents in three years. However, figures from the respective embassies revealed the number of work-related deaths to be higher. The Nepalese embassy alone revealed that 191 workers had died in Qatar in 2010 (one of the years that was part of the report sent to Human Rights Watch). The individual research noted that 19 died of work accidents, and 103 others of cardiac arrest, though workers did not fall within the typical age group for risk of cardiac failure.

The disheartening thing about most strikes in the UAE is that barely a handful of work stoppages have achieved their objectives of a pay rise and improved conditions of living. The government relies on its police and courts to crash any strikes before they can gain momentum for success. And the threat of deportation burdens striking workers. Once a few workers who lead strikes are put on a one-way ticket out of the UAE, others quickly report to work on time the following day. However, these failings are only temporary, as more workers are learning their rights, realizing the exploitation around them, and seeing that the justification of "this is not your country" is no longer credible. It is then that workers become emboldened to challenge the status quo. Then authorities will not be left with any alternative but to address directly and with sincerity the underlying grievances of all workers.

There are no trade unions in most GCC countries, and where they do actually exist in countries like Bahrain, Kuwait and Oman, membership to these unions is only for the GCC citizens not the migrant workers.

2.9 The Workers' Dormitories

Regarding the GCC labor issues, most journalists and researchers have found living conditions in workers' accommodations or labor camps to be abominable. The descriptions have ranged from squalid to dormitory-style – congested rooms of bunk beds accommodating as many workers as possible, along with filthy toilets.

Amnesty International researchers have also noted that in every camp they visited they found violations of Qatari standards, as well as recognized international housing standards on habitability.

The researchers described the workers living in squalid, overcrowded accommodation with no air conditioning, exposed to overflowing sewage or uncovered septic tanks; several camps with no power and large groups of men living with no running water.[117]

The team has documented in its visits that some companies house workers in rooms without windows. Toilets in the accommodation do not have ceilings, bunk beds are used despite this being illegal, and the limits on the numbers of workers in a room are not complied with.[118]

Though there have been efforts by some GCC countries to try and rectify the workers' living conditions, the responses from the GCC governments have always been defensive in tone, accusing the journalists and researchers of jealousy because of the GCC's economic progress.

While most journalists have concentrated on the workers' labor camps, living conditions of many single men is almost the same or even worse. The men that rent out bed spaces stay in rooms across the cities in groups of ten per room, sharing a single bathroom or two for the apartment complex. The congestion is a result of high rent costs that force desperate men to make do with accommodations in large enough numbers in order to pay the prices required by the "Arbab" or landlord. I lived in a group accommodation of a dozen people sharing a single room and a bathroom in Deira Dubai in my earliest days in the UAE. Rooms in my Ugandan boarding primary and secondary schools had more spaces with beds of sufficient size and comfort. In these cramped accommodations, a single television set became the source of bitterly contested rivalries among roommates, with each trying to control the programs or music CDs the others could watch. A roommate caught a cold whenever just one person sneezed. And we would not complain because we stayed in buildings that kept many other people like us staying on flat rooftops or verandahs without the comfort of air conditioners that we enjoyed indoors. Often, immigrants early on move from one place to another within just one week. When the lights start to go off in the city one can see workers clearly preparing their beds for the night's sleep. It is easier for the buildings that allow single men to sleep in dozens to a room so that others could sleep outside at a certain fee that "Natools" or "Arbabs" collected.

The first sign of a room being occupied by many workers is always the dozens of the pairs of shoes at the entrance. Add in the deafening noise of music, conversations and arguments that fill up the rooms and corridors every evening after work. These characteristics are among the reasons authorities in various emirates have been keen to separate the poor single men from residential areas mostly populated by local citizens. Municipalities often launch campaigns to hunt for single men that are staying in residential areas. Housing segregation is strictly enforced.

I remember numerous stories I did in Sharjah about bachelors being evicted from areas such as Halwan, Samnan and Al Leyyah. In one such story the Emirati ruler Sheikh Sultan bin Mohammed Al Qassimi responded to a local radio caller's complaints of bachelors living in his neighborhood and immediately issued an eviction decree for all bachelors in residential neighborhoods. The affected individuals were given only hours to gather their belongings and leave their current residences and find new ones in industrial areas or labor camps. The ruler visited the areas to inspect the eviction process in a crackdown that lasted well over a month. There was a shortage of rental accommodations in the bachelor buildings located in industrial areas and commercial centers. As a result, rents for workers skyrocketed while those in residential areas reserved for families plummeted. Streets were left in the dark, as most buildings were evacuated completely. For anyone to stay in any of those areas they had to produce a marriage certificate at the municipality before signing a house or an apartment contract. All single men in the Emirates were in trouble and for a full month I was doing only their stories trying to put myself in their place, because a few years back I had also been single like them, sharing an accommodation in an area from which I would have been evicted had the law come earlier.[119]

Drawing up similarities is always an impetus in covering such stories. A single Emirati woman – a reporter in a rival newspaper – must have had trouble with her editors for failing to keep pace with the follow-ups I was making. She was a woman and an Emirati, so why did they expect her to visit the bachelor workers' quarters to ask how they were coping with evictions. However, she finally came up with an even better story idea that dwarfed the whole month's bulk of stories I had pursued on the bachelors' evictions. Her idea landed her in trouble with the authorities and, most significantly, the ruler. She interviewed single women about how they were affected by the law and most of them told her that when they turned up for tenancy contract registration, they were turned away because they did not have a marriage certificate. The story was headlined, "Sharjah landlords claim single women cannot be allowed in the city."[120]

The focus turned to single women's plight for accommodation, as truly they would not go and stay with single men in labor accommodations. Once her story was published my tough local editor was so annoyed with me for not thinking about women and doing the story first. He demanded with his usual threatening language that I find single women in trouble and get back on top of the story. However, the authorities were not happy with the popularity the story had garnered and they dismissed its credibility. The municipality issued a press release rejecting the whole story. Some other local newspaper carried it but I refused to carry it intentionally.[121]

Authorities also called the reporter with all the usual threats and demanded her to hand over phone numbers of single women she had interviewed, the same way they had demanded me to hand them phone numbers of residents who spoke to me about my troubled Al Majjaz project story some years back as I have detailed elsewhere.[122] In the UAE, most people will not speak with a reporter because they know the potential implications if the story displeases the ruling elite. My reporter colleague persistently sought my advice and sympathetic ear. And I would always encourage her not to give her tormentors any source phone numbers, as this would be betraying an important journalistic standard of professional ethics. I told her she was an Emirati and that she would not be deported anywhere but the poor single women who talked to her were foreigners, and their deportation would be swift.

The authorities then came out to clarify for the first time that single women could stay in family-designated areas and did not need a marriage certificate for a tenancy contract. The story became popular in every office I visited, so long as the correspondent came from an English newspaper because officials viewed such affiliations with some trepidation. Many mentioned how the ruler himself had been offended by the story and they queried me about why English-newspaper journalists always wanted to antagonize the rulers. At the end, my female Emirati colleague was relieved of covering Sharjah, relocated to covering Dubai instead and eventually promoted to a senior reporter at her newspaper. All of us in the reporting circles congratulated her for being an Emirati. Otherwise her punishment would have been hard if she was an expatriate.

My experience of staying in the GCC squalid accommodations reiterated the dire circumstances many immigrants endured. After arriving in Doha, I stayed for three days in a hotel I had booked as part of the package to come to Qatar. Once my hotel stay expired, I asked around for a cheaper bed space among the Ugandan people living in Doha. My new roommate asked to meet me at the Hamad International Airport where he worked. He agreed to show me a room which would cost 700 Qatari riyals per month (US $192). He seemed trustworthy, as he was smartly dressed in the airport white uniform complete with tie and jacket. His appearance was far more respectable than the appearance of the accommodations that would become my home in Doha for several months.

The price might have seemed a bargain but the condition of the accommodations was dispiriting. The villa was partitioned into several other rooms and outside were two other annexes constructed from plywood. In one of these annexes I stayed with four other Africans. We were the only Africans to stay in these premises but there also were several Africans staying in the neighborhood. The whole villa compound hosted about 50 expatriates, most of them employed by Qatar Airways or the Hamad International Airport. They were all refugees from the company's accommodation that had slashed almost half their earnings just for a bed space.

My roommates had the barest of bedding. They would sleep atop a single bed cover on the floor. I was the first occupant to purchase a mattress and eventually we managed to upgrade to bunk beds after a few months. My roommates worked mostly at night and slept throughout the day, rarely venturing out even for meals. They often took advantage of free light meals at work and the company had slashed yet another portion from their monthly salaries for what it deemed as meal expenses. The problem with the meals, as one roommate told me, was that they were not foods identified with African cuisine but were instead Indian or Filipino. The Arab meals closely resembled the contents of most African meals but still Africans were given tokens that did not allow them to go for Arab meals but only Indian and Filipino ones.

A roommate said he just decided to eat whatever he could lays his hands on. When they were still living in the company accommodations about three quarters of their salary had been cut by the company to cover expenses for accommodation and food. My roommates were desperate. One had resigned and was still trapped waiting for an exit stamp from his bosses whom he presumed delayed giving it to him as punishment for his early resignation.

Even after I was hired as a local newspaper reporter, with a salary less than half of the lowest salary paid for a reporter in the UAE, I knew this deplorable bed space was the best bargain for me to stay in. My two immediate fears after moving into these accommodations were being able to escape if there was a fire and the sanitary conditions of the bathroom, the sight of which was enough to make me sick. In school we had a sweepers' roster where each student had a day assigned for the task of sweeping a classroom, or a toilet-cleaning roster where two or more people were assigned to clean school bathrooms. The accommodations in Doha reminded me of what we would have in school back in Uganda, but without a schedule of cleaning responsibilities. Cleaning tasks were handled voluntarily, as everyone was stressed or exhausted from their work.

Also, the cramped bathroom served three separate rooms that were only separated by plywood and were intended to serve 10 residents. Some people were responsible about cleaning up after a shower or laundry but even then the conditions were so deplorable in appearance that an individual could only do so much. The toilets were so old with tiles which obviously had been soiled for many years with every imaginable form of dirt.

Likewise, one could expect little or no privacy because the toilet was literally in the middle of everyone's living space. There were strange moments of odd humor. Semen stains were common on the bathroom tiles. After a month, I became accustomed to the sight, joking, "Whoever murdered his sons and daughters in the bathroom should show some respect to pour some water on them until they are fully buried in the holes. Those babies you display forever one will complain against you on the Day of Judgment and if you were destined for paradise God will be there and then reverse the decision and you will go to hell."

Yet, one could see that these also are the signs of the holistic starvation many immigrants must cope with in the GCC region, as later sections of the book recount, not just economically but also emotionally, socially, and even sexually.

We called our space "the dark room," as we agreed to keep the lights off so as not to disturb an exhausted roommate who was trying to catch up on his sleep. My roommates worked different shifts at the airport and often the shifts alternated between daytime and nighttime. Thus, at any hour of the day, at least one roommate was sleeping. We also did not see a reason to buy a television set and throughout the months I stayed there I had to forgo watching news. Roommates resorted to their mobile phones with headsets for entertainment while they lay in their beds. They played films and local African music that carried them back to their home countries for some modest emotional and cultural connection.

But even these arrangements were not enough to bring comfort into the room. There was one roommate who always called his wife in the early mornings when he returned from his night shifts and the calls always disrupted everyone's sleep in the room. Some roommates wanted to speak to him about the disruption but I pleaded with them to give him this small liberty to enjoy the chats with his wife. It was the thing that gave him happiness.

In the shared accommodation there were many sad stories about living and working in Qatar. One roommate had resigned his job three months previously and could not leave until he had received an exit stamp from his former employer. Of course, he was exhausting his limited savings that he accrued during the two years he worked in Qatar. Every time he visited his former employer's office, they told him to return the following week. There was a neighbor who told me he had also left the company's accommodations in a bid to save some money but for three months his company had continued cutting his accommodation expenses. Meanwhile, the HR people were always promising him that it would be reimbursed in his next month's salary. After three months they were able only to give expenses covering one month and when he tried to request reimbursements for the other months, the HR people told him they could only cover the current month. Convinced the company was cheating him because he was not a Muslim, he asked me why "Muslims are so heartless as to steal from the poor," and whether "these actions are condoned in Islam if the victim is a Christian?" These questions trouble me, as a faithful Muslim, and the only answer I can muster is to explain that these are an individual's independent actions, not ones rooted in or inspired by Islamic teachings. But for most Christians, especially from Africa, such an explanation is never satisfying. For them the Arabs and their *kandura* robes represent Islam and whatever they do is Islamic as well.

Nearly every colleague at the local newspaper stays in these old partitioned villas as well, even the editors. In my neighborhood a Sudanese journalist who works for an Arabic newspaper also shares a room in an old villa with two other men. The pay for journalists and even other professionals in Qatar is lower than anywhere else in other GCC countries. It is even poorer than in less wealthy areas such as Bahrain where I had worked for a few months and this low pay condemns journalists and other professionals to stay in these squalid accommodations.

Some colleagues, especially editors, live with their families in these shared accommodation villas. Every time there was a press release from the municipality about the crackdown on people staying in these squalid villas, all of us in the office were concerned. I remember one time after the municipality had issued a press release that it was cracking down on all these old partitioned villas we agreed to write a rebuttal with the headline, "Stop crackdown, say villa owners."[123]

The global media scrutiny on Qatar's squalid living conditions for its migrant workers had worsened and created more cramped living quarters outside the labor camps. Once the government inspectors stepped up their surveillance on the labor camps the companies made changes to the expense of workers' salaries. They reduced the number of workers that could stay in a room, and provided some cleaner facilities for toilets and kitchens, but they also increased the wage portions they deducted from the workers' salaries. My roommates complained their companies had increased the amount they charged them for the bed space they shared in a company's accommodation to almost 50 percent from about 30 percent earlier. They had no other choice but to leave the company's accommodations and go to find some other squalid accommodations elsewhere they could afford. The workers are in Qatar to save and provide some living allowances for their families in their respective countries. No one can spare that amount if he wants to live in more suitable accommodations.

No one could answer why the rich Qataris appeared unable to provide their workers with decent accommodations without cutting into employee wages and salaries. The unhygienic, squalid accommodations in the company-sponsored labor camps are barely improved upon in the old repurposed private villas. Meanwhile, inspectors and the media focus their attention on the labor camps and the private villas are free of any meaningful scrutiny. Thus, all forms of human violations are on display. The rooms are small and overcrowded. In our small villa there are about 50 people staying in different rooms. Even the kitchen is a room for sleeping and instead propane gas cylinders are placed in the small verandah which are intended to be used for cooking. There are about ten gas cylinders and on a Friday when most people stay home and cook the verandah is always crowded and busy. The risk of a fast-moving fire is always present.

The whole area called Mattar Al Qadeem or old airport area is largely inhabited by expatriates in skilled and semiskilled jobs who have escaped the large cuts in their incomes that would come in living in company accommodations. Most of these expatriates work for Qatar Airlines or Qatar Civil Aviation Authority at Hamad International Airport. All the roommates I have had and all my neighbors are working at the airport for these two companies. At all shift times one can witness many airport employees standing on the roads waiting for the private buses that pick them up. My roommates pay 150 Qatari riyals (US $42) a month for the bus pick-up and drop-off.

The area is a shame to the prestigious five- or seven-star accredited airlines but it is stunning evidence of how little they value their staff. It is not natural that such a large number of employees would opt to go and stay outside company's accommodation and in squalid conditions. There is something clearly wrong in the exploitation and extortion of their meager incomes.

Mattar Qadeem has not yet come into news as part of the stories about the squalid living quarters of prosperous companies. This is because many international journalists are looking to enter into labor-designated accommodations for their camera shots and news. Nonetheless this virtually open area, where a reporter could knock on each villa or house and enter at will with no security guards to check if one has a camera or not, contains many, if not more, tales as compelling as those to be found in the labor camp accommodations. As if that is not enough, the inhabitants of this area are largely skilled people working as engineers, journalists, and in other service fields. The stories would be a huge black eye for Qatari's polished, manipulated PR image.

The degradation of workers' rights as well as exploitation in most GCC companies is common where the management is of Indian origin. Despite the fact that most of the exploited and abused workers are Indians, these managers could only say yes to the abusive policies, as dictated by the Qatari or Emirati business owners. The rights of workers are much respected if the company managers come either from Europe or America and many workers, even Indian ones, have expressed preference for having a British boss, as opposed to an Indian supervisor. There is a misconception, represented mostly by Indian managers, that saying yes in a worshipful manner to their patrons is the only way to preserve their jobs. Indian managers say, "yes, sir," as if they have graduated with honors from a school specializing in sycophancy.

Even in the newspaper offices where I have worked, our Qatari editor-in-chief is revered like a god. Every time he comes to the newsroom he is blessed with affirmative responses in every regard. The Indian editors say yes to whatever he says and even when he is still thinking about what to say, they say yes before he finishes his sentences. Because he is often cut off in the middle of his words with the reply of "yes" he often has to say phrases such as, "what I wanted to say…" and again they respond with, of course, "as you want it, sir." When he leaves, they start thinking about what he was saying and complain in his absence.

So it is just normal that journalists under such managers also have signed contracts that dictate 48 hours of work per week and instead they end up working for six days per week and some even going for several weeks without taking a day off from the office. Even on public holidays like Eid when the whole country rests for days the journalists here report to work without a single day off and without compensation. There are no questions; it always has to be done that way.

The Indian managers have redefined the role of manager to a dutiful servant who says repeatedly, "yes, sir." In fact, they readily accept even the worst conditions of work for their own people. It is so rare to find one "yes, sir" staffer standing up for the rights of people under his management. Getting to the managerial position is often a matter of luck in most GCC countries but there also is a need for rights activists to target mostly the Indian managers and enlighten them as to how they should stand up to protect the rights of the people under their aegis.

This task is crucial in the fight against slavery in these GCC countries. The managers must be told their positions represent and are legitimized by the people they supervised. They are expected to honor this role by standing up to the interests of these people but not by joining the business owners in sucking their blood.

2.10 Justice for Money

For workers in the GCC, the most important unanswered

question is where to find justice in a region where their honor has been violated, their salaries withheld and their passports confiscated. It is true all GCC countries have tasked judicial and law enforcement institutions with procedures of relief and redress, have enacted laws, and ratified international agreements on human rights, but still justice remains out of reach for foreign workers.

The abuses that cannot be contested in GCC courts start in the recruitment process. According to UAE labor law, employers or sponsors must pay certain fees to the government for each foreign worker they bring into the country. They include a visa fee of 200 dirhams (US $55) and an employment visa issuance fee of 1,000 dirhams (US $273). In addition the sponsoring employers must also provide an airline ticket to migrant workers to travel from their home countries to the UAE. The law also forbids recruiters from collecting any fees from prospective migrant workers but, as suggested already here, the UAE recruitment agents openly violate this law, charging workers these fees instead of prospective employers.[124]

Human Rights Watch asked some recruitment agents in the UAE about this practice, and one response was, "For unskilled workers, we don't charge the employers anything. The candidates will pay for visa and transportation costs."

Even Human Rights Watch confirmed that in every case of a worker interviewed, the immigrant had been required to pay up front travel and visa fees to recruitment agents.

These fees – rising quickly, for example, to thousands of rupees or shillings for many Asian workers – constituted a main cause of indebtedness to workers entering the GCC. Many workers speak of ordeals in taking loans at high interest rates or having to sell some of their precious possessions such as land in their native countries to raise the money.

Lori Noora, writing for the Center for Migrations and Citizenship, also found that while the visa costs must be paid by the sponsor, in most cases the sponsors were passing these costs onto their workers. Some private companies deduct the payments in installments from a worker's monthly salary. In cases where the sponsors wanted this visa fee paid upfront the workers incurred heavy debts that were mitigated by selling their property at home in order to satisfy these fees.[125]

This exploitative, illegal levying of fees is not over even after the recruitment process has been fulfilled. Once the recruitment agent hands off the worker to the employer, the employer also claims the worker owes money spent in the recruitment process and as such starts deducting money from the monthly salary.

The employers also require old workers who have been with the company for three years to pay the fees for their visa renewals.

The Kafala protocol is set up so that the employer is financially responsible for repatriating the worker as soon as his or her contract is fulfilled or terminated.[126] However, there are many workers stranded in the country who face illegal status because of expired visas or because their sponsors fled and they had no recourse for getting a return ticket home.

There are several labor laws that protect foreign workers, enabling them to sue their employers, but because the employer and sponsor often are the same person, it means that while the trial is pending, the plaintiff is unemployed and forbidden to work for anyone else. Even if a foreign worker successfully wins the case against the employer, the outcome of the conflict will mean the termination of their employment and hence their residency visa. The worker would therefore have to return to their home country and repeat the costly process of recruitment to return.[127]

The reluctance of expatriates to seek legal redress in the GCC courts is recognized by Abu Dhabi authorities. Nasser Al Ghaith, the head of customer service at the judiciary, called upon expatriates to come and register their complaints, as he has promoted the judiciary as a transparent institution where the staff is willing to listen to and act upon foreigners' grievances. However, in the last six months of 2013, out of 118 complaints filed in the judicial department only two came from non-Emiratis.[128]

A Human Rights Watch report also found the requirement of courts in Qatar for workers to pay a deposit of 500 Qatari riyals (US $137) was prohibiting many workers from seeking legal redress. Most would turn to the courts for complaints about nonpayment of wages that spanned months but, unfortunately, they could not even afford the fee to have their case processed against their defaulting sponsors.[129]

Even those bold enough to report their exploitative or abusive sponsors are not only hurdled by the long and ineffective road to justice but by the only alternative of deportation. (If one reports his sponsor then the individual risks not having anyone else to sponsor or guarantee his capacity to remain in the GCC region.) For it is not the government's responsibility to replace sponsors, as one can only stay in these countries with a sponsor.

Qatar has enacted provisions for the workers to be able to transfer their sponsors in cases where authorities found the sponsor abusive. This provision is, however, unknown especially among the workers who need it most. Official figures from the Ministry of Interior's Human Rights Department for 2012 reported that 607 people made requests to transfer their sponsors, but only 49 were allowed to transfer permanently and 211 to transfer temporarily.[130]

The problem is many GCC families that employ domestic workers still view their housekeeping staff members as slaves, despite statements to the contrary that the ruling powers have issued. And others still believe some people should work for them for free whether it is domestic work or business tasks and assignments from corporations. These stereotypes of workers in the region formulate the basis of unfair legislations and massive abuses, underpayment of wages, and, in all-too-embarrassing frequency, no payment to workers in these countries.

Stereotypes drive this form of institutional racism – biases against anything non-Arab, anyone with a different color skin or someone who doesn't speak the language, regardless of whether that person is a Muslim, Christian or Hindu. In fact the most common victims of these abuses are poor Muslims from Indonesia, India, Bangladesh and the Africa subcontinent – the kinds of Muslims who leave their countries in search for a better life in countries of people they believe are brothers in faith. They often are moved by the expressions of equality preached in their native countries' mosques that Islam has brought to their lands, liberating slaves such as Billal bin Rabah and Zayyed bin Harith who despite their skin color had ascended into special ranks in leading the region's armies. These preachings give immigrants hope that the countries they are about to go to will give them a chance to prove themselves, tap into their potential and be on the ladder of economic mobility.

However, those delusions evaporate as soon as the plane bringing the immigrant lands at any of the airports in the GCC. Their dreams are soon replaced with nightmares when their new GCC employers treat them less like humans, disenfranchising them from their freedom by confiscating their passports and making them vulnerable to abuses and assaults of all kinds. The immigrant searches for justice only to discover it will never arrive. They soon learn that everyone is a conspirator in abuse and exploitation – the people who would have protected them, whether it is judges, imams and even news editors, have signed salary contracts with the abusers and exploiters. The immigrant discovers too late that these so-called friendly stakeholders are no longer the right people to contact for help. The government makes laws to protect the wealthy employers, and the religious scholars whom they would have turned to have become government employees, at work defending every governmental policy over the needs and petitions of the poor. These are the new desperate realities in the FCC. From the top scholars they call Mufti and Kadhis to the mosque imams in these countries; they are now all government employees. They are tasked with supporting and finding justifications in Islam for every policy or any action of government that has been dictated.

Nothing has compromised more the independence, credibility and conscience of religious scholars in the GCC countries then salaries and benefits these religious figures take from their governments or businesses for whom they work. In the so-called Islamic Banks in the region, the scholars eagerly articulate justifications that approve every bank product, which, in turn, is sold to masses as an Islamic product even if that product was as exploitative as the interest terms themselves. Before the Great Recession, personal loans were illegal in all Dubai's Islamic banks. After the crisis that spared no financial institution, banks were desperate to sell consumer product services and the innovations steamrolled. The Islamic scholars employed in these banks accepted the task to help the banks regain their profitability through every means possible. The scholars identify an Islamic justification for selling loan instruments with high interest rates to a conservative Muslim population. Previously banned products such as personal loans are reengineered with new Islamic names and blessings. Meanwhile, fatwa after fatwa comes out proclaiming their religious legitimacy and appropriateness.

The religious scholars subtly substitute the word "interest" for "profit." Once the product launches successfully, the scholars receive a bonus for their work. The newer generation banks attract more clients from conventional banks that had been providing interest-free Islamic personal loans. In my own research, I consulted various banks about the new generation of consumer banking products. I found out that if I borrowed a loan of 60,000 dirhams from an Islamic bank for two years I was to pay back the loan and interest – a total of 72,000 dirhams –with the

12,000 dirhams representing a profit to the bank. In a conventional bank I would pay back 71,000 dirhams in the same period with 11,000 dirhams as interest.

The findings intrigued me as much as they disturbed me. I could not distinguish who was being exploitative and who was not or whom they were fooling. I asked one bank sales representative about the Islamic personal loans: what was the difference between their loans and those of other non-Islamic banks? He told me it was about interest. The conventional banks took interest while they did not take interest but profit as allowed in Islam. I told him that I thought the two were the same with just the names being changed. Clearly, the salesman was on defense, explaining that for them they would be buying gold on my behalf and selling it to me at a higher price as a profit. This he said was a legitimate trading practice which is allowed in Islam by the same text that prohibits interest and the higher extra amount I would pay to them thus would be profit.

I queried him that the Islamic thesis of business always has been that we share profits and losses, but the bank in this particular set of circumstances wants profits in the first month of the loan regardless of whether I make a profit or not. Also I wanted to know about a profit that I have not already made, so I asked why the bank is stipulating that it's going to take its profit share from me each month. Again, he was defensive, arguing that it was perhaps too sophisticated and layered to explain to a layperson like myself the full details of the deal but he also was convinced it was an acceptable Islamic practice and that all popular Islamic scholars even in Mecca endorsed it. I was still not convinced, as I mentioned the reason Islam had abolished interest was to prevent exploitation by way of extracting money from the poor, Now the conventional banks extract less money in the form of interest but the bank in this instance is poised to extract more money in the name of profits. I waited for him to explain, as I did want to hear in all its sophistication how fair this practice was and then if I didn't understand the sophisticated nature of this financial instrument, it would then become my problem. But he had already blanked out of the conversation, being interested to know if I would be taking a loan or not.[131]

And, how did the scholars, the vanguards of Islamic principles of justice and custodians of God's word, come to this? Everyone who shifted from a conventional bank to an Islamic financial institution was looking for a fair deal, running from exploitation. They had been preached to and had believed that God the Almighty, Creator of all, had no reason to favor the rich GCC ruling families over the poor immigrants or to exploit others. And now the custodians of God's word unashamedly offer confusing interpretations and sell out the masses in order to reap meager earnings on behalf of the banks' big daddies. The banks paid their salary and had their loyalty, and it is that salary which is more important than the justice embodied in the Word of God. The regional religious scholars had no problem prostituting God's message, only to be rewarded with fat salaries.

If justice is a delusion to reckon with even from articulations of religious scholars, then expecting the media to present a picture of justice sounds even more delusional. We were in a reporters' brainstorming meeting called by *The National*'s then editor-in-chief, an American Iraqi national. It was the first ever meeting in the three years he had been editor-in-chief (and it was also the last one). Most of us thought he had convened the meeting for a major announcement about newspaper operations. Instead it was as a brainstorming meeting for gathering good story ideas.

Racism emerged as a topic and Hassan listed it on the whiteboard. I raised my hand and told the team about an incident involving an African neighbor who was harassed at a shopping mall because some eyewitnesses had reported an African man had stolen something in the mall. So if he was not the one, the thief was a brother, as the shop owner allegedly reasoned.[132] The story had been censured by the local desk editors and the US Iraqi editor corrected me twice by replacing the word "censure" with "*held*." This was how editors always consoled themselves with self-censorship. They deceived themselves that they were simply "*holding*" on stories and it stayed that way. The media tales continue to pile up, showing how the journalist's voice is so widely censored, not just for the helpless and miserable workers but for every other imaginable type of story that would be considered essential to a community's livelihood and informational awareness.

2.11 Visiting the Labor Disputes Section

The Sharjah Ministry of Labor office is one of the most hostile places for media in the emirate. Though the offices have a department dedicated to media communications, reporters cannot ask questions that will be answered satisfactorily. In fact, the department issues virtually no news releases. I have long tried to work on several stories that required their input but as always the response was along the lines of a bureaucratic put-off, as they would not answer anything. One day I tried to establish how the department handles labor disputes, and I tried to explain to the media section chief that, well, this is a good story, a kind of positive tribute to the work ministry staff members are doing. I was looking to gather the usual type of background any reporter would do in researching a story about a government entity.

After being frustrated by their lack of response, I turned to the Sharjah Media Center, formed two years earlier to function as the spokesperson outlet for the emirate. First, I asked an Emirati young woman who was handling the journalists' requests about interviewing the chairman of the media center, Sheikh Sultan bin Ahmed Al Qassimi. Besides being a relative of the Sharjah ruler, the chairman also was husband to the ruler's eldest daughter

Sheikha Bedour bint Sultan Al Qassimi, who led Shurooq, the investment arm of Sharjah. Instead, the Emirati media representative suggested I interview another senior official, citing the Chairman's official duties as a Sheikh as the reason why it was always difficult to schedule an interview. I insisted that I would wait until an opening popped up in the Sheikh's schedule. I merely wanted her to forward my request to him. A few days later, she got back to me with another suggestion: that I should submit the questions so the chairman could review them prior to an interview. A week later, instead of fixing my appointment day she sent me answers to my questions with photos of the media center building. I responded to her email with laughter and a Shukrani. Then it was her Turkish colleague to whom I wrote to in detail, explaining my dissatisfaction with their answers. I indicated that the answers were very general and that some were off topic from what I asked. I added that the responses suggested the media center had helped to improve relations and interactions between government officials and the media, but if even the SMC chairman was unreachable then how would it make other government departments officials accessible?

I decided to be as emphatic as possible in my request and I was grateful when she did respond that the interview would be arranged as soon as possible. Another week later I was in the chairman's office with my photographer, a South African man of British origin. The Sheikh, like most royal family members, is American-educated, and he spoke good English and was comfortable in the language. I did mention that arranging the interview had been a real trouble and that I was grateful to the Turkish staff member sitting beside him who had managed to fix the meeting after more than a month of back-and-forth communications. I mentioned there were a lot of good stories that could be written about the emirate but it was unfortunate the different department heads still distanced themselves from media even when they were being contacted on what would purely be a positive story. He admitted that Sharjah was known for being a closed emirate where no helpful information went out to any media but he and his colleagues were trying to change that by offering adequate media training to governmental department heads and spokespersons. I told him about the frustration of trying to get answers from staff members regarding the labor dispute story I was working on, adding how important it was to have the Emirati officials fill information gaps rather than leaving it to public and foreign media speculation. The Sheikh regretted being unable to help, as the arena came under the federal government's jurisdiction.

We chatted for about a half hour. He recounted how they had built the Sharjah University in only nine months, and I told him that people refer to it as the Sheikh Sultan's version of the "Burj Khalifa." We both enjoyed the joke which demonstrated how to differentiate Sharjah and Dubai people in picking their priorities. At the end of the meeting even my photographer was surprised at the ease with which the interview came off. "The way he spoke freely to the media and even admitted their shortcomings in dealing with the media was unprecedented," the photographer told me as we headed back to our car. "I didn't see any Emirati being as free as he was in his words."

Indeed, I was likewise stunned. I heard him previously in public speeches, and he did a better job of it than most members of the ruling families. He had paid handsomely the best speech writer in the world. After this meeting I was convinced he was among the new breed of ruling elites who had been educated in America or Britain and who are more confident than their predecessors in communications. I complimented him after the meeting as we took a picture of remembrance together, emphasizing that the ruler of Sharjah must be very proud of him, to which he responded with a knowing smile. This was especially true because the ruler had given his elder daughter into marriage. It was the only royal couple in the emirate in which the husband and wife led high-profile government departments and were known for their accessibility to the press. The Dubai ruler also once had a vibrant daughter who seemed quite at ease in public but once she was married, she left the public scene, a common occurrence. Bedour, despite his marriage, was still making public speeches, but the only problem was her PR insistence of not allowing photos to be taken of her by any man other than her personal photographer. The PR representative would make annoying calls after every press conference or event she addressed to remind us to wait for her single official photo which all newspapers were supposed to use. Few entertained even the thought of testing the waters by using our own media photographers to snap the images, who accompanied us to the events. I always wondered why they did not ban photographers from taking her pictures when they had the authority to do so.

After the interview I told the local desk editor about the interview and the media center chairman's comments about improving transparency in governmental department communications. He said, "We've got to pass on this, Yasin. Our readers are not interested in such stories."

Of course, the readers were (and are) interested. Who is not interested in reporting about transparency? *The National* editor would be interested if the pitch had come in the first days of the paper's existence when it enjoyed some independence. But now he was only trying to censor even before he read the story because he assumed it would be a hit piece. I had fought so much to get this interview and now I was fighting to have the story published. I thought the issue was too important to compromise my credibility, considering the effort expended to land the interview, a difficult achievement by any standard in the UAE. I thought of just writing the story with a positive angle, cropping out everything to do with Sharjah being a closed emirate, and I thought they would take it. My cluster editor reviewed the piece and returned a draft, and I noticed he had tweaked the piece's positive spin but still the editors in the final decision-making line would not green-light it.

And if just a story about transparency involving governmental efforts in communicating to the public was considered troublesome to land in the paper, think of what would happen to the main story I was chasing about the workers' disputes. The desk then wanted a year-ender story, a profile about an individual who had achieved so much during the past year. I rewrote parts of the story into a profile of Sheikh Sultan bin Ahmed, simply hinting at his desire to change the old stereotypes of the emirate being considered media unfriendly. It was finally published in the paper on December 29, 2013 with the headline "Man at the helm for Sharjah's big year."[133]

I met Eric (a pseudonym) at the metallic benches near the entrance of the complaints section at the labor office. A Filipino national in his mid-thirties who had worked as a baker in Sharjah, Eric had lost count of how many times he had visited the offices in the last three months. He was trying to resolve a dispute with his employer when his contract expired and instead of renewing the arrangement he preferred to join another company and do something else.

He had already landed a job as a sales assistant in a garment shop when he turned down his previous employer's demands to renew his work permit. As a result the employer had refused to give him his passports or even a release form.

"I wanted to leave after one year but he blackmailed me that if I left without completing my two years' contract he would ban me for good," Eric told me. "Now I have completed the two years and he still doesn't want to release me to go and work in a better paying job."

Eric was earning 1,200 dirhams a month as a baker. With the new job, he would be receiving a monthly salary of 4,500 dirhams, nearly quadruple his previous wages. He could not start the new job or receive a new visa until he had his passport in hand and a No Objection Certificate (NOC) signed by his previous employer. Eric claimed he did not tell his employer that he was going for another job but once he asked for a release letter the employer swore he would never allow him to work in any other company in the UAE.

"I begged him again and again to let me go and he played a good guy who wanted to know where I was going and cared about my safety and that if I told him the truth of my next destination he would give me a release letter and passport," he said.

But once Eric had opened up to his former boss, the employer became angry, telling him he would never allow him to resign voluntarily and go to work for others.

Eric's friends advised him to seek arbitration at the Ministry of Labor offices, which they refused. Oddly enough, Eric was perplexed because ministry officials seemed to be powerless in the situation. In the previous three months Eric earned no salary and was living on handouts from friends. The assistance did not come solely out of compassion. Eric said his friends blamed him for his condition and spoiling his own chances of future employment. His friends advised him to apologize to his former employer and beg for his original job. Eric's visa already had expired and he now was living as undocumented.

"The only chance I have is I submitted my case to the Ministry of Labor and as long as this case is still in the process I am not an illegal," he said. However, the legality of his stay by virtue of his complaints status did not help him. Meanwhile, his family in Manila was irritated that he was no longer remitting any funds back home.

At the labor offices I also talked to Mohammed, a laborer from India who had turned up to seek help after his sponsor cancelled his visa and reported him as a runaway because he was sick and had not reported to work for almost three weeks.

Mohammed said the high medical costs prohibited him from seeking treatment from the hospitals because his employer did not provide health insurance cards.

"At first I went to the hospital and they charged me 700 dirhams, almost half of my [monthly] salary," Mohammed explained, who was getting 1,500 dirhams every month. "And the sickness did not go away completely so I stayed weak and unable to go to work."

Instead of going back to the hospital, Mohammed periodically purchased a few medicines that were earlier prescribed to him by the doctor from a pharmacy near the neighborhood in which his accommodations were located.

Mohammed claimed he told his office by way of his work colleagues that he was unable to come to the job. His supervisor, also an Indian man, had turned up in the room to visit him and gave him 100 dirhams to buy some medicines.

Once he recovered enough to move about, he went to an ATM to collect some money from his account but he discovered his bank card had been invalidated. The next day he turned up at work and the supervisor who had visited him earlier said to first see the manager before he could resume work. The manager had few words: "You ran away and we cancelled you, so get out of my sight."

Mohammed now connected the dots between his invalidated ATM card and his dismissal from work. Once the sponsor reports an immigrant as a runaway, the government responds by canceling his visa and bank account. He is now considered an illegal who could be detained and deported once the authorities locate him. His bank account had most of his savings for the year he had worked in the country and he did not even know how he would be able to retrieve the money. But Mohammed refused to take in the harsh reality of his new status and hopelessness, instead seeking help from the Ministry of Labor office. He had filed his complaint and after a week his manager had yet to be notified to report to the labor offices. Mohammed visited the offices to see if ministry officials had already summoned his boss. The ministry advised him to wait for the call once he would be needed to provide any new information. He was worried because he did not know how long it could take to resolve his problems and to get the money that was in his account. One thing that gave him hope was that he was now not deemed a fugitive or illegal who could be arrested by any passing police officer. Mohammed believed he was immune from trouble, as he had a pending case against his sponsor at the ministry.

2.12 Legally Beyond Reproach

Working for the ruling royal families in the GCC can be a dream for many workers. The families are so secure in their wealth that they are not likely to default on the salaries. Instead they are presumed to be more generous. They take their domestic workers with them on luxurious foreign trips – an exceptional opportunity for a worker to see the world and stay in hotels that they otherwise would never be able to afford. All the signs of daily routines are encased in richness and abundance and workers in such environments might feel very lucky if not blessed. The local media portray the ruling families with the iconic status of gods, as profoundly religious, merciful and wise. Though these families are also masked in a near-complete information blackout, with hardly any criticism arising in the local media, foreign media reports paint a bleaker picture about the workers' ordeal in the palaces. The reports emphasize how Islam is used as a tool to safeguard ruling elites from criticism, while fortifying legitimacy and inculcating in poor citizens and immigrants the near-blind acceptance of their subjugation and exploitation. To outsiders, the story is an open secret.

In Saudi Arabia the elites align with the holy places of Mecca and Medina as their "custodians" and, in GCC countries such as the UAE, they refer to themselves as the "rightly guided," a title that for generations was reserved for the four loyal companions of the Prophet, who were his duly ordained successors. One would think with such grand titles their primary objective is to serve God and be forever faithful to their religion but instead they enslave their God and religion into earthly service that contravenes the essence of the Islamic theological core. Similarly local radio stations will utter their names and follow them with eulogistic prayers uttered more frequently than for those dedicated to the Prophet, which is a religious duty for Muslims whenever the prophet's name is mentioned.

The rot in the subjugating treatment of other people has filtered down through the ranks into the communities of ordinary GCC citizens, who now enjoy immunity from exposure and prosecution of their crimes as their rulers have. Whereas laws protecting the local citizens are common and strictly enforced, the laws that protect immigrants are scarce and rarely enforced. It is easier for a local citizen, especially if one is a royal elite, to get away with serious crimes.

The case of Saudi prince Saud bin Abdulaziz bin Nasir, a grandson of Saudi Arabia's King Abdullah, is an exception that proves the point. He was jailed in 2010 for killing Bandar Abdullah Abdulaziz in a London hotel after subjecting him to a "sadistic" campaign of violence and sexual abuse,[134] an exception given the crime occurred in a foreign country. The Prince was convicted of murder and a second count of grievous bodily harm.[135]

Still there have been efforts by the government to play the diplomatic immunity card on behalf of a murderous grandson but with no success.[136] In a foreign country ruling elites would seek diplomatic immunity and if such a case ever became known to the masses in their respective country, they would call in the religious scholars to confuse the masses and provide some fuzzy rationale.

The case is the exception, because the prince would not face imprisonment had the crimes and court proceedings happened in any GCC country. Consider the case of a video tape smuggled out of the UAE which showed a member of the country's royal family mercilessly torturing a man with whips, electric cattle prods and wooden planks with protruding nails.

The UAE Ministry of the Interior told ABC News, which first aired the video, that it had reviewed the tape and acknowledged the involvement of Sheikh Issa bin Zayed al Nahyan, brother of the country's crown prince Sheikh Mohammed. "Over the course of the tape, Sheikh Issa acts in an increasingly sadistic manner. He uses an electric cattle prod against the man's testicles and inserts it in his anus. At another point, as the man wails in pain, the Sheikh pours lighter fluid on the man's testicles and sets them aflame," as noted in the ABC News report.[137]

There was a two-year trial, the first of its kind involving an Emirati royal family member, but the verdict shocked the world. The sheikh was acquitted and the people who smuggled out this video were found guilty and sentenced to five years in absentia.[138]

The ruling elites also play with the people by exploiting Islam even in such a case which was so blatantly a farce. According to Islamic law, as cited by the judge in the verdict, "[a] drunk person cannot be punished for his crimes if he did not know the content he was drinking contains alcohol and this drunkenness caused him to commit a crime while he is mentally unaware."[139] Now if any evidence was required for how these elite families relegate religion to a mere tool of their own to subjugate others, this case was compelling. And one wonders why they should insult religion with such a case so blatantly seen on television across the world of raw sadistic aggression. These countries have both religious laws and secular civil laws, and, in most cases, religious laws are only used in family matters while all other cases are handled on the basis of the country's secular laws. However, why this specific case was handled by Islamic laws demands an answer. Even in secular courts he would have been acquitted, given the ruling family's power. The case demonstrates something much more insidious. The ruling elites believe they own the privilege of interpreting Islamic texts after buying off most religious scholars through generous salaries and benefits.

Winning over theological scholars in a region that values religion is important to the rulers. The scholars can manipulate the interpretation of the holy texts to justify even the most sadistic behaviors of their superiors and because the population believes them with little or no confrontation, this generates acceptance of the legitimacy of rulers even when they behave in the most inhumane ways. It echoes most disturbingly how terrorists use religion to justify the murder of innocent people.

There was a front page story run by *The National* announcing the acquittal – with the headline "Court Clears Sheikh Issa" – but the agency has since removed the story from its archives and website. This included an image of the victim hugging the sheikh, congratulating him after the verdict was announced.[140] One can only imagine that if the Saudi prince who murdered his aide in London had been tried in the UAE, the victim's family would have been required to hug and kiss the murderer sheikh after another farcical verdict.

And there was another murder involving members of the Kuwait royal family in Sharjah that is still awaiting a verdict. I was on vacation in Uganda when the incident occurred and my paper *The National* relied on follow-ups by translating reports from its sister Arabic paper *Al Ittihad*.

On my return the local editor informed me to hurry up and catch up with the story they had missed during my absence. Mubarak Meshaal Al Mubarak, 19, a first-year student at the University of Sharjah, died in hospital on February 25, 2013 from internal bleeding after sustaining multiple fractures.

My first story came from an interview with the Sharjah Chief Prosecutor Rashid Al Omran who told me that they had recovered a six-minute video of torture that caused the young man's death.[141]

When I went out to talk to university students, their version of the story had not been reported in any paper. They claimed the victim had been killed for dating a sister of one of the Kuwait royal family members who was also at the university. This version became popular even amongst journalists who were covering the case. When we did put it to the chief prosecutor, however, he said he could neither confirm nor deny but advised that we keep it aside because it was highly sensitive. No one would disobey such a request – or, more realistically, an order – because that meant being cancelled out of other communications regarding the case and a reporter could face even more dire sanctions for violating the request. So we all reported that the investigators had not yet established the motive for the torture even after watching the video. Why the case was being treated so sensitively mystified me, along with the reason for the murder which apparently was well-known even by members in the community. It did little to anchor credibility about how the case was being handled. What the prosecutor officially told us was helpful – confirmation that a member of the Al Sabah family was being sought for involvement in this murder.

More than a year later the case came to court and there was relief that the usual pains of having to beg for interviews and keep ears open for any updates would no longer have to be tolerated. We would be able to get updates by sitting and listening to the hearings as well as talking to the lawyers of the defense and prosecution after every court session. A week before the first hearing, a court PR staffer told me and an *Al Ittihad* reporter that we needed permits to attend the hearings. This disturbed us, as we had never encountered this issue before, even covering murder cases. However, in this case, the Kuwaiti royal family obviously was involved and prior restraint became the rule of the day.

The PR staffer threatened to limit access only to local

reporters, unlike us national correspondents. Something similar happened with a high-profile case involving 96 political prisoners in Abu Dhabi.

My local editors decided to send a female reporter from Dubai to the proceedings, so I was now scrambling for my next assignment. Covering such easy assignments was a luxury I did not enjoy often even when I had managed to file the initial stories regarding the case. The editors would want me to believe some reporters were more senior than me, especially once a story gained prominence. Giving my colleagues easy page one assignments would reinforce this and I would be reduced to helping a colleague on correspondence and contacts related to the coverage. I had to share the contact information from police that I had cultivated during my tenure, as my colleague had not done the leg work on firming up her own network of sources. I knew she needed permission to be in court more than she needed police contacts, and I was surprised why she even thought of police contacts for a case that already had moved into the courts. Sharjah is an extremely hostile place to work as a reporter. Once a reporter identifies himself to any official, the relationship is cut off abruptly. Many reporters would take ownership of story assignments that I already had put effort into, and then half way into the assignment they would give up and return it to me. The editors without any apology or shame would ask me to pick back up the assignment. Meanwhile, my colleague would haunt me the whole day of the court session with calls asking me every imaginable minor question.

Covering scheduled events or press conferences always seem to be the reporter's easiest and potentially happiest assignments. There is a good bit of professional satisfaction in accomplishing the assignment and filing the story, knowing that it's not going to be trashed, delayed, or reassigned. Meanwhile, I would be doing the hard work of cultivating and expanding my beat and sources only to learn without notice that a particular story now was going to a favored reporter. The sting would be exacerbated when the reporter frequently contacted me to bring him or her up to date on the story while I would lose time on finding another story assignment.

Reporting in a quiet emirate such as Sharjah or the other northern emirates is different from the far more lively emirates of Dubai and Abu Dhabi. Covering a story in another emirate or being reassigned to a beat in a different emirate entails all sorts of professional sensitivities. A simple road project story in Abu Dhabi could rise to the level of a newspaper's lead story while the same story in Sharjah might barely make it as a news brief or, more likely, would be axed. That is why reporters in Sharjah make use of crime stories more than their counterparts in any other emirates. Because while crime reporting in Sharjah is generally tolerated by authorities, such stories would be heavily censored or blocked in Abu Dhabi. To balance the paper from being a mere chronicle recording the progress of governmental infrastructural projects, the papers in the larger emirates would take up coverage of crimes from Sharjah. However, this was not to suggest that information on such crimes was readily available to the public in Sharjah, as officials exercised restraint on talking about anything, like they did elsewhere.

Reporters in Sharjah would rely on informal sources in hospitals or police departments as I detailed previously.[142] This was a highly risky, unprofessional source option but we all used it with a great deal of care. Some reporters especially in the Arabic language press paid for this risk with serious penalties. For one of my colleagues, the Ajman police wrote to his editor protesting the use of unknown sources in his stories. The police argued that most of his stories jeopardized the investigatory process and they wanted him to wait until they completed their work, at which time they would issue a press release. The problem was that most of us knew this could even take a year with some cases never making it to the public's knowledge. The editor fired my colleague who was deported to his homeland of Egypt.

Another incident involved a colleague from Abu Dhabi who did a one-splash story about Sharjah's air quality. She wrote that the air pollution in the emirate is as toxic as in Beijing.[143] The following day an assigning editor asked me to do a follow up on her story, talking to people in offices about how scared they were about this new revelation as well as asking physicians if they were treating more cases of illnesses related to pollution. These stories would hammer Sharjah's image like nothing else, and one felt sorry for the PR people like those of police who told us they were under strict orders to restrict the number of crime stories going to press in order to preserve the emirate's image in the year it had been chosen as the Islamic Cultural Capital. Before I could start calling doctors about the air quality story, I received a call from the staff at the Sharjah Media Center asking me for the mobile number of the reporter who did the splash story. Obviously they wanted to know her sources. I told her to call the news desk directly as I could not give her the mobile number myself. In another call, the media center spokesperson wanted me to listen to an Emirati radio talk show in which the source quoted in the original story denied stating that the air quality was bad. The media center wanted me to write a story refuting my colleague's earlier piece.

I emailed the assigning editor, copying the correspondence to my cluster editor and mentioning that I could not go ahead with a follow-up when the Emirati authorities had queried the credibility of the first report. More emails came in, including one from a deputy editor who summed up everything, adding that the newspaper would stand by the reporter's original dispatch and that any critics who had information that could be shown to be inaccurate in the original story should contact the editors directly. That evening my friend sent me a text that was making rounds among Sharjah reporters and which had been written by the media center chairman, who, as mentioned earlier, is son-in-law of the ruler Sheikh Sultan bin Ahmed Al Qassimi. The chairman had asked *The National* for an apology and a clarification of their reporting but there was no response. In the *Al Ittihad* office everyone asked me for updates about the apology but I had no information to share. I told my colleagues in the *Al Ittihad* office that *The National* would not have published such a story had the study been conducted in Abu Dhabi. The editors in Abu Dhabi had a knack for carrying primarily negative stories from the small northern emirates in detail while putting more positive coverage in news briefs that were buried in the page.

However, we debated whether they could get away with this now that even the Sharjah royal family was demanding an apology. All I could say was "thank God" that my byline was not on the story, because then I would be unable to get even the support of my deputy editor. In the *Al Ittihad* office we agreed *The National* could, at best, only delay the inevitable apology. At that time we had a new chief editor, an Emirati former diplomat in his first newsroom post at an executive level. Every morning he tweeted the stories of the paper, the only thing I noticed he did at the paper for the first few months. I stopped following his Twitter account after a month of realizing I could read the paper. He engaged in no social media interaction. Yet, this story's crisis would be his biggest challenge, as it needed an executive fortitude much stronger than the responsibility of posting tweets. Thus, it would test his loyalty to his rulers, employers and the owners of the paper versus the professional expectations and ethics surrounding the paper's credibility and his as an editor.

On March 3 another story ran on the front page, with "clarification" appearing in blue and the headline, "Air quality high in 'environmentally aware' Sharjah."[144] One of my colleagues, a female Emirati reporter, said it read more like coercion than an apology, adding she quite disagreed with the strong arm tactics exerted on the paper. "People will not believe this apology is true and their fears about the Emirate's pollution will continue," she explained. Over the following weekend the media center sent another release with the boss Sheikh Sultan thanking *The National* for responding "to a request by SMC and correct[ing] an article it had published about air quality." I forwarded the release to the news desk but was unsure any newspaper was going to carry the press release in the next day's paper, more so if *The National* itself would carry this appreciation stunt in its pages. An Egyptian colleague in the *Al Ittihad* office said the story received more attention than he thought, adding he believed if an African (referring to me) or Arab had done the story, the reporter would have been on a one-way ticket out of the UAE now. The usually correct belief is well known among Arabs that Europeans in their countries get away with things that they cannot as Arabs. This Egyptian friend also always joked whenever we shared a car to go on assignment that if he ever saw a black GMC with tinted windows following behind us he would know they were after me and *The Ambitious Struggle* (my first book). He said that he would gladly park on the side and hand me over to the authorities.

But the media center boss's new concerns and advice to the media about reporting fairly and accurately were the same that his father-in-law – the ruler of Sharjah, Sheikh Sultan bin Mohammed – had raised earlier while inaugurating the International Government Communication Forum in Sharjah that I covered.[145] He said:

> The Arab world today stands at a critical phase. Things are changing at a rapid speed. The regional landscape is in a state of flux – making it difficult to differentiate right from wrong. We see the enlightened moving towards darkness. Honesty is being taken over by falsehood … The question is – where is the media in this chaotic landscape and what is its role? Propaganda, dissemination of false news to mislead the

> public, validation of sources of information and respect for privacy – all of these are serious components in the world of journalism that need to be handled sensitively.[146]

I had made it a point during the conference to balance the rulers' concerns about the content of media reporting with the journalists' perspectives and my follow-up story was headlined, "Regional governments cannot control the media, Sharjah forum hears."[147] And I quoted the BBC's Nic Gowing, among the presenters, accusing governments of living in denial, taking everything for granted and warning them that change could come unexpectedly so quickly that the ruling authorities could not stem or stop it. Not all of the material I wrote made it into the final published version. Among the pieces left out were quotes from Saudi journalist Daoud Al Sheryan who lectured the governments that freedom of media comprises not only the practice of licensing media but also maintaining strict non-interference in the running of newsrooms.

The abuses of power by the ruling families in the GCC would make even the most liberal person hate the monarchic system. It's no wonder that the holy Quran, the most revered book in the GCC region, despises monarchism so much. In a verse in Surrat Al Naml, the Quran explicitly states that once the kings enter a country, they despoil it and make its most honorable people the lowest (Ch. 27:34).

One imam at a Ugandan mosque explained the meaning of the verse, adding that the primary target of all monarchies is always to degrade and dishonor all other people and make their families extraordinarily special. The most targeted people in dishonoring are always the knowledgeable scholars and thinkers whose knowledge and ideologies the ruling families want to belittle. Reflecting on his words, I now know why knowledge is so aggressively censured and why there is a scarcity of scholars in the GCC today. The region that once led the world in learning and was home to famous thinkers and scholars like Avicena today lags behind in knowledge. The scholars have been wiped out because they were the honored people of every community the Quran refers to and were considered as rivals dangerous to the monarchies.

In order for one to be successful, the importance of knowledge has been replaced with loyalty to monarchies. Even a small man like myself writing a simple autobiography can shake the thrones of those in power. They considered me a security risk and threw me out of the country before anyone even read my book. But it's not only the scholars targeted by these ruthless monarchies to sustain their grip on power but also the history and all the great men that have ever lived in that country that threaten them existentially. If they had not descended from their families they certainly would have their significance dwarfed. Once the Saudi family took power in Saudi Arabia, then called "Hijjaz," they changed the name and named it after King Al Saudi, disregarding all the other great men who once walked on the land including prophets.

2.13 My Work Site

It would be an oversight to close this chapter without talking about my personal work-related problems. I was glad to find a job as a journalist in the UAE, a profession I had trained for at university. Many fellow Ugandans came to the UAE with college degrees and worked as housemaids or security guards.[148]

Getting a job as a journalist is one thing but sustaining a viable, comfortable livelihood is another, a formidable challenge.

Despite having a professional job still there were many similarities that I and others like myself shared with those working in construction or as domestic household workers. However, my work was much better than theirs and always hearing their stories to be put in a newspaper was fulfilling both professionally and personally. The biggest challenge of working as a journalist in the UAE like anywhere else in the world is cultivating sources.

Hearing desperate stories of both immigrants and citizens and struggling relentlessly to find an angle that would not jeopardize their safety or mine while not compromising their voice presented complex challenges. Some stories resembled mine. However winning the confidence of a person to tell his or her story could prove difficult. I learned how censorship was not only a concern for journalists and editors but also virtually everybody else on the ground who risked the consequences of speaking up too freely or openly. One example came while interviewing an Indian immigrant in an elevator at Al Nahda where he and others had their electricity cut after a minor fire and power had not been restored after two months. He showed me electricity bills that still came despite the fact that he and others had to stay with relatives. Keep in mind that the UAE has sweltering heat during this time. The lift was the only thing that worked in the building because it was powered by a generator. As we talked another Arab man – either from Syria or Lebanon – entered the lift and followed our conversation. When the lift opened, he commented, "You Indians have no brain. How can you say all that to a journalist? Do you not understand the kind of problem you are putting yourself into or you call this Bombay as well."

His remarks silenced my interviewee who now seemed to regret everything he had told me. He begged me to kill the story or, at least, to never disclose his name, flat number or any other potentially identifying detail. I tried in vain to convince that he was safe but his concern was now about being deported. I filed the article without naming him and there was no problem at all.

Suspicion always came up once I identified myself as a reporter. Many compared reporters to spies, fielding potential sources who dared criticize the government. My most reliable journalistic tool was to show sources that I shared the pain of their problem – which was often true. That could spark the bond I needed, and often I could acknowledge similar details. Then I would convince them we shared concerns about facing possible deportation because I would be the first to go if someone wanted to squelch the story that I filed. I certainly had no desire to risk deportation because I also had a family to support. I reassured them that whatever angle my reporting took, I would handle the information with the utmost professional and ethical care, and always agreed to keep their anonymity or use aliases in referring to them. Once a source queried if I would keep him anonymous in the event that I went to jail for my reporting and if I would ever relent to authority pressure to disclose a source's identity. The truth is that every person is watched rigorously and censorship operates as if a dangerous animal is on the loose. The greatest fear is being misquoted, especially if the error leads to the direst consequences.

For me, getting a source to talk who does not immediately volunteer to do so always is a reporter's small yet significant victory. A source whose confidence I've won would often call back when another story emerged, willing to pass on important information based on our mutual trust. Being a voice for others is immensely fulfilling but also demanding, as I experienced the same distresses that sent me looking for a voice who could bring my circumstances to attention and resolution.

Likewise, the clash and intermingling of cultures affects the UAE journalist's effective capacity, with British and American editors on one hand and Arab sources on the other. I have to set aside my African culture, trying to play in both spheres of culture to survive. The editors are accustomed to the culture of accountability – of the public's right to know while sources are sworn to silence amid regimes with extensive police presence. I have to wear a mask, too, at various times, to show to my editors my understanding of digging in depth while demonstrating my understanding of withholding information when dealing with sources. One initiates story ideas because one knows what information sources will be able to provide without too much prodding, even if they knew the potential liabilities about being too open.

I was glad my editors – with just a few exceptions – were contented with a reporter's enterprising nature. Occasionally they would ask me to go and follow up stories, which they had seen other papers carrying in Ras Al Khaimah mostly. However, I always managed to cover my own beat. My biggest struggle was asking editors to hire a reporter in Ras Al Khaimah instead of having me taking on the work of reporting on other distant emirates especially after a Canadian journalist in Ras Al Khaimah was promoted and taken to Abu Dhabi. However, these pleas always fell on deaf ears.

Sometimes friends provided the most interesting news tips. One involved an Egyptian couple who had twins birthed in a Sharjah government hospital and were stranded with a heap of bills. The couple's daughters were born prematurely (at 27 weeks) in the Al Qassimi hospital. Though the delivery was normal, because the babies were immature they had to be kept in the hospital's nursery for at least six weeks. For each day in the nursery the charge for each baby is 2,200 dirhams (US $600). One of the twins died after nine days and the outstanding bill came to 25,340 dirhams (US $6,900). When we talked the father had collected the bill of the still living baby, who was in a pediatric intensive care unit, which came to 59,000 dirhams (US $16,000). The hospital told him the final bill after the baby was healthy enough to be taken home would likely be 180,000 dirhams (US $48,900).

The situation obviously stressed the parents. The father had worked as an attendant at a coffee shop until he was dismissed because he missed work to deal with his family's crisis. "We have already paid the 7,000 dirhams (US $1,900) for delivery and also secured the body of my other baby and buried it and that is as much as I have progressed so far," he told me as he shuffled through the hospital bills with an astonished look. He mentioned that the amount of money they needed was like a fortune, a sum he never thought of possessing in all his life and he said if he could have just half of it, he would be in Egypt living a very happy life.

He was disturbed by how expensive it was to be in a government hospital, saying that he had himself bypassed all private hospitals because of his low income and instead gone to a government institution. He was shocked that he could not even afford a public hospital.

Though he had been willing to talk to us on camera, hopeful that the visibility would move some charity to help, his wife warned him as my cameraman arrived with his big bag that it was dangerous to take his pictures and show them in papers. I told them they had nothing to lose or fear from having the pictures published, as we would exclude the wife and take only the images of the man. The couple hesitated, excusing themselves to chat privately. When he returned with his wife standing by his side, he said how sorry he was for putting my photographer and me through the paces. He said any press attention would cause him more trouble than he could handle and his visa already was set to expire. He needed to be discreet in order to keep whatever good relations he could muster with the UAE authorities.

I talked to the hospital physician who was caring for the infant and he said the couple's case demonstrated how important it is for every resident in the country to have health insurance. This is what officials could easily answer, but what they failed to explain was how the UAE's poor or unemployed could gain access to coverage. He also mentioned how costs for the nursery incubators had risen from 100 dirhams per infant to 2,200 dirhams in just one year. With rising costs, he knew what was happening. However, most of the immigrant workers, even in Dubai where carrying health insurance is mandatory, had policies with restrictive access and price ceilings. Even professionals such as journalists had insurance policies that did not cover healthcare services like maternity and dental care.

Even though the government hospital's nursery fees for premature infants were expensive, private hospitals were more so. A Syrian family, who spoke to me on the condition of anonymity after a charity referred me to them, also said they had to pay daily 3,200 dirhams (US $870) for their prematurely born babies to stay in a Sharjah private hospital.

"The only thing that helped us were charitable companies otherwise all our family could not raise all that money for two months," he said.

Upon filing the story, my cluster editor said he liked it, but when he forwarded it to the deputy local editor, he told me to go back to the guy and pressure him to pose for the pictures or no story. This was a part of the dilemma of working under British editors, as they never understood how threatened the Arab people felt by their governments. After a call to the father, I offered to give him other journalists' phone numbers who might carry his story without pictures. And then he suggested that we take the pictures of the babies in the hands of their parents without showing the parents' faces. My cluster editor was willing to help but I also was growing restless and didn't know if the editor had even read the story to realize that one of the twins already had died.

I thought of a way to rephrase it to the father who also was tired of my persistent calling. I asked him if he had any available photos of the twins but he responded saying that was impossible because mobile phones were not allowed in the ICU. The battle was tough, as I explained that the story would not run without photos. Actually, Arabic-speaking people, in general, regardless of their nationality, often shy away from having their names or photos published in the press, especially on sensitive topics. With Asian nationalities or those from the Indian subcontinent, this would not be a concern. Of course, the common Arab hesitation is justified, as many know that only in praising the ruling elites will a published identity be merited. With some, their sense of pride is too great to be seen in public pleading for assistance. Some cite their religious faith as the reason for the utmost discretion. Whatever the reason, here it was exceedingly difficult to make an editorial case for publishing the story without disclosing the parents' identity in full.

We tried different angles. The cluster editor suggested concentrating on making health insurance mandatory in Sharjah, as in Dubai, and using the family's story as a case example. Despite the story not being published, I went back to the hospital to see what came of this Egyptian family's circumstances. My concern was how health care is not even affordable in a government hospital. That is why I hesitated to follow my cluster editor's suggested angle. It was not an effective solution. In fact, I thought I would fall into an exploitative traps set by ruling sheikhs who governed and owned these insurance companies. The solution, as I saw it, was to alert the public to the skyrocketing costs of health care as unacceptable, not to boost the bottom line of the insurance companies. Whether it was money paid at insurance companies or hospitals they ended up in the same pockets of the ruling sheikhs. Mandatory health insurance was not even helping the unemployed and many workers would still be cheated on what could be covered and what would not be. Dubai's mandatory policy allowed providers to cut out employees' dependents from being covered, which, of course, would do nothing to alleviate situations like those the Egyptian father experienced.

In the end, I wrote the story that was required of me.[149] And before it was even published, the second baby also died. The family's story ended up as a small sidebar below the main piece.[150]

Many sources relayed their stories where racism played a role. Unfortunately most papers that I worked for in the GCC could not carry such stories. It was in Doha, Qatar where I managed to publish some of these stories for an online news outlet called *JustHere* designed as a news source for a community without borders. In June I had gone to Doha after my expulsion from Dubai to find another job in the newspapers and as I was working for free as a tryout for two newspapers, an Indian woman friend who edited content at *JustHere* offered to take some stories from me on a freelance basis.

Among the first stories that I pitched were some that concerned racism and discrimination of Africans in Doha. I had interviewed several African cab drivers working for the privately franchised taxi companies and many of their stories about discrimination followed a common path. They told me of passengers who waved them down but changed their minds when they noticed the driver was black. An African cab driver would watch from his side mirrors the same passenger waving down another taxi driver, this time of lighter skin or Asian origin.[151] (I always used the pseudonym Abu Taqiudin in filing my stories for *JustHere*, as I did not yet have an employment permit, but I also was evading UAE authorities to ensure they did not discover my whereabouts and put pressure in Qatari officials to expel me.)

After *JustHere* published my first story, the editor told me another African staffer in the office had problems with some taxi drivers who also did not want to transport black passengers. It was a similar story to those I heard in Dubai and Sharjah while working there. Black Africans had to wait longer for a taxi driver who would take them as passengers, including those whose cabs were empty.

As I continued investigating racism in Doha I came across a Kenyan woman who was working in a women's hair salon and told me how most Arab women who came to the shop always preferred to wait even longer for a light-skinned Filipino or Indian to serve them rather than a black African woman. "If the employer told her there was no Filipino or Indian in the next several hours, she would demand that the African lady first washes her hands with soap before touching her hair," she told me. She said the extraordinary demand humiliated her as well as an African colleague who worked in the salon. The other employee refused to wash her hands insisting they already were clean. The employer fired her, and she was asked to purchase her own air ticket back to Kenya.

Meanwhile, other sources turned out to be disappointing and unreliable. Some would cancel appointments while many others withheld information fearing governmental retribution. Sources from government departments were the hardest to crack. After an interview, many wanted to review a story draft prior to publication, something no professional editor would allow. There were call backs, especially from police and security, to delay or withhold publication. This request even came if the story had arisen from a press release senior officials had distributed but now they had a change of mind, claiming the information was never intended for publication. The problem with this patronizing was mostly if a story had been already uploaded online, given the cut-throat competition of claiming first credit for breaking news. My editors decided that a story would not be removed online but it would not be published in the print edition. The good thing was the police PRs just checked the papers, never online, but several times I would have been punished by being blacklisted if they had found this insubordination was sanctioned by my editors.

It was always a challenge informing British editors that a source cancelled an appointment or refused to speak; or that a story was delayed because the government departments needed to obtain approvals at several levels before certain information could be passed along to the media. The editors would be hardest to deal with when they were especially new in the country or when the newspaper was just starting on the British standards of what was considered newsworthy. A reporter could explain only with the most delicate tone to sources what is involved in professional journalism. If a source blacklisted a reporter, an editor had no sympathy, as expected. Missing a story that came from a police public information could lead to being fired. Yet, still editors pushed reporters to dig aggressively and in depth, even knowing that there was a strong likelihood of the story being nixed. Then editors, showing no true signs of being chastened, would push for softball stories to idolize the ruling elites.

The most stressful thing personally was to go even just for two days without a byline in the paper. In fact some reporters could miss for a week without becoming dismayed but two days made me feel sick. I did not have to compare myself with them, as that would have been a dangerous undertaking.

Sometimes officials simply expected journalists to toe eulogizing lines even when there was nothing frankly to praise. In fact, there were plenty of instances where worker exploitation would make the most compelling copy. Once I was invited to an open session with the staff of a major Sharjah hospital. As a journalist, I asked if I was in the right place, because as the questions were posed to the hospital directors it was clear most involved internal problems. The staff were asking for pay rises, wondering if the hospital's new management would honor earlier promises. The chairman told me I was in the right place, as they wanted the media to show the excellent services the hospital offered and its commitment to transparent accountability. I asked if there were actually pay problems at the hospital because we had reported that low pay had led to high staff turnover. The chairman quickly became angry. He did not expect a journalist to ask about pay problems, because his previous media experience had been about showcasing the hospital's strengths. He said in a patronizing voice that every company had its own problems and theirs were none of my business. It was clear that I was going to take the pay rises query angle in my story despite his threatening tone. He could count on the Arab reporters to write warm appraisals of the hospital's management taking the time out to hear employee concerns.

I had one final question: Why was the hospital charging so expensively compared to other hospitals; was it targeting only the rich families? The chairman referred me to the hospital director who calmly answered that the costs were actually cheaper than comparable hospitals elsewhere.

Another journalist asked about the relationship between the Sharjah Health Authority (SHA) and the hospital. In a clearly amused tone that made everyone present laugh, the chairman replied, "the hospital is a private business owned by the government and independent." I sent the confusing quote to my editor, who also was troubled about how to classify the hospital ownership. The hospital had been established by the emirate ruler on spacious land granted by the government-run university. Now it was going to be run by a government authority, but the boss of SHA was saying it is private. In the conference I was tempted to ask him to stop confusing us and simply say that the hospital facilities belonged to the government and the profits were private (but I controlled my urge and kept quiet). My story, though severely cut down, appeared in the paper with the angle I had intended to use unchanged.[152]

The problem of drawing lines between what was private and what was owned by the government was extremely blurred in the GCC. Companies were first formed as government entities; then they would be called semi-government and eventually private, and no one would question the process of these transformations. But even as a private entity they would still get government support like other government departments. The media company I worked for was also affected by this dilemma of identification. Sometimes it is government and other times it is private and it will be government again and henceforth.

My best satisfaction came from uncovering stories behind the official farce. When the Emirate National Oil Company (ENOC) group started closing its fuel stations in the northern emirates, the official version they gave all newspapers was that they were doing maintenance work.[153]

I was the only journalist who drove to every station that belonged to the group in Sharjah and Ajman to discover there was no maintenance work taking place at any of the locations.[154]

The company's PR rep called to chastise me after the story, claiming the official version was that of maintenance and I was supposed to mention only that as the reason, like other papers, but I did not budge. An Emirati friend in office also warned me that ENOC and Emirates Petroleum Products Company (EPPCO) belonged to the second highest ranking sheikh in Dubai and that I should take their official version as they could take any action against me. And I told him that maybe these managers had deceived the Sheikh as well that they are doing maintenance work and thus he would be glad to learn it from me that the opposite was the truth. Deceiving the public was shameful, and I would recall that in every follow-up story I covered about the fuel crisis in the emirate that year. Finally, both companies confessed a deal with the government had failed to raise fuel prices yet the group was instead buying fuel at higher prices in the international market.

It was also cathartic for me to write stories about citizens' social problems, such as covering increasing costs of rent, utility bills, and basic foodstuffs, while contending with stagnant salaries. These were stories representing not only my sources but also my own experience. I remember the stories of people living in cars during the property boom of 2008 that I told during my earliest days at *The National*, as I went early in the morning with a photographer to take their photos.[155] In Abu Shagara there were many cars idling in order to keep the air conditioning on even late at night when the day's heat was slow to moderate. One story told of a Palestinian man who had died in his car where he had stayed for several years.[156]

These stories returned with a vengeance in 2013 as rents recovered from the recession. I found many residents in Sharjah with similar fears that they might be forced out of their homes into their vehicles. Rent went up even faster than the costs of food and utilities.

But it was also painful when I felt like I might have to do this monotonous work all my life for a living. Unlike others who would be promoted to become editors, international correspondents or managers, I was not among them, being an African immigrant. I had seen many other veteran reporters whom I found doing the same work who were still stuck in the same position or reporting the usual routine of fire, accidents and other local stories. It is not that they are all unambitious or not smart enough and, in fact, many told me they are trying so much to do something else but the circumstances did not permit mobility for immigrants. Now six years in the same position, their fate appeared to be becoming more likely mine.

Today's reality suggests an inflexible, uncompromising reality that appears to be the more common story heard around the world. Sadly, even immigrating from the poor economies to the richest countries is no longer an assured route for one to escape poverty. The sacrifices of living away from home, family and dear relatives are substantial but still not enough to transform one's self-actualization and bring about prosperity. There is more evidence of one escaping from African or South Asian impoverished environments only to fall into stiff exploitation by rich ruling elites in the GCC region that is destined to make poverty a permanent condition for many. Poor people continue to invest their youthful lives and energetic years into developing economies that ultimately will disown them at will and in old age. This is dictated to by the knowledge, labor and experiences of immigrant expatriates who are starving while others bid mercilessly to keep up in the race to build the tallest tower and longest bridge or to buy out more companies from failing entrepreneurs, all in a bid to expand an empire that has little respect for the individual. Amid such a race, expatriates can only sell their skills and labor so cheaply or be replaced with others willing to come at whatever price is offered.

The managers who report their business performance to the ruling families would watch in astonishment the enormous magnitude of income being handed over while an ever-diminishing fraction of the profits are plugged back in to the wages and salaries of workers who toil at great expense to their bodies and souls. They would learn that these ruling elites and business owners can get away with the exploitation and middle-level and upper-level managers would, in turn, try it themselves by pocketing most of the meager turnovers in their own huge salaries and benefits while cutting the pie into smaller slices for working expatriates. Where it is possible they would push to cut the number of employees and expect individuals otherwise to do the work of perhaps five, with no increase in wage or benefits.

In the workplace setting of a newspaper with which I am more familiar, the management wants a reporter to cover the police, courts, civil defense, executive and consultative councils (a form of parliament, but with no legislative power), municipalities, educational institutions and universities, fisheries, road projects and infrastructure programs in all of the northern emirates of Sharjah, Ajman, Umm Al Quwain, Fujairah and Ras Al Khaimah.

Threats of being replaced and deported back to one's impoverished country of origin provide the unfortunate incentive to work. The race to be rich traps innocent expatriates and most of the citizens in a relentless cycle of exploitation and abuse that is difficult to break. The expatriates must bend to cut-throat competition on who stays when a business downsizes in order to provide greater margins to rich owners and managers. Workers offer themselves to do what is not humanely doable in order to beat a waiting sea of potential rivals.

This ruthless competition occurred among reporters, which extended to paying informants to tell journalists anything in hospitals or police departments before the officials announced it. There was stiff rivalry among reporters for an informer with each trying to win favors while at the same time requesting the informer to block other rival reporters from access or even worse withhold information that was part of the public's right to know. Of course, the problems of discrimination and racism occurred, in part, because of this competition, as reporters tried to get exclusive stories on a daily basis, worrying any time a single story was missed. Still if the managers or editors were looking for a reason to pay some people less than others in order to retain a larger slice of the salary pie, race and nationality always became more significant in the consideration.

As in the circumstances involving domestic and construction workers who I interviewed regularly, professional staff members like myself were scaling down or putting aside altogether the dreams we held when we arrived to work in a foreign country. All of us dream of working abroad for a few years and going back to our countries financially able to run our own businesses and be assured of a stable and even thriving economic likelihood. Dreams of being well-off and living like those who employed or supervised us at work have become more distant each day. Some construction workers aspired to the hopes of being supervisors in their own right, perhaps even getting the necessary education to become engineers and others managing large-scale construction projects. In the meantime, one could perhaps justify the differences in wages and salaries because of the skill levels required in certain roles. However, the income inequality at my place of work was different. There were differences of income even with the people who worked in similar roles and capacities. In fact, some with inferior education and experiences could as well earn double the salaries of those who came from nationalities and races that, truthfully, were viewed by the ruling elites as inferior.

Now I saw myself in the same predicament as my sources, nearing the point of giving up the dream just like my fellow country men and women who had high expectations in coming to the rich emirates.

Once I asked the chief editor, local desk editor and his deputy to give me a recommendation letter for a media fellowship application. The Iraqi-American chief editor was the first to respond, promising to give me a letter, adding he was so happy I was making efforts to improve myself. A day later the local desk editor and his deputy – both British and close personal friends with each other – replied with laughter, adding they could not in their right conscience give me such a letter. The response disturbed me deeply. A week later, I checked with the editor-in-chief to see if he had written the letter as he had promised but there was no response. Clearly, the response of his two juniors had become his as well. This would be humiliating for any young person, ambitious and ready at the age of 30 to make his mark in a different society and culture and to validate the training and experience he has received in his faraway homeland, all in order to gain yet further experience and training to improve continuously. Here, others thought nothing about putting up a roadblock to one's potential and aspirations. One could dismiss such statements as prejudiced but still the feeling of non-accomplishment always returns to haunt the individual. I recalled that while I was working with *The Gulf Today* an Indian editor had given me a recommendation letter to attend an AIDS conference in Toronto so easily without even giving it a second thought.

Now, working in a paper for six years, a request for a recommendation was treated as a luxury only reserved for certain individuals. These British editors held themselves in high esteem, of the sort that suggested no one else could share that level, even with training and further education. My work performance and output spoke plainly on my behalf. I had tolerated several instances of name-calling and demeaning emails from them. However, one day I blurted out to one of them and responded to his email that the difference between us was that I was hired when the company was still strong and hiring the cream of the crop from all over the world, but now he came onboard when the newspaper turned desperate, taking everyone who applied.

2.14 Detained for an Hour in Doha

In Doha, journalists risk a lot while doing their work more than in any other place in the GCC. Despite being home to the popular Al Jazeera broadcast network and the Doha Center for Media Freedom, the country's relationship with local journalists is largely one of a patronizing master. At the local paper where I work an editor enjoys telling his tales of troubles with the Doha cops and the time he was almost deported for stories that were considered too critical. I had escaped arrest after authorities wondered why I was photographing workers who were taking their lunch served in dirty containers. The photos ran with a story I wrote for *JustHere*.

After I was hired at a local newspaper and started chasing stories more aggressively I would soon land in more trouble with Doha cops. I was working on a story about the hardships for expatriates getting married in Qatar and the skyrocketing costs of weddings in the country. I had collected input from Islamic scholars about how expatriates' marriages are organized to become binding and now I was looking to cover the story from the angle of Christian expatriates. I set up an interview with a Catholic priest and when I tried to arrange for photos, the local news editor told me the paper did not take pictures of other priests apart from the Qardawis, referring to adherents following the popular Islamic scholar Yusuf Al Qardawi, a spiritual leader for the Muslim brotherhood organization based in Doha.

In the morning I showed up at the gates of the church for the interview. The Religious Complex in the Mesaimeer area is guarded heavily and it is home to five religions outside of Islam. Security is extremely tight even on days when there are no services, as evidenced by the presence of several police vehicles. Each gate has a police vehicle stationed and as I entered through one of the gates, a cop stopped me, asked where I was going and said that I looked like a Muslim. I did not argue but I told him I had an appointment with a priest at the complex. He first tried to tell me Muslims are not allowed to enter the premises and then demanded to see my ID or documents.

I then identified myself as a journalist, which alarmed him. He called his boss immediately in a manner that sounded like he had just identified a terrorist. He then led me to a small police unit office in the church complex where his superior was on the phone trying to sort out the details. It was as if a journalist had never entered the church complex. The superior took my wallet and rifled through all my documents and IDs, reading them one-by-one to the person on the other end of the phone line. The call ended, and the policeman did not return my driver's license which I had obtained in Dubai and my Qatari ID. I was not sure of my fate so I texted the managing editor that I could be in trouble, and that he should keep checking my phone and once it is off he should try to find out where I was being detained.

My managing editor contacted me after 20 minutes, advising that I should not worry but simply cooperate and they would let me leave. This is what editors almost always advise journalists in these predicaments: just cooperate with those authorities who are trying to prevent them from doing their work as reporters. I started to wonder to what extent an editor would cooperate with the authorities. Would he agree not to disclose my whereabouts if I went missing for days?

I texted another friend in Nairobi, Kenya and asked him to keep trying my phone every hour until I informed him I was out of trouble. In case my phone cannot be answered or if it gets switched off and he doesn't hear from me until the evening he should post something on social networks, especially my Facebook page, saying that I had been detained trying to interview a Catholic priest in Doha, Qatar.

Meanwhile, I started deleting the texts in case the phone also became an object of investigation. The cops returned to me after about an hour and they asked me what I was trying to ask the priest, where I had written my questions and how I knew the priest. I called the priest who offered to talk to the authorities but they refused. I had not written any questions so the police gave me a sheet of paper to jot down the questions. I was unclear about where all of this was heading.

After about 30 additional minutes they told me I needed to bring the questions written on letterhead stationery from the newspaper along with a letter from the priest requesting to do the interview. They then let me go. I returned to the office and everybody was curious about what happened, especially all of my Indian colleagues. For them, the story seemed like a part of a Bollywood movie.

During my stay in Qatar's newsroom I have seen many topics subjected to the red lines of censorship. This includes racism. Because we worked mostly at night and left the office around midnight I discovered many migrant employees slept at construction sites and others in open-air verandahs. That too is off-limits for a story. Even reporting on traffic jams caused by road projects in anticipation of the World Cup is forbidden. And this is the editorial policy for a newspaper that claims its boldness in journalism, championing past stories that were published despite them being considered taboo for Qatar. The

Qatari editor-in-chief once sent a message from his hotel where he was vacationing in Europe to his Indian managing editor that read, "Don't carry even a 0.01 per cent negative story in the paper while I am away." The message was passed on to all reporters with a warning that a negative story carried a personal risk. A few days later the country's ministry of interior issued the Qatar Cybercrimes Law in which it announced prison and financial penalties for even those who published what it called "false news" online.

The new law included the following provisions:

Article 5 indicated punishment of up to three years in prison and a fine of a maximum of 500,000 Qatari riyals (US$138,000) for anyone who creates or manages a website for a terrorist association or organisation on the Internet or any other media or assists in communication of the heads of the organisation or any of its members or spreads its ideologies.

Article 6 states punishment of up to three years prison and a fine of a maximum of 500,000 Qatari riyals or either punishment for anyone who creates or manages a website on the Internet or any other media to publish false news with an intention of jeopardising the safety of the state, its general order and its local or international peace. A punishment of up to one year in prison and a fine of a maximum of 250,000 Qatari riyals ($US 69,000) or either punishment for anyone who broadcasts or publishes false news on any media.

Article 8 carries punishment of up to three years and a fine of 100,000 Qatari riyals (US$28,000) or either punishment for anyone who violates the social values or publishes news or pictures or records a voice that violates the private or family life of individuals even if the content is true or if it slanders or libels another person on the Internet or any other media.

That same week the Qatari editor-in-chief returned from Europe and asked us to do an extensive follow-up story to be published on the weekend, saying he preferred it be critical. I worked on the story with two other colleagues and they both kept praying that the story be cancelled. They told me they had seen critical stories pulled out of the pages at the last minute disregarding all the effort they had invested in them. However this story was not cancelled but what happened was that it was edited heavily and made much softer than it had been intended. Two days after it had been published some of my sources wanted to see it online and its earlier link was no longer active. We searched it again and again but in vain. I then asked my news editor what had happened and he said was surprised that I was asking. "Don't you know the problems that story has caused with the government?" And that was the end.

It is these restrictions by the GCC countries that completely kill the functioning of local media in their countries and relegate the newspapers and televisions to mouthpieces for the government PR machines. Unfortunately a non-functioning media is not even effective in doing PR work for its ruling patrons because the whole society knows the media are dead and no one cares to read local papers.

Even the journalists are reluctant to ask any questions because they will never get any answers from either the government or even private companies that are well connected with the rulers. I was thrown out of an office of a franchised taxi company that was just across the street from our office on D-Ring road. I wanted to interview taxi company administrators about why there were so many complaints about their taxi services in the city. I was shuttled from one office to another and along the way everybody asked why I didn't just wait for the press release to arrive in my email. Finally I landed in the office of the Qatari manager who ordered me to leave the company's premises immediately, adding they never entertained journalists in their offices.

Because of similar instances journalism has become a lazy profession in Doha. At the two local papers where I have worked, rarely do reporters go out to work on any story other than a press event. They arrive in their offices sometime between 5 and 6 p.m. and ask the translators what stories have been carried by the Arabic dailies that day. They go through the list and each chooses a story that pleases them and the translator will relate the story details and they will file that very story for the following day. Translators will again check the Qatar news agency for government releases and the next day's paper will be full of translations and press releases. Only on Saturdays did the paper where I worked carry a special story, compiled mostly from tweets and a few quotes from old press releases of community members. This story would take a whole week's enterprise from two or three reporters.

When I started working in Doha, I panicked about having to go out and cultivate sources and one reporter told me confidentially they were all capable of doing what I could do but they simply chose to give back to the company what it paid them. "If you are going to run around for stories even the whole salary they give you will not be enough for taxis alone," he told me. "You just need to learn the politics of survival here; it's all about turning up for work and being good to the editors and you take whatever they are giving you." There were no further explanations of what low pay means to any kind of worker. I am worried if the construction workers and engineers of those tall buildings have the same spirit as journalists at their work because, after all, they are the most exploited. One wonders what the risk for calamitous carelessness could be.

The GCC rulers have managed to make their local media almost worthless and now they are extending their wars into the Western media. Unfortunately many respectable journalists and researchers in Europe and America have been recruited into this war of tiny countries, just for money. There are many fake blogs,

Twitter accounts, websites and even human rights organizations being set up by these Western elites on behalf of their GCC sponsors to attack and tarnish the name of another GCC country.

The managing editor of a local paper I worked for came almost running to the newsroom announce to the news editor that he had found a story in the US media speculating the UAE had paid journalists in the US to write negative articles about Qatar in order to tarnish their image in the wider public opinion arenas of American and European people. The news editor, an Indian in his sixties who was mainly the man in charge at the newspaper, dismissed his boss the same way he dismisses a reporter with a bad pitch, telling him the editor-in-chief would never allow such a report to be carried in the paper. The managing editor returned to his office but the debate was just starting in the newsroom among reporters and their subeditors about the rivalry of the two countries.

One reporter offered a perspective of the GCC rivalry suggesting the GCC governments were traveling on the same ship but in different decks. One government trying to sink the other's deck is simply being myopic as the whole ship will sink and all GCC governments will collapse in unison. Another colleague asked why the UAE was going to bomb Islamists in Libya and Syria but did not bomb its immediate neighbor who sponsored the Islamists. Another one suggested they were trying to replay the old US–Russia Cold War, exchanging words in the media and fighting on the battlefields of other Arab countries. Then we all agreed on the role of money in the world geopolitical map that tiny countries like Qatar and the UAE were destabilizing governments of big Arab states such as Syria, Yemen and Egypt. And even though our newspaper was scared to carry any story on the rivalry, the online Doha news published a story on the same rivalry.[157]

One might ask how these governments benefit from sidelining their own local media in their proxy media wars, and the answer is simple. It is only the opinions of Americans and Europeans that matter regarding the conduct of these GCC governments, not the already suppressed opinions of Emiratis or Qataris.

A few months after starting with the newspaper in Qatar, the editor-in-chief was relieved of his duties. The editor was a civil engineer who rose to the post almost exclusively because of his Western education and perceived knowledge of English. However, he was not so fluent, as his opinion pieces were written in Arabic and then translated into English, and I had translated a couple of them. But he also had a positive personal touch, making bonds strengthened with a sincere sense of loyalty. Some colleagues talked about him as kind compared to other Qataris, as he quietly assured his staff always had tea without needing to pay. We missed this greatly after he was dismissed. I realized I had taken on average three cups of this free tea every day and now I would have go to the cafeteria and start paying for each cup, a discretionary expense that was pretty significant in an already tight, limited budget. Indeed, small gestures like this made a difference.

But what bonded me to the outgoing editor was not his free tea; it was his willingness to stand up to the opposition of a newsroom, heavily represented by Indian nationals, in my getting hired. Initially, when I applied, the response from the Indian managing editor was lukewarm and the aging news editor – who was in his mid-sixties – told me outright they did not need Arabic reporters. As I exited the premises, I met the editor-in-chief who was impressed with Arab language fluency. After going through my resume, he confidently announced that he was hiring me. Landing a job on my first day in Doha was a major achievement. Meanwhile, the old Indian news editor insisted he wanted me to work on a trial basis for one week before a contract would be offered. I was given an article from an Arabic newspaper to translate, and a group of Indians in the newsroom including the news editor stood behind me as I typed, watching every keystroke carefully. They would point out a mistake as soon as it was typed and make comments in Malayalam, a local Indian language, which sounded like "OMG, he can type." There were a couple of sabotaging and blackmail incidents in that one week and the reports they always gave the Qatari editor were not good, but then in another meeting with the editors in my presence, he insisted that he needed someone who understood Arabic and could also write some clear English. He also pointed out to them that there were many stories that an Arabic speaker could go out and get as original rather than relying on translations from competing Arabic papers. This threatened the stance of the aging Indian news editor, as he was the main person served by three Arabic translators. The translators were good in Arabic but they could not write English, so they always told him what was in the Arabic papers verbally and he would recycle the stories without verifying the information. He had served at the paper for 37 years all along recycling translated Arabic stories and as I would learn from even Indian colleagues he apparently enjoyed the game of kicking out bilingual reporters fluent in English and Arabic.

Because my experience had not been good in that first week, I went to another newspaper and offered to work on a trial basis. After two weeks my visa was due to expire but the second newspaper was less political than the first and they agreed to take me on but they told me their recruitment process required several more weeks which would have meant me returning home and waiting for a contract that was not guaranteed. Meanwhile the Qatari editor-in-chief at the first paper called me back and I signed the contract before leaving Qatar. I learned later that my residence visa was passed on to the Indian secretary who delayed sending it for more than 20 days. Almost all GCC entry visas require someone to travel within 30 days of issue or the visa becomes invalid. I wrote to the Qatari editor-in-chief again that I was having another offer from a Qatari newspaper in case their visa did not come in time, but then the Indian secretary, who previously had refused to respond to my queries, sent the visa to me, which, incidentally, carried a date several weeks prior.

The editor-in-chief's departure now meant that I had lost one of my strongest allies in Qatar, which left me in a bit of a panic. However, the new editor proved to be as friendly and we became good working colleagues. He also encouraged more enterprising journalistic opportunities, asking me to redevelop the paper's website into an aggressive news portal that would be a reference for all the news in the Gulf Arab region. He asked for a proposal and once it was accepted, I was offered the opportunity to be the new web editor. The news was good but my mind also was locked on the inevitable day he would call me to give the bad news of dismissing me after publishing this book, on the orders of his government, the same way the editor at *The National* had responded in April 2014 after my first book was published.

Section 3

Enslavement: Losing Human Dignity

3.1 More than Slavery

To comprehend the treatment of domestic workers in the GCC, one must first read the history of these countries. Slaves initially arrived in the UAE, mostly from Zanzibar but also from other African countries, and were received mainly at the Dubai creek.[158]

Like all other slaves, they would be in chains when they arrived in the UAE and they would remain so until a buyer had completed the transaction. The prices differed from slave to slave, according to sex, strength and area of origin.

The male slaves mostly did fishing and pearling, which occurred during the hottest months of the season. The male slaves also worked as guards to the sheikhs, or as gardeners and other household servants. Female slaves worked as housemaids.[159]

A slave called his/her male master *Ami,* or "paternal uncle," and the female master was called *Amati, or* "paternal aunt." In some families a slave would take the name of *Khali,* which meant "maternal uncle," and the female slaves would be called *Khalit,* meaning "maternal aunt."[160]

Once a female slave had children from the *Ami,* the children would take on the father's surname and while the offspring were identified as sons or daughters of a slave they would inherit part of the wealth, and they would be free. The mother would also be free. Such children born to masters, however, would have problems marrying free spouses despite their freedom and carrying the name of their father. They would be discriminated against on the grounds that they were *Biyisra,* meaning "sons of slaves without a clan." *Biyisra* was a term applied to someone who didn't know their roots. A slave could also buy his freedom those days; on such an occasion he would call residents of the area to a party such as a luncheon event called *Walima* and attendees would serve as witnesses.[161]

The faces of slavery slowly changed in the GCC countries with the arrival of Iranian women who also looked for domestic work as maids. The Iranian maids were also working in shops during mornings and in the evenings would return to their masters' homes. The Iranian maids worked alongside the black slaves but their rights in society were different. They were paid, unlike black slaves. These changes evolved and around 1952 Indians started arriving on boats into the UAE to look for jobs in large numbers and they were cheaper than the Iranian maids. They entered without passports or documents, and soon after Pakistanis arrived in similar waves. The Indians and Pakistanis mostly worked as housemaids and didn't go fishing or pearling as they didn't know the art of these professions. It was Indians who changed the words of *Ami* to an Indian word *Arbab* for a male master and *Bibi* or *Mamma* for a female master.[162]

It was after the discovery of oil when the faces of slavery changed. More nationalities started flowing into the GCC countries, including the UAE, where immigrants did everything from domestic work to sales and fishing. At this time slavery had already been abolished in most countries and the GCC countries followed suit. The UAE's Sheikh Zayed banned formal slavery in Al Ain and Abu Dhabi in the 1960s, for example. Most GCC families replaced slaves with maids or domestic workers. What remained uncertain was whether the long-standing ingrained culture of enslavement would also be replaced or if this was a mere reengineering of terminology. Offices dedicated to bringing and distributing domestic workers throughout the UAE and other GCC countries started opening more frequently during the 1980s. The business of maids had been taken over from slavery and it was highly profitable as well.[163]

As maids and other workers continued flowing to the Gulf the local natives became more uncomfortable with them:

For a certain time after a new batch of people arrives from

> elsewhere, unless they are manifestly wealthy; they are dirty, they are noisy, they steal, they will not work but just want to live on welfare, they will fill up the hospitals, they crowd the schools, they will not adopt our ways, they live in overcrowded houses ... If they are wealthy; they are buying everything up, they name prices rise, they look down on us, they think they are too good for us, they have got the ear of the government.[164]

The difference here is that foreigners are no longer looked to as new batches of people in all GCC countries even though many governments have refused to naturalize even the longest staying amongst them. The problem is this discriminatory attitude, as described above, has become permanent.

One of the most comprehensive studies examining domestic household workers in the UAE was published by the Ministry of Labor and social affairs in 1994. The study, written in Arabic, criticizes everything to do with the presence of maids in the UAE. The project was titled "Domestic workers in the UAE" by Mohammed Eissa Al Suwaidi, Abdullah Mohammed Abu Shihab and Twaha Hussein Hassan. Seif Ali Al Jarwan, the Minister of Labor and Social Affairs at the time, warned Emiratis in a foreword about the bad impact foreign domestic workers were bringing to their country, culture and language. It is not surprising from this report that the researchers also pointed out the objective was to establish the negative phenomena posed by foreign domestic workers.[165] The research concluded the foreign domestic workers were responsible for most of the wrongs occurring in local communities that threatened Emirati families and their future. The researchers said that even previous literature on the subject had found similar results and their findings reflected a common opinion held among most Emiratis. It also warned that if nothing was done to stop the inflow of maids, the forthcoming years would see more foreign workers coming into the country and their negative impacts would multiply.[166] I was struck by passages suggesting how the Arabic language had been affected with many words infiltrating either from Urdu or English, and one could feel the pain of the author who clearly loves his country and language dearly. Besides that I didn't find anything practical that justifies stopping the influx of immigrant domestic household workers.

Despite the research's dated origins, one is shocked to learn that such perceptions about foreign domestic workers in the Gulf countries are still alive and kicking in the hearts and minds of most GCC nationals. This is striking in the age of globalization and internationalism, as it is not at all possible for Emiratis or any other community elsewhere in the world to be capable of thriving alone. Emiratis can no longer live without maids or drivers and local Emirati people could not – and would not – take up these jobs in other households. The best way to preserve a culture or language was not to close doors from foreigners, as that is cowardly. Even traditional Arab cultures have assimilated contemporary evolutionary aspects. Emiratis could do better by befriending the foreigners especially those working in their homes and teaching their culture.

The problem with most Arab families is that domestic workers are always segregated or discriminated against. Even on family outings in parks one finds maids will be in their own circles, eating with fellow domestic workers or being alone. Maids can only associate with children, not adults. Government-supported studies such as the one cited above might serve desired nationalistic purposes but they are hardly realistic because domestic workers cannot be seen as standing exclusively for negative effects and impacts. It only heightens tension between local citizens and foreign workers, which explains directly the bad treatment of maids in the UAE and other GCC countries. Locals might be persuaded to believe that domestic workers are responsible for the misfortunes in the country or even in their own families. That is categorically wrong not just on a hypothetical basis but also on an empirical one. It is disheartening to see the ruling elites mobilize biases and prejudices among the local citizens against their own sponsored migrant domestic workers. It is the same emphasis that would explain the government's reluctance to address adequately migrant grievances, especially serious crimes such as rape and murder involving their citizen sponsors. Governments do little to raise the awareness that would integrate migrants into the local society. Instead, they rely on discriminatory propaganda that regrettably has poisoned the attitudes of local citizens toward their own household workers.

There is no study that has been done in the UAE to distill the contributions and the economic contributions of domestic workers who have come from abroad. No one has dared pose the empirically tested question of what would happen if there were no domestic workers to fulfill the service needs of Emiratis. The same goes for all other working classes heavily populated by migrants, who have done much to bolster the UAE's economic position in a global economy. Confirmation bias was rampant in the study, as researchers failed to show any data suggesting domestic workers were interviewed or surveyed. This is reprehensible on so many levels but it most compellingly illustrates the greatest error in neglecting the recognition of domestic workers as human beings who should be allowed to have their own say in their lives. There are no safe, open channels for domestic workers to address their concerns or to seek fair relief on grievances.

Unfortunately, the disregard is so common in this region even among non-GCC nationals. One personally embarrassing incident occurred when I wrote a story about an Emirati mother, her three daughters and two housemaids dying in a villa fire in Ajman. The story was published in the newspaper[167] as the lead story with the headline, "Fire kills mother and three girls." The story carried details about all of the casualties, including the domestic workers. It was only when a reader pointed out in an email that the headline was "racist": how could it talk about only Emiratis as if the maids' lives were not important? I was embarrassed to be called out on something like that. Of course, I had no control over the headline. The only good thing was the clearly angered reader copied the editor-in-chief who responded with an apology, requesting the reader did not have to pass sweeping judgment on the newspaper's capacity for being respectful toward all individuals, regardless of origin, race, and nationality.

3.2 Hate Propaganda

An Emirati colleague in the *Al Ittihad* office talked to me about African housemaids and said something that was not only racist but also showed the misinformation so rife in local GCC communities. He asked if I knew of a culture in Africa in which if a housemaid killed a child of her GCC employer, she would be blessed by an African god and become rich. He said there were many variations of this story being told in GCC courts, especially in Saudi Arabia where Ethiopian maids had murdered several Saudi children. The judge would ask the maid why she killed the sponsor's son or daughter and she responded that her mother called from Ethiopia instructing her to kill the baby as a sacrifice to the African gods so that would grant her the wealth that Arabs had experienced up until now. It was terribly twisted propaganda perpetrated shamelessly by the authorities to discourage their citizens from hiring African maids or to justify the mistreatment and dehumanization of these poor maids in their homes.

I suppressed the urge to tell him that I have covered several courts in the UAE and with only the few exceptions of a handful of European nationalities, most poor Asians and Africans in the courts are not even allowed the chance to give their version of the case. They are simply presented to the court, read their charges and then dismissed to wait for another hearing or verdict. The prosecution and defense of these poor people is pinned down by the prosecution and such versions of the mythical "African Culture" must also be a work of unprofessional, lazy prosecutors who are intent on spreading hate propaganda against all Africans. Instead I told him that Africa was as big as the Arab world and embodied many different cultures, as even in my small country Uganda the cultures and practices of different groups are anything but uniform.

He showed me a video of African mob men in the Central African Republic (CAR) who had assembled three Black Muslim women and lynched them. As the women sat down on the orders of the mob, one man jumped and kicked one of them, truncheons with the widths of trees were used on them, coupled with stoning. I asked him to stop the video in the middle, because it was too graphic for me to watch but he refused and continued letting it run. I watched him, as tears gathered in his eyes. He commented on every move and act as if he was broadcasting a football match. "I think one is dead now; there is no one to stop them. What kind of people do this to women and no one stops them? They have started burning them. *Subhannallah,* they killed three of them and that's not enough to cool them; they are burning them now. Yasin, come and see this."

I screamed. "I don't know, you are simply relating me to those people just because I am black but you are forgetting that I am also a Muslim like you and the women being burnt." After the words sputtered out, I was near tears and embarrassed to be losing my composure in the office. He immediately apologized, adding he was not relating them to me; that I was a good and disciplined person, not like other Africans. It was bizarre how even his apology that sought to explain his experiences with me excluded other Africans.

One had to be alarmed how quickly violence inflicted on

Muslims in the CAR had found its viral route to Blackberries, WhatsApp, and other mobile platforms in many Arab communities. Videos such as these propagated dangerous ideas and distorted generalizing information about all Africans or black people. The Arab communities that watched them thought the Africans were in arms against Islam. I remember another video that was passed on to my WhatsApp by another Arab colleague, which showed a mob circling off a man's car. Meanwhile others pointed accusing fingers toward the man proclaiming he was a Muslim, while he desperately tried to deny it in his incessant pleas. The video carried translated subtitles of what the crowd and the man was saying in English. The man begged the mob not to burn him in his car, but instead to take him prisoner and let his car be free, the only property that he had to leave to his family and young children. The mob told him not to worry as they would also burn the children.

3.3 Stigmatizing and Subjugating Others

I got a call from a friend in Uganda who had a sister (Hajara) working as a maid for an Emirati family in Ras Al Khaimah. Hajara had called them within about a month of her coming to the UAE to complain that she was being exploited and abused in the sponsor's home and she wanted the people in Uganda to help her return home. The friend recollected a lot of ordeals, all familiar abuses recounted by many other maids working in the GCC, and ended with: "She told me she was even feeling shy to tell me all what they have done to her because I am her brother but she wanted me to know that everything bad in this world has been done to her," he said. We both interpreted "everything bad" to refer to sexual abuse. She had no one to turn to in the UAE and that is why she was calling home. She had attempted to escape but she didn't know anywhere to go for safe haven and was afraid of worse ordeals once she escaped.

The brother wanted me to go to Ras Al Khaimah to pick up her sister and put her on the quickest flight back home – as simple as that. That was always the delusions carried by people who have never been to the UAE. They thought a flight was like waving down a taxi and telling the driver one's final destination. He did not even consider that his sister already had her passport confiscated by the abusing sponsor. I asked for the young woman's number so I could talk to her and ascertain what could be done. She did not have a mobile and she was making calls in the presence of her sponsors at night on a landline, but she had advised them to call on the landline during the day between 10 a.m. and 1 p.m. when she was home alone. Though she could answer calls she could not redial to call any number except with the permission and in the presence of her sponsors.

I called at the specified time the following day, and Hajara came online. She told me the other Filipino maid she found in the house had escaped and she was alone taking on all the work from cleaning a two-storey home to cooking and every other domestic task. Her recruitment agency back in Uganda had told her she could work in a shopping mall and get around US $600 and now she was working at home getting 800 dirhams (US $220). This was her first month but the salary had already been canceled because in the previous week the sponsors (or someone acting on their behalf) had beaten her severely to the point of bleeding. She was taken to hospital and the sponsor paid 1,000 dirhams (US $271), all of which would now be deducted from her salary starting with that month.

Hajara told me they beat her regularly and the father as well as the son had both attempted to force themselves on her. She had managed to fight off the father with screams that sent him running out of her room for fear of being noticed by his children and wife. But when the teenage son attacked her in the same room even the screams were not a sufficient weapon to send him away. She was only saved when the mother heard the screams and came to the room and asked in a loud voice what the two were doing. Without saying a single word, the boy who was nearly 18 at the time, left the room. Then it was left to the maid to explain to the mother what happened and as a way of consoling her she chided her, warning her not to repeat the story in the home. She could not bring herself to tell the woman about her husband also attempting to do the same.

She also told me that her sponsors never wanted to see her even taking a brief rest; they always wanted to see her working even when there was nothing to do or if she already had done everything. She said after they ascertained she was a college degree holder they did not hesitate to ask her to do all the homework for their grown children and to teach the young ones English as well as do their English language homework. The two grown daughters just left their books on the table but their brother brought the books to her room and would again try to force himself on her. There was one small girl about seven years old whom the sponsors insisted that the maid sit down with every evening to do the homework and teach her. Whenever she said anything this girl didn't want or asked her why she didn't remember what they studied last time, she would simply slap her and go. There would be more slapping from the mother in the morning if she found out that her daughter did not do the homework.

I told her to let me brainstorm with my office colleagues and see how we could help her return to Uganda. To be sure there was no one in the office I considered brainstorming with, and I didn't know what to do myself. The next day, I asked for her recruitment agent's mobile number in Ras Al Khaimah who I called. I explained that I was calling for a newspaper and was following up a serious case of human trafficking involving a maid he recruited deceptively and who was now being abused by members of an Emirati family. I told him lying to someone about the job type and salary amount while recruiting was defined as human trafficking in all legal books and that not helping this girl out of her trap even when she reported abuses by her sponsors constituted a conspiracy. He promised to call me back and begged I would not go further with the investigations until he responded.

I could sense the fear in his voice. He called the maid first and she told him all she wanted was to go back home and then called the sponsor explaining the media was investigating. The sponsor booked the maid on the next flight, paid all her dues and before he took her to the airport, he called his wife and they both apologized to the maid, asking her to accept their apology so they would meet in the face of God as friends. The next day the agent called to beg me again not to write anything as they had resolved the case amicably. He was acting as if he knew I was working for free media in Europe where such allegations would easily have been published.

One day in December 2013 a friend in Dubai called to tell me of a relative Sharifa (name changed to protect individual's anonymity) who had been working as a maid also in Ras Al Khaimah and had just fled her sponsor. She was being mistreated, which was not surprising. I told my Arab colleagues in the *Al Ittihad* office in an attempt to get a quick fix for some advice. The consensus was that she was now a runaway who could not be helped. She would have to turn herself into police, where she would be detained for just a few days and then she would be allowed to go home, one Emirati colleague advised. However, everyone was against her decision to escape. Everyone considered the word "runaway" to be dirty and runaways had to be incarcerated regardless of the reasons behind their actions. One of them wondered why maids actually did decide to run away instead of asking their sponsors politely for permission to go back home, as if the sponsors did not treat them as their property and would simply relent to such requests.

Another one recalled a maid who had asked to go home, and

once she was in her home country of the Philippines she called back and requested to return – but she had long ago been replaced. Another asked what if the sponsor says she ran away with her gold or money; that it is not allowed for a maid in the UAE to have any relative or anyone she knows in the country besides her sponsor because she could run away and steal household valuables. These were decent people in the office that I had respected but this also was the image the local ruling elites had perpetrated through all media channels. They had become prisoners of ill-advised thinking about foreign domestic workers and they saw no reason to question the justification of any abuses. Once I couldn't get anything helpful from them I neglected their conversations and started making calls elsewhere.

I tried my contacts in the Dubai police, as it had been six years since I last worked with Dubai police and every number I tried in the human rights department had long ago been silenced. I then tried to email the human rights office in the region, but the response was also going to take time. Meanwhile we needed to race against time, to report that she had left her sponsor's home before the family could report her as an absconder. I tried the contacts of the Ugandan embassy, my friend (the first secretary) and his assistant but neither of them were in the country. My friend Ismail worked as a journalist in Abu Dhabi but did not have the ambassador's number because she was a new officer. Instead she advised they report directly to the embassy, where they would be able to help her.

Finally through the embassy's landline I learned the ambassador was also in Uganda. How this embassy was operating disturbed me, I told the phone operator. Because I had identified myself as a journalist she had some respect and did not exchange the same harsh words. Instead she told me there was one new Ugandan official (Araali Mbabazi) at the site and asked if I wanted to talk to him instead. Mbabazi was new but he was welcoming and kept cracking jokes about the maid's plight in the country as we talked. He advised that I send all of the case details via email along with contact information.

Now I set out to gather the details of Sharifa's case. Ashley worked for the local Emirati family for five months and reports having been beaten and abused regularly. On one such occasion she was pushed by the wife, falling to the ground and injuring her eye along with leg wounds that bled profusely. The family took her to the hospital where she had eye surgery and her leg plastered. Still when she returned home the abuses continued and the family refused to return her to the hospital as the doctors had asked. Instead the wife turned herself into a nurse, removing the plasters on her eye and pouring iodine on the wound.

Ashley spoke of another Ethiopian maid in the house; they were fed with small rations of food at lunch and bread at night to just keep them alive. She had lost weight and grown weak but she was supposed to do so many house chores even when she was sick. Because the small amount of food they had been allowed, she had developed stomach complications that suggested ulcers and perhaps other more serious problems. The wife again stood in as a nurse and forced her to swallow Panadol. Her pleas that Panadol could not be taken on an empty stomach were reciprocated with slaps on her cheeks and warnings of cutting her salary.

Her contract entitled her to 800 dirhams (US $217) in a monthly salary, but only one month did she receive that salary. On other occasions she was forced to simply sign for it.

She also claimed to have contacted her recruiting agent and at first the recruiter told her she would have to pay large sums of money to win back her freedom. When she insisted on paying and leaving the country the recruiter changed the story, now threatening her with imprisonment and blacklisting if she did not complete her two years' contract. She had escaped in the morning hours when the husband left for prayers. She then asked a passer-by on the road to help her with a phone to call her relative in

Dubai. She stayed in the relative's shared accommodation that housed 10 male friends.

I emailed Mbabazi and two hours later he responded to me with another set of questions that simply proved his willingness to help:

Thanks Ndugu for the details. We are registering them as made by your godself on her behalf, until she submits her own.

1. Have these been given to the police yet?

She has not yet reported to the police, though I have queried some of my contacts in human rights. They also recommended that the embassy should be the best place to take action for now.

2. Are the details/contacts of her recruiter Ugandan or local?

She has the contacts of her recruiting agent, a Sudanese man.

3. Does she still have her passport? Is it valid? With a valid Residence Permit... labour card... etc.

Her passport has been confiscated by her sponsor, like it's often the case in most cases in this country. It's still valid with a residence visa, until the sponsor reports her as an absconder. As noted, she just escaped this morning.

4. Does she still have a copy of her contract?

She was not given a copy.

I am asking these questions just to try and understand more so as establish her preferred course of action going forward:

5. What does she want to do now that she has left the "employer"?

She simply wants to go back to Uganda. If the authorities here can help her get her pending salaries with the employer, good, but she is not placing it as a priority. She needs her passport and she can mobilise an air ticket from her family in Uganda to go back.

6. Does she have/can mobilise from relatives & friends a

ticket back home?

Answered in the lineup.

7. Does she require an exit visa approved by her Employer?

Here in the UAE there are no exit visas like in Kuwait and Saudi. However she still needs her passport back from the employer and this is going to take an intervention of authorities.

Just to cap it: What is her immediate action and how can the embassy be of help, excluding funding?

In the past we have helped a similar case with Mr. Tushabe, the course of action was the embassy officials (Mr. Agrey and Tushabe) escorting the girl to the human rights department at Abu Dhabi Police. The department asked the sponsor to bring the girls passport and pending salaries. It was much simplified than any of us expected.

When they reported to the embassy together with his cousin brother they found the new secretary cooperative who offered them a letter to take to immigration authorities in Ras Al Khaimah. They found another woman with the same problems after running away from her sponsor in Ras Al Khaimah as well. It could be that Ras Al Khaimah has been more hostile to Ugandan maids as even maids of other nationalities in other emirates had similar ordeals, but most Ugandan maids were first brought into small emirates by their recruitment agents. In Ras Al Khaimah the immigration authorities asked them to first go to the police where they received a letter to return to immigration and now the authorities demanded a representative from the Ugandan embassy to accompany the maid in Ras Al Khaimah. When my friend requested that I talk to the new secretary and ask him to go to Ras Al Khaimah, I was afraid, as it was so demanding, even after they had received a letter. I wrote to him though and asked for his advice. Two days later I had yet to receive a response so I advised the maid to go to immigration on

Sunday explaining that no one would be coming from the embassy because the diplomats had considered the letter as sufficient. I suspected the new secretary was alone at the station and that leaving to go to attend to a single maid's case in Ras Al Khaimah was too much. This was understandable because the embassy did not have enough staff to personally attend to the case of every Ugandan in UAE courts or immigration.

The sponsor had also failed to turn up on Wednesday when Sharifa met the immigration officials for the first time. On the following Sunday morning he turned up, accusing the maid of running away with her own passport, 300 dirhams and a handbag from the wife's collection. He also showed the salary receipts he had forced her to sign to indicate that she had taken all her dues even though she simply signed by coercion and only received one salary. He also showed a document written in an Ethiopian language that Sharifa had used to plot her escape, which contained the details of the stolen property. It seems the sponsor was even not aware that his maid was from Uganda not Ethiopia or he perhaps thought that all of Africa had the same language. She broke down in tears when she responded to the allegations in front of immigration officials. She testified that she did not speak or write in an Ethiopian language, that she did not steal anything or take her passport, and that she simply wanted her passport to go home. The immigration officials asked her to stop speaking and instead listened uninterrupted to her sponsor in Arabic. She noticed they were having a heated debate but eventually the sponsor softened the tone and was shown out of the chambers. The immigration officials turned to Sharifa, requesting her to come back any day with an official from the embassy, as only a staff member from the embassy could resolve her case and make way for her return to her native country.

She also told me her concerns about retrieving her passport and it was evident the process had become far more complicated than either of us had expected.

On Sunday also the second woman who had been with Sharifa in Abu Dhabi also called me. Faridah told me she had been asked by RAK immigration to go to Dubai instead.

As she recalled her case, which was almost identical in details to what the first maid Sharifa had tolerated, Hasifa shared her own accounts of small food rations, name-calling and other verbal abuses.

Hasifa told me that often her sponsors denied her the food she had cooked and forced her instead to gather leftovers from their plates and eat the scraps after their meals. This had started as chastisement one day when the sponsor found her eating a small amount of food which had been left in the saucepan before she washed it as she was still feeling hungry after having consumed that day's rations of food. The sponsor declared that from then on the maid would wait for them to finish eating and she would only then be allowed to eat what they had left on their plates. She did this for three days, reiterating that she would return frequently to the practice especially when she was paranoid or if she had visitors and worried that the food they had cooked might not be enough to serve guests.

The woman also endured various forms of psychological abuse from the sponsor and her three daughters. They claimed she had body odor despite the fact that she bathed. Whenever they came near her in the kitchen or when she was cleaning the house, they would ask her to stop whatever she was doing and take a shower, sometimes two or three times in a day. The daughters doused themselves in perfumes to the point of obsession, so the maid assumed they had lost all sense of what ordinary people smelled like.

The maid asked police to pressure the sponsor, an Emirati widow, who convinced the authorities to return the domestic employee to her home. The abuses went on for another five months before the maid attempted again to persuade the police to let her leave the country in safe passage. This time the police advised her to contact her embassy as there was nothing more they could do to force the widow to allow her to return to Uganda. The embassy took up her case, and staff members discovered that her visa had been cancelled six months earlier. The immigration authorities called her sponsor several times a week but the old widow stubbornly refused to take the calls.

A desperate Hasifa now sought my help. I queried Human Rights Watch about helping to resolve the case but the staffer said the organization could not intervene properly on her behalf. I went ahead and called the sponsor. She answered the call and as we spoke in Arabic she occasionally added in English phrases such as "Me no problem at all. Why she run away I don't know?" I asked her for Hasifa's passport and she said immigration authorities had taken possession of it. The widow demanded that she be reimbursed the 6,000 dirhams fee that she paid to the recruitment company. The contract she had signed was for two years, the widow explained, adding that she was too poor to pay for another maid to come to the UAE every six months and risk losing her again before the contract expired.

The sponsor sounded genuine enough, as she made a justifiable claim for a refund because the contract terms had not been fulfilled. However, the question was whether the sponsor was justified in holding the young woman's passport hostage. Hasifa had also paid a recruitment fee of 1.5 million Ugandan shillings (US $600), and there was no reason why she would be required to pay a penalty of 6,000 dirhams (US $1,630) in order to be able to leave without any further problems.

The law made clear that the recruitment company could not charge legally these fees. Sharifa also mentioned the recruitment company claimed that probation was for only three months but during that time she could not leave the sponsor's home under any circumstances. In Ashley's case, she had already served nine months and had made two unsuccessful attempts to get the police to intervene.

Hasifa's case appeared to be hopelessly complicated with a cancelled visa and the police's refusal to investigate the circumstances any further. Immigration authorities were demanding Hasifa to pay the outstanding fines, which now were registered to her name, not the sponsor's. Her passport was missing and the sponsor was stubbornly refusing to answer immigration summons. I queried HRW and the Ugandan embassy to see if they could help. I said that if matters were not resolved, I would have to publicize her case, either in the UAE as a staff reporter or in Uganda as a guest journalist.

For almost two months both troubled household servants tried unsuccessfully to resolve their cases but even the legal system in the UAE did not acknowledge their standing right to seek redress on the same level as any citizen in the country. Their sponsors refused to hand over to the immigration officials the passports they had confiscated, despite extensive pleas by the authorities. Immigration authorities seemed powerless, as sponsors could not be pushed or pressured when they failed to appear. The only possible option to free the logjam was to take the women's stories to the public through the media. However, I had to deal with editors who had their own rigorous gatekeeping agendas. I wrote in my editorial query that I would highlight the illegal withholding of passports that has become so common and the pain it caused to the immigrant victims. I outlined all of the failed attempts, including talking to an immigration official familiar with the cases who did not want to be named. I had asked him why they did not use force in getting the passports back into the rightful possession of the individuals, but he replied that this poor woman likely would want to remain in the UAE for work and that otherwise she would risk never being able to gain employment.

Editors always take their time in responding to a story query which is potentially sensitive and controversial in challenging conventional UAE norms. My cluster editor finally responded saying that while he liked the idea it could only run with an official Ministry of Interior quote. In the end I only was allowed to mention their plight in a single paragraph in a story I did about a conference eulogizing the treatment of maids in the UAE.[168]

The women's desperation was obvious. They struggled financially to sustain a livelihood and had incurred substantial expenses to process their cases. I wondered how they had managed to survive. Sharifa shared her story with an HRW staffer who asked me to intervene. The truth was that they were far more cases like Sharifa's and finding support to resolve them became more difficult. In some moments, I helped as much as I could.

Sharifa was dressed in a full Islamic *abaya* dress and spoke with words that invoked Allah in almost every sentence. I asked her if her sponsor had ever considered her piety while mistreating her or if they were simply a non-religious Emirati family. Sharifa recounted the family practiced the faith regularly, following strict prayer protocols and tithing guidelines. Eventually, my contact with the beleaguered migrant workers became less frequent until the point when we would not speak for weeks. Then one evening I broke the silence and called Ashley, who said that she and others had given up the possibility of seeing their case resolved. Unsurprisingly, there were many others without their passports in the UAE and their hosts had counseled them to work, get some money and plan their exit like all "*other people*." The phrase *other people* became the comma and full-stop of every sentence she uttered. I asked her what she was doing and she said doing what *other people* are doing. She had been introduced to other people's workplaces when she had no transport and food and she followed what others in her predicament decided. There were no more questions, and I wished her luck. However after ending our conversation, guilt about failing them grew in my mind. These two young women had both contacted me for assistance and now that I could not help them, they decided to join the *other people* who never asked for any assistance. The dismay was significant, because so many had heard their story – my newspaper's editors, the UAE police, the country's immigration authorities, the Ugandan Embassy and even international organizations such as Human Rights Watch. Individually or collectively, not one entity could break the unfortunate, soul-draining stalemate of their circumstances.

Their case had not gone as smoothly as an earlier one when just by my mentioning "media" the recruitment agent quickly relented and processed the request to let a maid return to Uganda. Now in these two cases, not even my calls to the sponsors or officials could help. A few weeks later there was a YouTube video which went viral about a Ugandan maid who was sick and trapped in a home in Sharjah. A friend in Ajman brought the video to my attention. It showed a Black Muslim young woman in black *abaya* and blue scarf, who was wary and clearly ill in her physical appearance. The video was recorded on a mobile phone and I could tell that she lived in the Al Qassimiya area of Sharjah. The video was shared extensively in Dubai's Ugandan community, where two individuals asked me if I was responsible for the video and if I was able to help the ill woman. I had never met the woman and I hesitated to get involved given the failure to help Ashley and her friend. I told them that I was sure where the video was made but I had decided not to intervene. I had not yet been able to relieve myself of the guilt over raising up someone's hopes for being rescued from a bad situation only to see them dashed and forgotten. The video did indicate a contact's phone number in Uganda, likely the person who took the video and wanted his or her anonymity preserved in some small way. Few housemaids in the UAE had their own mobile phones or Internet access, a clear sign that sponsors intended to cut off their workers from any outside communications. It was the digital manacles for today's slaves.

The problems were stark. No freedom of movement or communication. Starvation in homes of enormous wealth. Media reports about "runaway" maids almost never mentioned allegations or evidence of abuse. They focused exclusively on how the sponsors were impacted. Any suggestion of mistreatment was strictly censored. Likely, few GCC citizens were aware of these problems that echoed the most insidious aspects of slavery. Media were busy reinforcing tributes and positive imagery ascribed to the ruling elites and to carefully constructed illusions of their piety and allegiance to the central tenets of Islamic charity. One risked significant consequences for suggesting otherwise.

3.4 Torture and Murder in Homes

Maids staying in the homes of their GCC sponsors have endured terrible treatment. Some have been beaten to death or given incapacitating injuries. The female sponsors inflict the beatings more often than their husbands, who are complicit in their tacit endorsements. However, husbands have also been responsible for some of the most vicious attacks.

These are just a few representative examples of the abuses reported in the GCC press. A body of an Indonesian maid was found naked in an Emirati home after she was hit with a frying pan by an Emirati woman sponsor and a male Emirati neighbor.[169] An Ethiopian maid neighbor told the court the Indonesian maid was regularly beaten by her sponsor. The court sentenced the woman to 16 years in prison and the male neighbor to 13 years.[170] Set aside the court sentence for a moment, and ask what satisfaction did this Emirati woman derive in having the male neighbor joining to strip naked this woman and beat her to death. To the people who forbid a man from seeing an Arab or Muslim woman's hair, why would it not be forbidden to see the naked body of an Indonesian maid as well?

What else could explain this madness apart from a complacent belief that dehumanizes people as slaves; this man would, of course, not join in with the beating if the victim was an Arab woman, especially if she was undressed. And what of an Emirati woman who beats her maid like a slave and undresses her in front of men? Is there no propriety or chastity in respecting the humility of the *abayas*? While the reporting of these cases does elicit sympathy for maids, few bother to consider how such incidents can be prevented from recurring. A maid cannot tell who will be cruel or not. She does not have the privilege of asking for references about her employer. The police did not even have a reason to let the people know of her death in the daily press releases it sends to the media about murders, as she was killed by a local woman and that is sensitive information. Most of the murder cases the police report involve Bangladeshis, Indians or other nationalities killing each other but not those involving Emiratis. If there is a mention of a case involving an Emirati, the police then refer to the individual as being of Arab origin.

Cases only become known in court proceedings and if the reporter is not keen that day to hear a murder case readers likely will never hear of a victim's tragic fate. And one then learns that many have suffered similar fates and their attacks and deaths are ignored in police reports. So long as she is in the UAE, the maid belongs to the sponsor precisely in the way a slave once belonged to his master. The court's judges who handed down a verdict of 16 years in prison to the sponsor would give a sentence of life imprisonment or even death for a similar offense if a non-Emirati committed the crime. Or compare that sentence with one that Rizana Nafeek, a Sri Lankan maid, received in connection with the death of her sponsor's four-month-old child. The maid said she had been bottle-feeding the baby when he choked and died but her male sponsor said she had strangled the child after an argument with the sponsor's wife. She was arrested, sentenced to death and beheaded.[171]

As for the Emirati sponsor, don't count her to be in prison for any length close to the 16 years she received. She may be out the next Eid or Ramadan because the rulers of her country are generous about releasing prisoners, mostly Emiratis, on major occasions. Probably she was given a lenient sentence because the sponsor told the court she had beaten her maid to discipline her, not to kill her. One can only pray she does not "discipline" other maids once she is out of the prison.

Then there was another case prosecutors brought before the Dubai criminal court in which a housemaid died after being locked in a room and starved for almost two months by an Emirati woman.[172] The dead maid identified as Khadija Kamel was starved and abused along with another Filipina maid who survived the ordeal and testified to the abuses carried out by various family members, ranging from forcing maids to drink detergent and stuffing dirty underwear in their mouths, to slamming their skulls against the wall and beating them with wooden sticks. Maids would be stripped naked and videos taken with mobile phones. She testified they were locked in rooms for days without food. One maid, desperately hungry, had to watch others eat. The family, she explained, got away with these degrading and humiliating incidents because the father was an influential police official.

Khadija became weak and lost weight. She weighed just 38 kilograms when she died. The surviving Filipina maid also mentioned that even though Khadija died, she would occasionally receive favors of eating because she was a Muslim and she was forced to watch while starving as punishment of being Christian. Now that might sound like a Hollywood or Bollywood ordeal but the actual events were far worse than in any fictional portrayal. It is distressing to the greatest extent that someone with some semblance about the existence of God could cause so much pain to a human being like that. How someone praying five times a day could starve another to death when food was abundant in the house – the same food she herself would eat. And her husband was with her in court, accused of being an accomplice. According to the story, the police official prepared the room where the two maids were incarcerated and starved. However, there was no mention of how he participated in the more intimate tortures of stripping and sniffing the wife's dirty underwear. Perhaps these acts of torture were acceptable as along as his wife was inflicting them upon female employees or slaves and not the male drivers or garden boys. It doesn't matter whether the wife is stuffing her underwear in the mouths of female maids or garden boys, the act could never be construed as one rising to even a modicum of justifiability. But right and wrong have no meaning to this family. They were married and in love, their marital oaths were not for good or bad, weak or strong alone but also for torture and exploitation, enslavement and dehumanization of other people.

In Abu Dhabi, an Ethiopian maid died on September 4, 2012 after her female Emirati sponsor poured boiling water over her. The sponsor also beat the maid with an electrical cord from a hair dryer and put pepper in her eyes.[173]

"Her death was the result of several burns all over her body that had become infected. Her eyes showed evidence of bleeding from the torture, which a doctor concluded had taken place over 'several periods' of time," a published report in *The National* indicated.

The Emirati woman was jailed for three years and gave blood money of 200,000 dirhams to the victim's family.[174]

I also covered numerous other cases of abuse toward maids and domestic household servants, including one who had been admitted to the Al Qassimi hospital in Sharjah. The hospital PR spokesperson asked reporters to interview a housemaid who had been burned with cooking oil by her Arab employer. The patient, a shy 23-year-old Ethiopian maid, preferred to look down or on the walls as she recounted her ordeal to the team of reporters while our photographers persistently reminded her to look into the camera as they snapped images.

"She was angry and poured the cooking oil on my head as we were preparing a meal in the kitchen," she said. "This was not first time she did pour burning things on me; every time she was angry she would do it, whether boiling water or whatever and she would ask me not to tell anyone."

Dr. Faisal Salman, a consultant from the hospital's department of plastic surgery, said the maid had turned up last month to the hospital with burns on her face, back and foot that could be classified as first- and second-degree burns.

After reporters gathered statements from the maid and her doctor, the ward went silent while we observed the burn wounds on the patient which were found from her head to her back and then legs. One could sense the emotional impact and tension in the room. An Arabic reporter broke the silence asking what we all thought would happen if that Arab employer was a leader who possessed nuclear weapons. We all laughed and another reporter reminded him not to talk politics in the hospital.

The lists of these abuses seemed endless in all GCC countries. In Saudi Arabia the BBC reported Sumiati Binti Salan Mustapa, 23, who was taken to a Saudi hospital with broken bones and burns over her body. Her employer was arrested for allegedly putting a hot iron to her head, and stabbing her with scissors. The woman was sentenced to three years in jail but was acquitted soon after.[175] Another Sri Lankan housemaid, LP Ariyawathie, 49, was found with nails embedded in her body. X-rays showed there were 24 nails and a needle.[176]

And the body of another maid (Kikim Komalasari) was found dumped in a garbage bin on the road in a Saudi town called Abha. Her neck had been slashed and she had severe cuts to the rest of her body.[177]

In Abu Dhabi an Emirati sponsor confessed to police beating

her maid to death with a wooden cane because she was lazy.[178] The maid's dead body was found in a bathtub and forensics investigators found fractures to her head, broken teeth and bruises on her arms and legs.

Another Arab family murdered an Ethiopian maid and even burned her body before throwing it in the Ajban desert of Abu Dhabi.[179] Col Rashid Mohammed Bou Rashid in a police press release said the maid's body was found in the desert wrapped in a cloth with burned fingers. The maid, unfortunately, was living illegally in the UAE and working without documents for the Arab couple who murdered her. The husband told police his wife had battered the maid to death because of a domestic dispute in Khalifa city where they stayed. The husband then stripped the body and poured a corrosive substance on it to obscure its identity. He carried the body to the car and later dumped it in the desert.

If one tallies similar abuses inflicted on maids that have been reported in the local papers, one quickly would be fatigued in discovering an obvious pattern. The unfortunate surprise is learning how many more abuses likely go unreported under cover of the region's dark secrecy. The GCC should be declared the most hostile place to work as a housemaid.

HRW found women migrant workers in Saudi Arabia were literary locked into their workplaces and residences for the duration of their employment. Their forced confinement exposed the cruel intentions of their private employers and how government authorities tolerated the circumstances, further aggravating their vulnerabilities for even more heinous abuses. The HRW report recounts a series of housemaid rapes perpetrated by Saudi sponsors. Funny how police always found these women "on the run" and chose to return them immediately to their abusive sponsors. The report also compiled newspaper accounts about migrant women who reportedly committed suicide by leaping from buildings. However, those reports were not accurate. More likely the women were in the midst of a desperate escape, not trying to end their lives.[180] As the report summarized: "The denial of the right to freedom of movement, combined with oppressive working conditions, leaves many of these migrant women in situations that arguably constitute servitude or forced labour under international law."[181]

3.5 Maids or Slaves?

In the UAE the mistreatment of maids has been attributed to a country's legacy of slavery.[182] Rima Sabban, one researcher who has studied the history, cites maids who suffered verbal abuses being called "animal," "donkey," "crazy," "stupid," and "trash," to name just a few examples. She also cites physical abuses: a maid who was smacked with a ring and sustained a red bruise on her face, another attacked with a plate. However, the most striking accounts are of the sexual violence that Sabban attributes to an old slavery culture of Arab men taking sexual pleasure from their slaves. According to the tradition all women in the house are "harem" meaning forbidden from anyone outside but allowed for the husband who is protector of the home.

Sabban goes so far as to compare Female Foreign Domestic Workers (FFDW) in the UAE to the African-American slaves of the U.S. South.

"The characteristics shared by both groups include numerousness and limited personal or collective rights," she notes in her work. "Differences between the two groups included the fact that African-American slaves lived with their families and worked in close proximity to them unlike the FFDW who left their families in another country, Secondly, FFDW are not enslaved all their lives. They work under a contract that theoretically is supposed to have a specific duration."[183]

Maids in the UAE have responded to their sponsors'

mistreatment with violence and some have taken their own lives along with those of their sponsors or their children. Some do manage to escape unharmed.

Ibrahim Ahmed Ibrahim Ali cites an incident in 1988 when a maid waited until her sponsors left the home, poured kerosene on the floor and set the home on fire along with her and the family's two children, aged two and four.[184]

These practices have long been entrenched. In February 1987, a judge gave an interview to a paper concerning a case in which a wife with three teenage boys had brought a pregnant maid to court. The maid was asked who was responsible for the pregnancy and she said she was not sure, as the four men in the house (father and three sons) had each had forced sex with her.

In March 1984 a married policeman in Sharjah had sex with a maid while his wife was away, and afterward the maid ingested kerosene to avoid pregnancy, based on the man's suggestions. She experienced immediate stomach problems and when she was taken to the hospital she told doctors what happened. The man was arrested and sentenced to death, the standard penalty for an adulterer but with the intervention of an influential person the punishment was reduced to just six months in prison.[185]

3.6 Runaway to Safety

Runaway, escapee or *huroob* are the most commonly used terms in the Gulf countries to identify immigrants who have fled their sponsors. The term "runaway" has long been associated with slaves escaping masters or subscribers. Amnesty International has likened "escaping," the term mostly used in Qatar, to the language used in cases of "convicted prisoners or people in conditions of debt bondage and slavery."[186]

Today, the term is used frequently regarding domestic workers like housemaids who are sponsored by individuals, not businesses. An immigrant in either Saudi Arabia or UAE is more likely to run away from their individual sponsors than from companies who abide by at least a modicum of the rules. However, not all companies can be assured of even caring to follow the basic letter of the law. Companies also default on payments, but the individual sponsor is more likely to be culpable in beating employees, denying them food, or, worse, forcing sexual activity with those under their sponsorship. (NB: The governments do not keep statistics regarding abuse incident reports.)

There also are reports of slaves running away from their masters and going to a British representative in Sharjah who would provide some sanctuary. The British representative would also give the individual a letter testifying the person is free.[187]

No doubt some maids are also guilty of abusing their work. Some are guilty of assaulting a sponsor's children and these cases are covered in the newspapers. There are also stories that every community will witness – even in my home country Uganda – where maids often are treated more like family members.

In Uganda, I remember an incident in which my mother became exceptionally annoyed with her maid. My mother came home one day without notice because she forgot something and found me sad-faced, sitting in a corner. The maid had just beaten me and, as on previous occasions, ordered me not to tell my mother about it. Violating this order would mean another severe beating the next day and she even threatened to cut off my mouth. My mother asked me what happened and when I refused to respond, she sensed something was terribly out of sorts. She took me to her bedroom and asked again. I whispered into her ear that the maid had beaten me and that she would cut off my mouth if I said a word about what happened. She counseled me that no one could ever cut off my mouth in her house and that no one should ever stop me from telling her anything because she was my mother.

She summoned the maid, demanding to know why I had been beaten. The maid responded that I did not rinse the dishwashing soap off the dishes completely. In Uganda although maids are expected to do house chores, the children in the house also are expected to help or participate and parents prefer maids teach their children how to do ordinary household tasks. My mother told her she was fine with my beating but she wanted to know why she would threaten me not to tell her. "If you are beating Yasin for a genuine reason or disciplining him, why should you shut up his mouth even to his mother?" she asked. The maid had no response to this.

I wish today I would tell the same to my children. That all parents should win their children's confidence to tell them everything, even acts of abuse. Far too many homes do not champion or cultivate a transparent, open communicative environment. If the parents treat the maid well then there would be no reason for the person to mistreat or abuse the children. And, even in cases of abuses, children who trust their parents should be able to report without fearing retribution or vengeance.

Almost every month, various Emirati police agencies in the UAE issue press releases, announcing the arrest of hundreds of runaway maids. In 2009, the immigration department changed its name to "foreign affairs," and now the only news reported to the public consists almost exclusively of the arrest of runaway maids whose documents and visas had expired, and who did not have in hand their passports. Awareness campaigns are launched periodically, urging residents not to employ the runaway maids. They emphasize that runaway maids are bad peopled, undisciplined and likely to carry transmittable diseases such as HIV/AIDS. Individuals who employ runaway maids could face fines of up to 10,000 dirhams for each undocumented worker. However, the information that all of these campaigns lack is why the maids or other domestic workers are running away from their sponsors. In the decade that I have been in the UAE, not one campaign has reiterated to Arab sponsors the basic acknowledgement that maids are human beings who have the right to their own personal dignity, respect and freedom. Nor have they encouraged sponsors to tell maids that in their sponsor's home their rights are still present and they should not be afraid to report any incidents of abuse inflicted by their sponsors. Of course, one can see clearly why a government-funded awareness campaign should do anything to even hint the slightest at empowering what undeniably is one of the country's largest labor pools.

Unfortunately, running away aggravates a desperate maid's circumstances and has potentially severe consequences. The body of a Sri Lankan maid was found lying next to its newborn infant in Ajman near one health center. The incident first had the appearance of a rumor but when we called a police PR spokesperson, he said a release on the incident was forthcoming. The police release indicated that she was a runaway maid, one of the many who tried to give birth at home because individuals who have defaulted on their Emirati sponsors, whatever the reason, cannot go to a hospital for delivery as they are undocumented and face the risk of arrest. Lt. Col. Abdullah bin Saif Al Matroushi, the director general of the Ajman Police CID, said the woman attempted to give birth with the help of her four friends in Abu Dhabi, but she consequently experienced complications including severe bleeding. The friends panicked and attempted to take her to a private hospital in Dubai where they knew a Sri Lankan midwife who had agreed to help. The midwife administered drugs to stop the bleeding, but she could not admit the woman to the hospital because of her undocumented status. The group and the ailing mother were on their way back to Abu Dhabi when she died en route. Now the friends were stranded with a body in their car, so they drove to a remote emirate in Ajman and dumped the bodies of both the mother and the baby. An eyewitness saw the group removing the bodies, recorded the license plate numbers, and reported the incident immediately to police.[188]

The police mentioned the woman was unmarried and thus could not be admitted to a hospital. The four suspects told prosecutors the woman was married to the baby's father who was in Sri Lanka. The truth was the woman could not have had a hospital-supervised birth with her status as a runaway in any location because she would have risked arrest and deportation immediately.

There also have been stories where runaway maids have successfully birthed infants in their residences outside the hospital but they dumped the baby's body somewhere. Stories of abandoned babies in mosques, public parks and roads are common in Sharjah and Ajman and although the authorities categorize them as births outside wedlock, they also carry another similarity – almost always, the story involves a runaway maid. A Filipina mother threw a newborn infant from the ninth floor of her residential building through a garbage chute to the aluminum rubbish container and the baby miraculously survived.[189] It was the building watchman who found the baby while doing his daily rounds and alerted police. Brigadier Abdullah Mubarak Al Dukhan, deputy director of Sharjah Police, told reporters the police arrested the maid and the couple she was working for because the couple had employed her illegally after she had run away from her official sponsors. However, consider this case in another perspective that comes to a different conclusion other than direct blame for the maid. She was willing to work as a maid even though she had run from her sponsoring employees. Does anyone ever wish to know why she was a runaway maid in the first place when she loved her work?

There are several stories of maids jumping from the buildings of their sponsors to end their lives, but the editors at *The National* shy away from carrying these reports, and, thus, I would neglect covering them. However, why do stories of maids stripped naked and beaten to death, stories of maids being raped, stories of helpless bodies found lying in pools of blood or children surviving falls from garbage chutes not move policy makers to revise the sponsorship system? Why do editors keep watch at the gate, failing to address the ruthless, callous and inhumane nature of sponsors? No one dares to ask the questions; much less, seek the answers to redress the situation.

The stories of today are barely different from those told in the 18th century. Runaway slaves relied on knowledge of geography, clever disguises, tips from conductors and their own "motherwit" to evade hunters and catchers.[190] Today, the situation is not much different for GCC runaway workers or maids who use various tactics to evade their sponsors, police and immigrants officials. Also interesting is how runaway maids would entice their colleagues to join them and stay in congested accommodations. The situation resembles the time when Harriet Tubman directly helped hundreds of slaves escape in a decade, and indirectly helped countless others. Many escaped slaves upon return faced harsh and horrid punishments such as amputation of limbs, whippings, branding, and many other unthinkable acts.[191] Today, the runaway illegals in the UAE face prison and deportation to their home countries, if they are fortunate enough to escape even more physically degrading and humiliating acts of punishment.

Almost every country which supplies the GCC countries with domestic workers and maids has expressed dismay about how their citizens are treated in GCC homes. Expressing dismay is not enough, while the desperation in these countries compels them to see the remittances these maids send home are justified.

Indonesia already has banned maids from going to Saudi Arabia after Ruyati bin Sapubi, 54, was beheaded for allegedly confessing to murdering her sponsor's child.[192] Sri Lanka also responded to Saudi Arabia's beheading of Rizana Nafeek[193] by requiring those who could work in Saudi Arabia as maids to be at least 25 years of age.[194] Saudi Arabia responded to the blacklisting of these countries by banning the recruitment of their respective nationals as maids in the kingdom.[195]

Ethiopia, another primary origin point for maids in GCC, has set laws banning its domestic workers from going to the GCC. Solomon Tesfaye, Ethiopia's minister of justice, planning and implementation, told the African Press Agency in Addis Ababa that its citizens could no longer be expected to work as "domestic slaves" in countries like Saudi Arabia.[196] Once Ethiopia tightened its rules regarding domestic workers going to the GCC, Uganda with its biting poverty readily opened its doors to its university graduates to go and work freely in the GCC region as housemaids.

It was not the desperation of governments alone seeing their citizens going to work in cruel homes or even dangerous worksites reaching hundreds upon hundreds of feet high where the risk of falling to death was ever present. The workers even in the most seemingly benignly environments such as a rich home were equally as desperate. Indeed many have heard of the abuses or have seen a neighbor's son or daughter who returned from the GCC with more ordeals of torture than tales of becoming rich, but even these stories did little to stop the flow of new migrants. Returning home was always on the table but also fears of finding a job even with meagre pay made reasonable individuals desperate in making rash decisions. Most governments have altogether given up on offering their citizens employment. Countries all too often resemble Uganda, with leaders who are installed for decades only able to hold onto the grip of power through military campaigns. Indeed, the military is often the only guaranteed employer for people in these nations. However, military jobs are just as cruel to women as to those who decide to become maids in GCC homes. Those brave enough to take up these military jobs also learn that when they go on missions in Sudan, Somalia, Congo or Rwanda they are not only blowing up huge and expensive weapons that take Ugandan people's money but they are also blowing up their own lives. Leaders like Uganda's Museveni would replace those blown-up lives with other poor people and allocate yet more people's money toward purchasing more heavy weaponry to be ready for another mission aggravating his international neighbors. Nothing seems able to stop a war-mongering leader's thirst for blood and violence.

The alternative in private-sector employment presents fewer job opportunities especially in a 21st-century economy where machine labor is rapidly replacing human labor at a torrid pace. The cut-throat competition for jobs is no longer only among people of basic or standard educational skills but also now graduates who have to compete with ATM machines that operate 24 hours for the once respectable teller jobs, computers for the secretarial jobs and other technologies. One can only imagine the frustration of a university graduate who cannot find any job in his or her country and chooses instead with an air of resignation to come and work as a housemaid likely for an illiterate family in the GCC region. In Qatar, I met a couple of African maids who told me their Qatari sponsors had not only confiscated their passports but also their mobile phones.

The motivation to work is to save some money and be self-employed once one returns home but one even finds after few years of work in so demeaning an environment the chances of returning home every year grow more distant. Reports of people who have gone back with relatively more money and started small businesses, only to go bankrupt in a year, always invite second thoughts and yet another year of delay. The future of self-employment now is a delusion not only in Uganda but also for others in India and other Asian countries.

One maid in Dubai told me how disturbed she felt with the world in which we are living. She gave up the comfort of staying at home with her parents and one child, hoping she would be able to support them and improve their living, but she has ended up in an Arab home where she is abused and paid very little. She told me how she does not know what she is going to do to survive and to support her son, as opportunities become bleaker by the day. She told me that even if she worked for more years saving every little penny she received from her sponsor, there is little chance she could become self-reliant as her own boss. That even opening up a small grocery shop in her country is now a waste of one's savings as gargantuan shopping malls owned by mega business people are opening in remote areas; and with more capital, they easily outcompete any small startup business from a returning immigrant. But even working in the GCC no longer seems to be a sure arrangement, as citizens of the GCC are increasingly tired of staying home and receiving government welfare that is not enough for various reasons. More are entering into the workplace than ever before. There is a growing sense of uncertain future for many immigrants, especially as GCC countries like Kuwait are now contemplating major plans for repatriation.

Section 4

Bureaucracy: "Eating People's Money with Greed"

4.1 Emirates Cards for Infants

GCC countries boast of being the world's most desirable tax-free haven but actually they take more from their residents in form of fines than other countries take in tax, according to a colleague of mine in the *Al Ittihad* newspaper office. He complained about having to pay for Emirates ID cards for his two young children, ages two and four, respectively. The Abu Dhabi Media Company, the parent company for *Al Ittihad* and *The National*, had issued a new rule that all employees must have Emirates IDs, required of all citizens and expatriates, for all family members before they could claim the health insurance cards from the company. Any member without an Emirates ID would not get health insurance that year.

My friend had to pay a fine of 1,000 dirhams for each child who did not have the ID, which would have been obtained at a cost of 500 dirhams each. He needed about 3,000 dirhams to settle the Emirates ID problem. He asked for 1,000 dirhams from me to help pay the fines, which he would repay at the end of the month.

"What I don't understand is how this two-year-old child needs an Emirates ID," he asked. "For what exactly when she does not even go to school?"

This represents a form of taking money from people the same way Allah had indicated in the Quran. My friend read the Quran chapter, translating and emphasizing the line: "*They are eating people's money with greed.*" Most Quran translations in which I have looked for the verse have not used words suggesting greed. I did not truly grasp his frustration until December 2013 when my family cards expired and we needed to renew them. This time I was supposed to pay a 1,000-dirham fine for my one-year-old daughter because we had not arranged for an ID card for her after she was born. I was reluctant to obtain the ID because the family was now staying more often in Uganda than in the Emirates, where they came usually for short visits lasting no more than a month or so. Soon, I received a stream of emails announcing the end of health insurance coverage which could only be rectified once I obtained cards for each member of my family. And, every time I looked at the emails, my heart skipped. I was not sure if I wanted to forgo the health card for my little one, as she would be in Dubai for the whole of January and return to Uganda the following month when her elder siblings had to go to school.

However, a month for a one-year-old child without health insurance was too much. I could imagine how much stress my colleague felt whose children remained in the Emirates all the time and why he actually even had to take a small loan from me. This whole thing of attaching the health Insurance with the Emirates ID was like a trap. In the UAE there are always many traps to have residents (especially immigrants) pay these dishonest government fees. I realized that even for my elder children who already had the Emirates IDs, they had never used them at all and, in fact, the cards stayed untouched in the white envelope in which I had collected them. The rich GCC states preferred to extract from their poor expatriates even the seemingly incremental amounts they have received through their hard work for the country. These extractions accumulate quickly through a burgeoning scheme of bureaucratic fees imposed on almost everything.

4.2 Discounts on Violation Fines

Fines for almost everything in the GCC comprise the second most common form of revenue collections for the governments. Almost every government department has its different sections for collecting fines, most of which are levied in excesses. The immigrations offices levy fines for staying beyond visa expiration dates, while the municipalities levy fines from delaying visa renewals to attesting an apartment rental contract to hugging clothes in the windows. The police constituted the most formidable levier of fines for all sorts of traffic violations. There were numerous stories of motorists accumulating fines running to thousands of dirhams. Among those fined was a Bangladeshi woman who accumulated 257 traffic fines, totaling 201,140 dirhams (US $54,760), in just three months.[197]

Statistics indicated other major traffic law offenders, thus earning the Emirate many thousands of dirhams, including a Syrian woman with 288 fines totaling 186,900 dirhams (US $50,885), an Egyptian motorist owing 169,420 dirhams (US $46,125), and an Indian national with combined fines totaling 137,400 dirhams (US $37,408).[198] Traffic fines constitute the largest share of income generation for the government from the residents and its figures of total collections per year have remained secret, though they would tell reporters the number of fines reported each year, but never the amount.

The government also treats traffic fines collections as a business, often offering incentives like discounts to erring motorists. The Sharjah police are quite generous, willing to offer violating motorists up to 50 percent discount on traffic fines paid in a given period of time, usually within a period of four months.[199] Still the ruling elites are among the main violators of these traffic rules and they accumulate more fines and benefit from the discounts. *The National*, for example, reported of a "high-profile" figure in Dubai who owed up to 9.4 million dirhams (US $2.55 million) in traffic fines for 12,740 traffic violations over 18 months. The driver topped a list of 33 VIP traffic violators who owed Dubai police more than 14.3 million dirhams (US $3.89 million) in traffic fines from 21,148 violations, according to a list published in *Al Ittihad*. The second offender on the list received 1,826 fines worth 2 million dirhams (US $326,708), while in third place was another driver with 731,900 dirhams (US $199,264) for 1,022 fines over the same time period.[200]

4.3 The Attestation of Everything

Wahab, my younger brother, had earned his higher education diploma in radiography, and he attested his certificate with the Ministry of Foreign Affairs in Uganda and the UAE embassy before coming. A director at Al Qassimi hospital had promised to help me place him in the hospital for the non-paid attachment when he arrived. The position would be at most two years for gaining the required experience and could be one year if he was really good. Personally, I did not find the offer attractive to work for such a long time without pay but there was no way I was going to convince my brother who like many eager Africans before him was ready to come to Dubai to carve out a promising livelihood.

The director showed me through the HR director who asked me to obtain written approval from the Dubai health ministry offices. Afaf Al Sayyed, the ministry official, regretfully informed us the nonpaid attachment was only for Emiratis and advised my brother to obtain his two years' experience back home before returning. Then I happened to meet Dr. Amin Al Amiri at a function in Sharjah at which the crown prince donated his blood. He advised me to come to his office with the documents and said that he would see what could be done. The next morning he saw all the documents were in good form for attestation and we went to see the Ministry of Higher Education about obtaining a certificate. The ministry of education required us to first return his O and A Level certificates to Uganda for attestation and the local offices of the ministries of Foreign Affairs and Education along with the UAE embassy would give us the approval documents. We returned with the attested certificates and the female employee first queried the system of two years at A Level, as she thought they were supposed to be three years' requirement in the UAE. She refused to approve the document and a supervisor intervened, indicating that some education systems were different but he also wanted to see the pass slips as well attested. Then we had again to send for the pass slips in Uganda and repeat the attestation process.

The attestation process was expensive but more cost-consuming was the long time it was taking when my brother's visa had a limited number of days remaining. Once the slips were returned we went again to the Dubai ministry office where this time there was a female Emirati officer who could read very little English and wanted help to identify which of the certificates was O Level and which was A. She also needed assistance on matching up the spellings of names. Finally, she said the approving certificate would only be ready in two weeks' time. Now, only three weeks were left on my young brother's visa which was only two months to begin with and we had yet to complete the first quarter-leg of the journey to obtaining the Ministry of Higher Education certificate.

My brother was distraught and he wanted to give up immediately. Many others have found themselves in the same dilemma in the race pitting the rapidly expiring time on the visa against the long lumbering pace of a bureaucracy that always is about waiting and then waiting some more. Most Dubai immigrants have given up on hopes of finding jobs that match their professional qualifications and seek work as security guards or other petty jobs that never required a lot of document attestation and bureaucracies in recruiting. But sending a radiographer to work as a security guard was a tough choice, not one I wanted for my brother. I counseled him to wait and see. Two weeks later the certificates had been approved but the approval had not yet been committed to final document form. It would take another two days of "come back tomorrow" to have it in our hands.

We now had to go to the Ministry of Higher Education in Abu Dhabi for the real certificate of equivalency that would complete this process. I knew from the start it would not be easy and a quick scan on the Internet showed many grievances from people who had struggled through the attestation process. One American woman wrote a blog after she spent more than six months trying to get the certificate.[201] If even Americans had struggled that much to obtain the certificate and they had not succeeded, one could only imagine the troubles for a national from a country that did not enjoy the same level of esteem as the United States. Yet, I told my brother to ignore whatever disgruntled experiences these online individuals had and to pursue the certificate.

This time it was an Emirati man, more confident than his sister workers in the Dubai ministry offices, but his message could not be deciphered. He first turned us away, insisting that we bring the official documentation of the curriculum, which would require another few days of asking someone in Uganda to get it and send it expeditiously. Then when we appeared a second time he still had other new demands, as he wanted us to go back and ask the Ugandan embassy in Abu Dhabi to write to the college where my brother studied. Then the college would get back to the embassy confirming the certificates were valid and the embassy should seal the response letter and send it to the ministry. I queried the man that these certificates and transcripts have a stamp of the UAE Embassy in Uganda, and they have stamps of UAE foreign ministry along with the official marks of the Ugandan foreign ministry as well as the Ugandan embassy in UAE. *What else do you need?*

"We need a letter that is sealed; without it we cannot help you," he replied, like he was tuned specifically to turn us away. I told him my brother's visa was expiring in two days and he was leaving, so I asked would he allow me to bring the papers on his behalf. He said, yes and turned away immediately, but I didn't trust him.

I told the first secretary of the Ugandan embassy, who also could not understand what the UAE official wanted. The embassy officer said he wanted to help me but the embassy does not take up the responsibility to correspond with colleges back in my native country. The embassy only stamps on transcripts and certificates as verification of the stamps of the Ministry of Foreign Affairs. Later I found online a Dubai-based university articulating guidelines to higher degree attestations which indicated that, indeed, the embassy had the responsibility of contacting the relevant college or university.

When I showed this to the first secretary, he was defiant. He could not believe they could make such a demand and he made it clear that he was not going to do it. I had to be creative in finding the means of going through this stupid process. I asked my brother to return to Uganda and take the papers to his college, asking them write to the embassy and seal the correspondence for mailing. A month later I carried the parcel from Kampala to the first secretary again and he was still defiant: the stamp they had put on the certificates was enough and he was not going to write anything further to the Ministry of Higher Education in Abu Dhabi. I went to the ministry, explaining the situation to a staff member who seemed to understand and he allowed me to proceed with the application online and then hand in the papers. He promised they would contact the embassy themselves directly and cautioned they could not do anything until the embassy issues a letter confirming the documents' veracity. After eight months I checked with the ministry and the embassy had never responded to their request to send them the papers. I was only glad that my brother had given up on working in Dubai and started doing something in Kampala, where he would continue his studies and pursue a degree in medicine.

And I was not alone in getting stuck with bureaucratic requests from the ministry that the embassy of Uganda's proud first secretary could not handle. Another friend Juma had patiently waited for four years to get the same Ministry of Higher Education certificate. With a master's degree in Education he had taken up a job at a local gym in Ras Al Khaimah, as he waited for his papers to be shuttled through the UAE bureaucracy. He was well known at the embassy, where he had worked part time as a translator. But after getting his equivalency certificate from the Ministry of Higher Education after a four-year struggle, the Ministry of Education that was supposed to employ him then required him to get a letter of experience from Uganda which would need to be attested. The foreign affairs office and the UAE embassy in Uganda stamped on a letter issued by the former school he had last taught five years back in Uganda and when it was the turn of the Ugandan embassy in Abu Dhabi to sign, the first secretary again refused, telling his former junior he does not sign on letters from schools. He even made a call back to Uganda, quarreling with the woman from the Uganda foreign affairs ministry who had signed the document.

One would wonder if these governments with enormous wealth could not hire someone professional to advise them on such simple things like attestation. Someone to mitigate their fears of forgeries, which could also be avoided by undertaking some simpler, clearer procedures. One can consider that a document does not have to be fully covered in stamps to be genuine. That there are some countries who make sensible requirements on stamps and have extremely low incidences of forgeries.

And, why all this bureaucracy? The system throws road blocks at every step attempted for individuals. Unless one is desperate, one easily loses patience with these bureaucracies and gives up. However, the problem is global desperation which is rising everywhere and many people have no alternatives. One of the main alternatives is having a *wasta* ("contact") with an influential Emirati man or woman. It is the simplest explanation to resolving the seemingly endless stream of roadblocks to scrutinize inefficient job seekers while there are still many inefficient personnel who don't understand anything about how their job is to be carried out through assigned tasks. A system that prioritizes *"know who"* over *"know how"* ends up blocking the qualified in an effort to cut competition for the unqualified people with good contacts, or *wastas* in the local language. As much as the bureaucracy is so burdensome to individuals and extracts a lot of money from the poor jobseekers, it is also unhelpful to the system's overall performance.

This kind of bureaucracy is also one way the system extracts money from its poor and the desperate expatriate community. Now imagine each stamp costs around US $30, and one has to obtain five stamps simply for the purpose of attesting a higher education diploma.

The UAE bureaucracy triggers much stress for expatriates. I recall the time when I wanted to purchase airline tickets for my family, an entitlement granted to every employee every year. It was in December and I knew the privilege would not carry over into the new year. One would have thought that a journalist would have little trouble in using the entitlement before it expired but I experienced the same types of roadblocks that others would encounter. The Abu Dhabi Media had put in place a system in which such applications had to be approved by almost six people before the ticket could be issued. I was fine until the third step for the approval process when the human resources office staff member had not yet approved my application, and she was not even answering calls. I even thought that perhaps she was on vacation but then I was getting frustrated trying to find out from others why the delay occurred. I asked my cluster editor to take a day off work and go to Abu Dhabi and stay there until she signed. He refused, adding it was a waste of time and energy for something that could be sorted out easily via phone or email. However, he would go and check on my application's status because he was in the Abu Dhabi office. Even after two days of trying to find out what triggered the delay, the editor still had no answer. Finally, we heard from an Indian woman junior HR who responded in the humblest of tones in an email, asking for the intervention of an Arabic female speaker, begging the senior HR to sign off on the application. She added that she was always slow and rude.

I could speak Arabic so I decided to plead my case the following day. The procrastinating staff member was in the office and I introduced myself, adding, "Taweel Umrikhi, please kindly approve my family air ticket request in queue" (*Taweel Umrikhi*, which means "may God extend your life," is a popular greeting in local GCC communities.) With just a nod of the head she opened the email, approved it in seconds as she did with all of the other pending requests, and I had the air tickets in few minutes. The crisis that had meandered about for two weeks was cleared in less than 10 minutes but I still struggled to understand why she had been so adamant about this simple bureaucratic procedure.

It was always stressful that when the one who had the power to approve such requests was an Emirati, the person making the request had to pray several times that, one, the staff member is available, and two, the individual is in a good enough mood to review the request as positively as possible. One could not push this individual because approving someone's company benefits like an air ticket was tantamount to granting a special favor, a gesture to be done altruistically not as the normal part of the job responsibilities. Rulers and the ruling elites enjoy warm, full tributes as a precondition to the actual request for the favor – a common part of the UAE culture. The problem, however, is that the act of offering tributes is not appropriate as part of the daily conduct of job responsibilities. These entitlements are predicated upon the basic acknowledgement of all humanity's right to respect, dignity and decency.

There was also a provision for children school fees allowances at the office, but the procedures for any child studying outside the UAE were as mind boggling a bureaucratic procedure as any other. For example, one had to get the school fees slips attested from the UAE embassies and then the Ministry of Foreign Affairs every year. Initially, there was no UAE embassy in Uganda so the executive editor at *The National* excused me and offered to do a phone check with the school. Once the embassies were established, unfortunately one could not avoid easily the bureaucracy. Shortly before being ousted from *The National* because of the controversy over my book, I submitted papers that required five signatures of approval. The first three signed off without incident but then the fourth person in the chain emerged, the same Emirati female senior employee that my HR representative had referred to as being lazy and rude earlier. She raised her usual questions about the stamps. I wrote back explaining it had been approved previously for my daughter without those stamps for the last two years.

Instead of stalling, the woman opted to just be an outright pain. She conducted some quick research, confirming there now was a Ugandan embassy in Abu Dhabi and the UAE had also established an embassy in Kampala. She wrote back giving me details of her research with orders of obtaining all of these stamps before coming back to her. She copied all of the correspondence to those individuals who already had signed off on my documents. She had no idea that the Uganda's first secretary would not sign such letters from small schools besides college and birth certificates.

It is always expensive, crazy and irrelevant bureaucracy. Each stamp costs money and the purchase must appear on every bank slip, so the slips page itself is not sufficient to verify that all of the stamps have been obtained. After going through the bureaucracy in obtaining the stamps, one discovers rudely that all of the school fees have been spent on getting the stamps and may be an additional amount equivalent to one-half of the fees just in terms of the time and effort to collect and deliver the stamps. I found it hopeless and thought I should give up the school fees allowance that year but I was not yet done. I wrote back, asking if she would need all those stamps from me every year to which she responded in her rude official English: "I would like to inform you that you have to stamp the papers every year and you can't ignored. Also, the company will not do the payments to the people abroad before completing these important procedures."

I sat down and started working out how many stamps I needed for attestation, starting with the Ministry of Foreign Affairs in Uganda, then the UAE embassy in Kampala, the Ugandan embassy in Abu Dhabi and the UAE foreign affairs office. This came to four stamps for each bank slip that would be paid. Each stamp cost around 150 dirhams (US $40) and there are three bank slips in a year. After jotting down all the sums and comparing them with what I was looking to be compensated for, I was furious. Almost all the school fees for my daughter and son for whom I was applying for the first time would be spent on stamps. I was further infuriated that I did not have the money to send home at the time to start the process; that I had been expecting to have my money I paid for school fees reimbursed as my allowances. The situation appeared somewhat hopeless, as I was angry at a system that had finessed the dubious art of heartless exploitation especially for those whose income was limited and barely reflected a modicum of economic justice.

How could one get a personal loan or even a charitable donation that would be justifiably simpler than reaping the rightful rewards of an entitled allowance at one's workplace in the UAE? And, then there is the demeaning scene of trying to explain to everyone from the child's teacher to the security men at embassies and then to the embassy officers why one needs a stamp on a child's bank slips. Ponder the circumstances for a moment and one quickly realizes that it's even worse than asking for charity.

The UAE bureaucracy in everything is persistently painful and exploitive – a system that excels in giving a benefit with one hand but then essentially taking away everything they have given with the other. This time I decided not to give them any more money and they could keep their allowances. It's all the same unfortunately, as the company I worked for belongs to the government. It's the government that gives and takes it all and unless one is keen to sit down and do some calculations, the government officials will take away more than what they have given, much to the surprise of the affected individual. What is the use of awarding allowances that the government is not willing to give to foreigner workers or that we the poor workers could not afford to have by our own means? If I could not afford to educate my children at UAE schools, I can only imagine how much more dire the situation is for immigrants earning much less than me. The company had stipulated a certain pay level per child which was less than half of what the cheapest schools paid a year. It's not an affordable venture for families with more than one child. And, then there were issues with racism in the schools. I needed to protect my children from worrying about their skin color while still young.

Ahmed, my Mombasa friend who in 2004 helped me secure a visa for Dubai, called to alert me that he was coming to the UAE. He wanted to collect a lot of money on behalf of a client who had died at work in the Hamriya industrial area. The man died after a coworker had started a machine while he was in the wrong place and it mutilated him. The court in Sharjah decreed blood money to be paid to the family and the company had notified the family that the blood money payment had been made at the court. However, that was two years ago and the family had yet to receive the payment from the Kenyan diplomatic mission. The family lobbied Kenyan parliament members and an attorney said the family could collect the blood money from the court.

Ahmed planned to stay for only two weeks or less. I told him it would be impossible in this country to process the papers in such a short time given bureaucratic madness. But he said the process had started about two years back, and the company had already made the payment. Likewise, the consulate was also following up the case and they simply required him to turn up to court and collect the compensation. A week after he arrived in the UAE, he was already certain his assumptions were wrong and was sure that even a month would not be enough for him. He had to complete the papers once again, including obtaining the death certificates, attesting all of the documents with embassies and foreign affairs departments and getting letters from companies. The stream of documents required seemed endless and every time he visited the court hoping he had everything, he was told something new that he was missing. Finally, the two weeks were only enough to compile the documents, and when the court finally accepted his submission, he was told they would need some time to go through all the paper work and get back to him. He asked if it would take simply a month and the documents recipient said not a month but more time. After a year he waited in Mombasa for a response that never came. I joked that he should be prepared that if we were to return, he would need to do the papers again. Ahmed replied that he had given up any hope and the poor family had also understood that they were twice unfortunate: their father was killed and the blood money stolen.

The Sharjah court have a lot of people attempting to receive their compensations and even though they are in a hurry to collect them from the offenders, the authorities are not in any hurry to make whole the rightful claims of migrant families. I wrote an article about a Pakistani man who was paralyzed in an accident and lost his job; his compensation had long been paid and the Emirati person who knocked him down already was released from prison. The court claimed he was released because he had paid the compensation but for more than a year, the court had yet to transfer the amount to the paralyzed victim.[202]

4.4 A Friend in Prison

Ibrahim, a friend at our usual Friday football games, greeted me with a stern face suggesting *nga kitalo* ("pretty sad"), a phrase for expressing condolences in Uganda, as he changed from his football kit to his street clothes at Safa Park where we always had our weekend football reunions. Hamza (pseudonym), a mutual friend who usually joined us for our weekend get-togethers, was a popular fixture at our games. His team already had been scored against several times and the other players complained the team's defense was lame without Hamza.

He had been imprisoned but no one precisely knew the reason. However, after his arrest he brought the cops at night to the location where he shared accommodations with his friends and they picked up another roommate. No one even knew at which station they were being held, and everyone thought he had contacted me after his arrest and they were waiting for me to tell them the details.

I spent two days canvassing different police stations but I could not find him. Hamza had called a roommate who said he was at the Naif police station, which was located right in the neighborhood of their residence. We never considered the possibility the police would have detained him at such a close location.

At the Naif police station in Deira visitors are welcome only on Mondays from 9 a.m. to noon. A large Arab man queried the name and case number before anyone was allowed to visit. I told him I didn't know the charges and he said just a word of advice like a brother: just say any charges, like check or illegal, just anything and it doesn't have to be accurate or otherwise they will turn away visitors. I followed his advice and told the officer who was taking down details and giving indications about a bounced check, even though I knew very well he did not even have a checkbook. There was also no way he was an illegal because he was working legally in a hotel.

After meeting him in the police cells with a large mirror separating us he told me he had been a victim of being merciful. The roommate who was arrested had an arrangement with a buyer in Uganda who purchased various items from an Indian salesman. Whenever the customer could not come to Dubai, he would send money directly to the Indian and, after paying, he would ask the roommate to collect the items and ship them to Uganda on his behalf. The Indian told the roommate he needed to have documents to pick the items but he was in Dubai without documents so he asked Hamza to represent him.

Hamza went to the shop in Bur Dubai, but was informed immediately he was under arrest and had to produce his ID. Hamza was confused about the situation; he did not even know the Ugandan businessman. But the drama had started nonetheless. They gave him two appointments to see a prosecutor which were then abruptly canceled. For a full month I had visited him in jail every Monday, as he had not yet seen a prosecutor. I asked the embassy in Abu Dhabi to help and simply ask the cops to let him see the prosecutor and be informed of the charges. A secretary called the police but the only response was that the case was still pending under investigation

Nothing was done to hurry the procedure. After a month a prosecutor came to the police and asked Hamza to respond simply "yes" or "no" to each of the charges. Hamza was astonished, believing he could talk to someone explaining what the exact circumstances were – that he was asked to help a friend. At court, the judge queried with some vague details indicating the charges were fraud but he refused to give Hamza a chance to explain the situation. He could either plead to or deny the charges and then be returned to jail. All along, he read the usual stories of confession in newspapers, which seemed to occur with all criminal cases in the UAE. He wondered if he was about to suffer a similar verdict.

Hamza tried to rationalize his predicament. The delay

occurred because the holy month of Ramadan was approaching when the rulers would forgive prisoners as a gesture of goodwill. A human resources representative from his employer, an Egyptian Arab, also tried to help Hamza's situation by applying for Kafala sponsorship but he was denied. Ramadan came and went, and still there was no amnesty for him. I urged Hamza to get a lawyer but he feared that he could not afford legal representation. I advised him not to say a single word about the pending case without representation. His incarceration was a prelude to a deportation hearing, a process that would be far more expensive, as I explained to him, than hiring a lawyer. A female journalist colleague who covered Dubai courts referred a Jordanian female attorney, who went to investigate the case and discovered some alarming details. Hamza was being charged for fraud, forging official government documents and staying in the UAE illegally. The last charge was clearly erroneous and I contacted his employer with the information. Obviously the police assumed Hamza did not have legal documents when he was arrested because he was black and African. The police asked the employer to bring his passport and visa but then they never bothered to change his status. It was as if the police were incapable of deciphering a legitimate set of documents.

The first lawyer told me to deposit 10,000 dirhams to start on the case but the costs could increase as the case progressed. I turned down his offer, knowing there was no way the fees could be collected. Then the Jordanian-Palestinian lawyer told me she needed 25,000 dirhams to start on the case.

Good lord is there no justice at all for the poor any more, I wondered. The judge doesn't speak, the prosecutor does not provide a lawyer and so all workers – who are the majority of this country's population earning about US $200 each month – can always simply accept the charges blindly once arrested even on false accusations, because not a single one amongst them can afford a lawyer.

When I visited Hamza to deliver the disappointing news he could not hide his shock upon discovering how few alternatives he really had, especially that the right to legal representation was not among his options. I told him he had to be sharp and stubborn when being demanded to respond "yes" or "no" to charges. Instead, he should tell the judge that he had a small request: *Talab Basitu,* which I taught him how to say in Arabic and to repeat it until the judge agreed finally to listen to him. Then the judge would inspect his passport and discover a legal visa. I told this to Hamza as discreetly as possible, because any prison officers overhearing this discussion would have laughed at me before ejecting me.

A week later, Hamza's verdict was announced, as feared. He was convicted on all counts including that of staying illegally in the country. He was given three months in prison and because the time already had been served, he was scheduled to be deported immediately. Hamza, though, wanted to appeal. "I think if I appeal they could have a chance to examine my case, starting with looking at my visa, and know that it was wrong to charge me for illegal residence when I had an employment residence visa," he told me. I interrupted him with *Inshaallah* – when God wishes an encouragement for him to go with the appeal even though I strongly doubted it could change anything. The chances were nil that an African expatriate could argue successfully for an appeal, especially when he did not even have a lawyer at his side.

My friend was behind bars at the same time when two other popular prisoners were making headlines – not so good for Dubai in the international media. A Norwegian woman who had reported a rape was jailed for illegal extramarital sex. The other was an Indian man who had filmed an Emirati customs manager punching an Indian driver on the road for a traffic violation. Authorities often feel shame once the global media picks up such stories and often pardon the victim, as in the case of the

Norwegian woman who was pardoned after getting her verdict of 16 months in prison.[203]

For the majority of prisoners such as Hamza, especially on clearly erroneous charges that are not investigated by their prosecutors, such gestures are as far from reality as can be imagined. Even when it looks like the cases are different, a prison term on whatever charges is self-destructive. In the case of my friend it also meant losing a job affecting the livelihood of dozens of people who depend on him in Uganda.

Local police chiefs have publicly praised the central jail located in the Al Aweer Desert at the outskirts of Dubai as having the amenities of a hotel with four or five stars. In the media, the chiefs insist on calling the cells punitive and rehabilitative facilities but not prison or jail. After Hamza was transferred to the central jail, it took me more than a month before I could see my friend again. Twice I was bounced at the prison gates: once because I didn't have a visitor's card, a requirement similar to that for parents visiting their children in boarding schools in Uganda. The guard could have easily rectified this. On the second instance the prison gates were locked an hour earlier than their stipulated closing time. They had closed by 11 a.m. even though they were scheduled to be shut at noon. I had arrived at 11:10 a.m.

On the third attempt I was at the prison gates at 8 a.m. Hamza was relieved to see me, as most of his friends were no longer responding to his calls from prison. I noticed he had lost weight and looked highly stressed. He told me the situation in the central jail was worse than the three months he spent in the jail at the Naif police station. The air conditioner was set at full blast, cold enough to make him shiver throughout the night as prisoners were not allowed blankets. The meals were meagre and disorganized. Prisoners received a small cup of tea in the morning at 7, then lunch at 11, and supper constituted only a small bread portion called *hubz* at 5 p.m.

"By 8 p.m. one would be already hungry but there would be no more meals," he said. "So those with money relied on buying a few things to eat at the prison canteen."

Also disturbing was the prison requirement for inmates to pay fees for products and toiletries for their personal hygiene. The prison charged a cleaning fee of 5 dirhams every week and if an individual did not have the amount, the outstanding fees would accrue and a person could not leave prison without settling his account in full.

Hamza had been preparing for his appeal to be heard in the coming week, and it already had been six weeks since he requested a hearing. He had written a letter to the appellate judge detailing his circumstances and he opened with the fact that he was not an undocumented immigrant, as he was gainfully employed with a legal residency visa in hand and his job was with one of the main hotel groups in the country. Hamza paid a small fee to have the letter translated into Arabic and he had memorized the contents of the letter, both in English and Arabic (his Arabic was fluent to the extent that he could read the language). He had spent his prison time to be as fully prepared as possible for his appeal.

I asked Hamza about the two others who were involved with the case. One was waiting for the embassy to secure papers to use as his passport and the other had become entangled in further trouble with the police. When he was arrested, he had 10,000 dirhams in his pocket and submitted it to the police safe custody as customary. However, the money was nowhere to be found when he was released at the airport. He had to cancel the flight and return to prison. They advised him to file a case to court and the dates had been set two months away. He was now considering going to Uganda and having someone attend court in his place and demand the return of his money. It was a good story. Unfortunately, the circumstances about police impropriety were such that I could risk trouble for my own status if I wrote about it in the UAE.

I told Hamza about the book and I added that I could not rule out the possibility of joining him in prison at some point. My time was growing short, as once the contents of the book were made public, the ruling elites would try to interfere with my attempts to leave the country safely and without incident. Hamza told me it was not about staying in prison but the worst experience is getting in a legal dispute in the emirate knowing the legal procedures are prejudiced and ineffective for an immigrant who is seeking relief and remedies for his situation. Hamza did not wish anyone to experience a painful legal procedure where judges pass verdicts before looking at papers of the accused and before they know anything about the case.

Unlike at Naif where we could give prisoners money in hand, in the central jail we had to leave the money with the police and get a receipt. They strip visitors to ensure that one does not even carry keys before entering the prison. I said my good-byes and added that I would leave him something at the police reception desk.

Hamza called me a week later to say he had been in the court and the judge listened to his appeal in a discussion which he believed was constructive. He had yet to hear the outcome. Then, one evening at about nine, he called me from a pay phone in Dubai, indicating he had been released and was hoping I could pick him up from the Nasser Square roundabout in Dubai. Hamza was dressed in a drab *kandura* and his only other possessions were an exercise book and pen. He told me the security men had called him (along with three other men) on the prison microphone, escorted them outside the jail and then told them they were free. None of them remembered to ask for their passports or other belongings, as they were all excited to run back into the world. They had no transport from the desert prison and had to walk about two kilometers to find a truck driver who would agree to drop them off in Dubai.

Forgetting his passport was a big mistake. I told him we should go back to the prison first thing in the morning to reclaim the passport. When we arrived, no one among the police officers seemed to have even an idea of what my friend was asking for. I tried to speak in Arabic but one cop would refer me to another without any guidance. No one could locate system details showing the case was closed and some even ventured to determine how he got out of prison. Finally another cop suggested we go to the public prosecutor's office and get a printed copy of the verdict and a letter indicating the case was closed and bring the documents to the prison officials. The prosecutors told us the letter would be ready in a week's time. Meanwhile my friend decided to let his employer know that he was ready to resume work. The immediate supervisor led him to human resources who told him all they wanted for him was to bring his passport and letter that the case was closed and then he could resume his work.

A week later he completed the bureaucratic hurdles but when he showed the passport to his employer, his supervisor had a change of mind. He now required him to reapply as a new employee and wait for approval. As a beginner, he would be paid 2,000 dirhams per month, half of what he earned before he was arrested. He asked his boss for some time to consider these changed circumstances. I advised Hamza to ask for his end-of-service benefit and he was told that because he left his job without resigning, he was considered an absconder and not entitled to such benefits. Furthermore, the company representatives told him that they had even been kind by allowing him to re-apply, that his visa had been canceled and would allow him to stay in the country for only a month. He had worked for the hotel for seven years and this seemed to be the end, leaving him as penniless as when he had just joined the hotel upon his arrival in Dubai.

4.5 Exit Bureaucracy

After my termination at *The National*, the HR assistant who had to handle my exit had many things she couldn't figure out how to do. Among them was how to sign out my apartment clearance with the office before leaving. I had simply changed my house contract to be paid by the office just a year before and human resources was finding it a big problem. She told me to go to the housing department and have this sign out explained to me clearly as they were having problems with all departing employees regarding the company's housing contracts. No one could explain satisfactorily why there were so many difficulties. The departmental staff checked my account and confirmed that my contract was expiring that month so there would be no need to renew it. It was the Canadian executive editor who wanted to know how I was progressing with the exit and she took me aside around the office canteen and explained to me the real problem. She told me the office required a clearance from my landlord that I did not owe him anything and that the apartment was in good condition. To get this clearance I needed to cancel my contract at the municipality and then cancel my electricity and water services with the respective authority and then leave the house to have the landlord issue the "no objection" certificate.

She told me canceling all these meant I would have to vacate the house for a few days or even a week before my departure. I was frustrated to learn at this late stage that I would have to figure out where I would be staying the last few days. The editor suggested a hotel or perhaps a friend's place. The idea set me off completely, as I was not planning on spending any money for a hotel or begging friends to stay in their sitting rooms. I was temporarily lost without a solution.

After discussing the problem with the real estate owner of my apartment, we reached a deal: give a deposit of 2,000 dirhams and he issues the clearance letter. Once the office cleared my dues and I was ready to leave I should then go to cancel the contract with the municipality and electricity authorities before collecting back my deposit. When I started canceling the contracts, I found that at the municipality I needed to pay a canceling fee of about five percent of the house contract value and the electricity and water authorities also charged fees for canceling their services. There was no end in sight for charging fees even to a fired employee like myself who was being forced to leave the country. And it took days of running up and down before it was finally done.

Then I called the men from the used furniture shops to come and buy all my furniture, only to learn that they were actually not buying but taking. One after the other would turn up to inspect the household space from the kitchen to sitting room and bedroom and then would make an offer of less than what is meaningful for even a single item. I kept turning them all down until the last night of my stay in Dubai, when I simply gave it all up together with my car. I couldn't imagine what kind of pain people must endure who are given 48 hours to leave the country, which is common for mostly Shia deportees. I had almost a month to dispose of all my household items and car and found it was not enough. For others it must be much worse.

However, the biggest challenge of clearing my obligations came with the bank and I only learned at the last moment just how much effort was required. The salesman told me there was a big problem if I was leaving the UAE without another sponsor or job offer. He went silent for a moment and then explained to me that my web shopper was like a credit card. It first had to be cancelled in about one week and then a clearance of my liability was to be issued in 45 days. He advised I should apply for the card's cancellation and then go to my country and then come back after that time to collect my money. The advice would have been fine if UAE was a visa-free destination or if I never needed another sponsor to return.

I became more agitated as I listened to his advice. I raised my voice in anger, explaining that "no credit was given on my web shopper; I always had to put money there in order to use it." And all he could respond was to calmly say: "Those are the rules." I gathered my ATM and web shopper cards, passport and other papers from his desk and told him I was going to see his manager. Even then I knew there was nothing the manager could do for me if these were the rules. I don't know how many times I regretted having not left the country and waiting instead for my money in Uganda, taking to heed the earlier advice from the HR assistant. I cursed the fact of this information gap – that no one, whether from my office or even among friends who had changed or cancelled jobs had told me about this rule in advance so that I would not have been caught off guard. I thought about my cancelled visa, and the fines I would have to pay if I insisted on staying in the UAE and the fact that if I left there was still little chance I would ever get another visa to return to the UAE. I knew the authorities were waiting for me to leave the country and block me for good. I also thought about my landlord who was daily demanding my exit from his house and I could not imagine where I was going to stay for the remaining time. I wondered how many people were trapped like me and wished I could go and speak out loud and warn everyone from taking any banks card or even loans in the UAE.

When I arrived at the branch manager's office, an Emirati woman like many others in the bank had witnessed my earlier outbursts with the salesman. She chided me initially, telling me to behave well in her office and then asked what the problem was. I opened my passport and cancelled visa and told her I had few days left in the country and I wanted to have my funds when I left, as it was the government that fired me and wanted me out of the country, so I conceivably could not come back to the UAE to collect my money in 45 days. She seemed to understand my dilemma but still she insisted the rules were firm. I wanted to ask her who devised these rules that were so distant from logistical reality, expecting people to first go back to their country and then return to collect their end-of-service benefits just because they had a credit card. Instead I told her that I had avoided taking their loans and credit cards and now I was trapped like people who had taken them simply because of a web shopper. She told me the only thing I could do was to go to the collections center in Dubai and talk to the manager there but the branch had nothing to do for me.

At least she had the courtesy to print out the directions. Already half of the day was gone when I set out to the office in Meydan. The manager's name was Khadija, the same as my mother and my infant daughter. I showed her the photo of my daughter which was the screensaver image on my mobile phone. She admired the photo, uttering traditional praises in Arabic. She listened intently as I recounted my troubles. Within minutes, she had cancelled the card and said I would be able to collect my funds the next day. If the credit had yet to appear after 24 hours, she advised me to contact her, and she gave me the number to her direct line.

I looked at her as a savior, who had solved the hardest imaginable mystery. I thanked and told her she had actually been like my mother and left.

Section 5

Sexual Starvation

5.1 Introduction

The Gulf countries were not only into building luxurious cities or malls, but also desperate villages exclusively populated with single men, the numbers enough to match that of a small emirate such as Umm Al Quwain. There was a Sonapur labor camp in Dubai, a Sajja labor camp in Sharjah, among others. Even driving in these villages with a woman passenger is enough to turn faces on the road throughout as if women were from another planet. And these are men who work as office aides or cleaners in big offices and malls. It really should not surprise anyone that the voyeuristic placement of cameras in female toilets has recently become a major problem in Dubai. That women in this modern emirate are not safe in hotel rooms, office toilets or even public spaces such as malls and metro stations. A woman has to look around and check to see there are no secretly planted cameras when she goes into a toilet before she can strip down to her business. She has to watch every square centimeter of the floor she is crossing.

Consider these headlines *The National* carried in the month between Oct. 8 and Nov. 8, which are only a small sample representing a potentially much larger number of cases:

> Dubai man jailed three years for filming female colleagues using toilet.[204]
> Man secretly filmed female flat mates in shower.[205]
> Man used phone to take up obscene clips of women on Dubai metro.[206]

This last headline highlighted a story about a phone camera zoomed in on women's cleavage or used to capture images and videos up women's skirts. Police found at least 13 obscene clips of different women.

One incident concerned a popular Ugandan traditionalist

named Mamma Fina, who calls herself a caster of spells and was photographed naked resting on a bed in a Dubai hotel that she used frequently for business.[207] The nude pictures went straight to Uganda's tabloids. However, these were not ghosts or spirits that took her nude photos, even though the self-proclaimed caster of spells would have many of her followers believe. It was the work of men notorious for hiding cameras to film women naked in the emirate. And, it was not only women that were filmed answering nature calls in GCC public or mall toilets; a Kenyan man also planted a camera in a men's toilet in Deira City Center.[208] The camera was discovered by a Bangladeshi cleaner and upon looking at the camera footage, police found the installer had also filmed himself during the process of placing the camera.

Illegally planted cameras concerned both women and men in the UAE, but also the legal security cameras in malls or traffic justifiably bothered some Emiratis. Covering the Sharjah Consultative Council session on April 18, 2013 as part of my regular beat for *The National*, I learned members questioned the Sharjah police about their policies and wondered aloud about their legitimacy. One of the council's most vocal members asked the police commander-in-chief why they were putting security cameras everywhere in malls, roads, banks, and virtually every other building. The question asked was why police were unaware these cameras were being manned by some Asian workers who decided to retain some photos for their own use or pleasure.

Furthermore, the council member added that the cameras violated the sanctity of Emirati women's culture and religion. Major General Humaid Mohammed al Hudaidi, the police chief, appeared eager to dodge the question and responded with a "wait-and-see" attitude. Visibly dissatisfied, the council member rebutted with even a more bitter-sounding statement demanding an end to the use of the cameras. The police commander was now pushed to the verge of apologizing for the tactic but instead defended his position politely and calmly, explaining the cameras were essential to the country's security and that police could not be everywhere. He tried to reassure the council, saying if there are some privacy violations the police could investigate them but they would not consider banning the cameras. Along with fellow reporters, I followed the inquisitive council member outside to gather a rounder picture of his views.

I trailed him to the mosque and we exchanged greetings of "Salaam," which triggered a snarky chuckle from two of my cynical colleagues. However, he was reticent and reserved, telling me that his comments at the meeting were not for publication. "Not everything you hear in that house you have to put in your newspaper," he said. "If you ever publish it I will deny ever saying it." We parted and I told my colleagues what he said. They told me if he doesn't want it published, then forget it, and write about other things. I wrote the story that was published three days later, as customary. The council session story always appears at the beginning of the week (on Sunday). While the story featured primarily the angle of the Emiratization of all police jobs in the emirate, I did manage to mention the discussion of security cameras with women in my story.[209]

5.2 Restrictions on Living a Married Life

If one believes the process of getting a residency permit is as difficult as has been perceived then those who have one will find that sponsoring a spouse is that much more disturbing. The emirate is a haven for singles and many hurdles have been erected that make one's dreams of living with his or her married spouse quite frustrating to achieve. In the GCC sponsoring a husband or wife requires one to have a certain income level. The levels change constantly according to the country and mood of the legislature but they are set much higher than what many laborers are able to earn realistically. In the UAE one has to earn more than 5,000 dirhams each month (US $1,350) with accommodations provided or a total of 10,000 dirhams (US $2,700) without accommodation. In Qatar one requires a monthly salary of 10,000 Qatari riyal (US $2,700) and an executive job, while in Saudi Arabia it's 3,500 Saudi riyal (US $980), and in Kuwait, between 450 Kuwaiti dinars (US $1,230) and 650 Kuwaiti dinars (US $1,770) That sum is not just prohibitive for unskilled workers but as well for many professionals in the emirate.

Qatar further complicates the lives of expatriates who want to bring their families, as it dictates that only those earning 10,000 Qatari riyals per month (US $2,750) and who have in hand a degree from an accredited university can bring a spouse to the country. At the newspaper where I worked many reporters and subeditors do not make enough money to bring their wives. The company occasionally raises one's monthly salary to the required level once the employee completes the paperwork for processing of visas. Yet, there also are other requirements that disqualify employees from being able to bring their spouses. Sometimes, the salary requirements could be larger along with the need to attest documents such as marriage certificates and diplomas.

It has always surprised me how they decided to uphold the degree requirement for someone bringing his wife, suggesting that non-degree holders do not have conjugal rights in Qatar. In the UAE, at least, the degree or attested certificates are required for processing a work permit or labor card for some professions but are never a requirement for someone to bring a spouse. In Qatar, officials processed my work permits, never bothering to inquire whether or not I had a university diploma. The only mention was if I planned on bringing my wife and children to Qatar. The requirement is unsustainable and irrelevant for all reasonable purposes. Rather, the authorities are simply erecting additional hurdles to restrict their immigrant expatriates from living a comfortable and stable life in Qatar, especially if they are married.

When I worked for *The Gulf Today*, I tried once to bring my wife with me and the response from the human resources office was that my salary was too low to sponsor a family. *The Gulf Today* quietly offered almost the same salary to all reporters which meant no journalist could qualify to bring his wife. Some reporters however were living with their spouses, and I tried to ask my editor how that happened. Instead he advised me not to go into the politics of those details. One reporter who had a working wife told me his spouse was on another job working visa, not his own. If a survey could discern how many expatriates in the UAE earned the required salary to sponsor their wives, the results would be shocking to many outsiders. My simple guess would not even put the number at one-third of total expatriates. The figures would be especially alarming among UAE's most despised nationalities of Asians and Africans.

And even when one was fortunate enough to pocket earnings of 10,000 dirhams a month there were other roadblocks such as having a tenancy contract in both names. One of my African friends who worked in Abu Dhabi had trouble getting his wife a visa because he was subleasing a room in a large residential building and therefore didn't have a tenancy contract. His woes were exacerbated when real estate agents wanted almost 6,000 dirhams a month in order to secure a decent house with a contract. My friend gave up that year and stayed a bachelor hoping his circumstances would change once when he changed his residency to more affordable accommodations in Dubai. Again he could not get a spouse's visa as there was another law he had broken: one could not stay in Dubai and work in Abu Dhabi. Many expatriates had exploited this opportunity by driving to work in Abu Dhabi which, in turn, left the capital city's expensive buildings persistently empty.

Saudi Arabia had similar restrictive rules for expatriates desiring to bring their spouses from abroad. I have known plenty of expatriate friends in Saudi Arabia whose wives regularly go for the great pilgrimage every year, not to participate in the holy rituals but instead to meet their husbands who have no other chance of sponsoring them to stay with them.

Arabian Business reported that Qatar Airways female employees are required to secure permission from the airline to get married or change their marital status as part of their contract of employment.[210] The rules read, as taken from the report published in the newspaper:

> You are required to obtain prior permission from the company, in case you wish to change your marital status and get married. And: The employee shall notify the employer in case of pregnancy from the date of her knowledge of its occurrence...
>
> The employer shall have the right to terminate the contract of employment from the date of notification of the pregnancy. Failure of employee to notify the employer or the concealment of the occurrence shall be considered a breach of contract.[211]

The National later ran an article about two major UAE airlines with the headline "Emirates Airlines and Qatar Airlines defend cabin crew rules".[212] In the story, Akbar Al Baker, the CEO of Qatar Airways, had an emotional reply to critics of the airline contracts that forbid female cabin crews from marrying within the first five years of their employment. He said the criticisms amounted to attacks on his country because Qatar had won the bid to host the 2022 World Cup. He said: "All this was a big sensational [effort] to target my country because of 2022, saying people have no human rights. It is not true ... You know they have come there to do a job and we make sure that they are doing a job; that they give us a good return on our investment."[213]

The Emirates Chief Commercial Officer Thierry Antinori

offered a less emotional defense, saying that cabin crews were expected to fly for the first three years and pregnant women could not work on board for health reasons. He also said the female cabin crew members who became pregnant during their first three years of employment were expected to leave. He added that such rules did not stop people from coming to work for them, as they had 129,000 applications for cabin crews in the previous year.[214]

Despite his explanation focusing on cabin crews, the reality I found in Qatar has been different. All Qatar airlines staff – whether cabin crew or ground staff and including those employed by the airline's subsidiaries – have consistently told me they are not allowed to get married. One Ugandan airline employee in Doha told me that every freedom is treasured once it is denied. That after their employer restricts their freedom to get married most of her female colleagues become so obsessed in talking about marriages that one would think they would all be married had they not been employed by Qatar Airways. They plan their weddings in advance so that once they resign and leave their jobs the wedding can be set in motion quickly. The policy is the same, regardless of years of employment, and even in those cases where employees request permission from their employers to be married, the company often denies applications from nationals who are always targeted for discrimination in Qatar. For example, it would be unheard of for a Qatari national to be fired from her job even if she decided to get married and pregnant early in her job tenure.

The region's leading airlines make it a point to recruit beautiful young women in their most sexually active years and, as a condition of employment, demand them to put off marriage; suppress their sexual drive or use birth control pills during the time they are working for the airlines. Not a very easy challenge to meet when one is young and beautiful with a lot of admirers and just even a casual glance into these women's lives reveals a difficult existence filled with anxiety and depression, as women refuse courtships and marriage proposals because of their employer's sanctions. And, for those who are already legally married, pregnancy would mean immediate termination.

Still a friend working with Dnata airline services in Dubai would often explain how difficult it was for a married woman to get a job in the industry. It was also difficult to get any solid numbers from the airlines themselves about how many employees working in plane cabins were married because they often hired pools of employees in the tens of thousands. The analysis or explanation often offered was as much rubbish as if one would suggest that all female employees receive free prescriptions of drugs intended to depress their sexual appetite and feelings. The company, despite claiming that, indeed, it did receive many thousands of applications from young, unemployed women, could not explain away its most obvious sexual discrimination policies. Women were forced to sacrifice their own freedoms and dress just in order to get a job that paid modestly and included benefits that were equally as modest, certainly not enough for those who hoped to get married and raise their own families one day. It is completely understandable that people could sacrifice their rights, not only for having a family but many others were forced to do so just because they dared to speak out about their employment conditions on the basis of a universal right to human decency and dignity.

Rarely discussed in public are the many sacrifices young women make in order to work for companies that like to present themselves as globally responsible corporations but instead do everything to cover up the process of draconian rules they use to subjugate their workers. The Qatar Airlines CEO who justified such rules because he wanted "a good return" on his company's investment did not even seem to acknowledge that such rules were unnecessary and counterproductive to a company's profit-maximizing goals. There certainly are many other businesses, including those in the airline industry, that do accommodate female employees, especially those who are married and who have children. The point is that this is possible, even in Qatar and other emirates which pride themselves as 21st-century vanguards in the global economy.

This draconian rule of essentially dictating when female employees can be married prevails unfortunately in many GCC companies and not just airlines. I interviewed numerous young women working as sales assistants in malls and in petrol stations and consistently I heard stories about employees being fired because they became pregnant. Even the married workers would tell me how they lied about their marital status to get hired because they knew it would be impossible otherwise.

And it was not only women who were tortured by these unjustifiably restrictive rules that banned paid maternity leave. Most GCC companies required even male workers to notify their employers before getting married. Even men could be fired for getting married. A friend working with a Dubai hotel said everybody was required to notify management of any intention of marriage, regardless of gender. Employees, especially immigrant workers, could only seek housing in the company-approved accommodations, which, as described previously, were as crowded as they were inexpensive. And companies found it easier to fire than keep an employee who was about to be married because the company would refuse to raise their residency allowances for accommodations outside of the compounds they have stipulated for employees.[215]

5.3 Children Born Out of Wedlock

Despite prevailing attitudes about sexual repression in the UAE, there is no shortage of children being born out of wedlock. The problem is most of these innocent children are victimized, abandoned and sometimes even killed. I covered one stretch in which three babies were abandoned in just four days in the emirate of Sharjah.[216]

Most parents resort to such desperate means taking the lives of their children to avoid being punished by the same legal system that repressed them and with insidious temptation opened doors through which desperate individuals seek to satisfy their sexual needs in risky, even illegal circumstances.

The penalties for having a child out of wedlock could carry jail terms, though the time of stay depends upon factors such as the emirate in which the incident took place along with one's nationality and race. There are no neat guidelines in the UAE. Some risk losing custody, especially for an expatriate who has a child born out of wedlock and the child is undocumented. In 2010, a Ugandan woman resorted to desperate measures after she was forced to leave her baby at the Dubai International Airport. She refused to part with her baby and called friends in Dubai and Uganda to help arrange documents of marriage with any man to prove that she was married and that her baby was legitimate.

The pains to avoid an uncertain legal process have forced many women to kill their infant children almost immediately after they are born. UAE local newspapers often carry reports of abortions gone wrong or infant deaths. In one gruesome attempt (mentioned earlier) a Filipina maid threw her baby into a garbage chute from the ninth floor, an hour after his birth and the baby miraculously survived.[217] The police issued a press release, explaining how the maid had gone into labor while the family was asleep and gave birth in her room. Afterward, she crept into the bathroom and cut the umbilical cord, wrapped her newborn in clothes and threw him into the garbage chute. In the morning the watchman found the baby and called police. The baby was only able to survive because the chute did not descend straight into the dumpster, as there were turns and twists which slowed the fall and mitigated the impact. The baby was admitted to the Al Qassimi hospital in critical condition and was monitored for any complications. The baby was fine and eventually transferred to the Sharjah Social Care Center. Not all cases ended the same; one baby was found dead after being thrown into a garbage pile in Al Dhaid district of Sharjah.[218] The body was found by municipality workers as they emptied the garbage bins. In another incident the infant's body was found floating on the waters of Buahirah Corniche.[219]

I was the reporter in several of these most unfortunate cases. In Umm Al Quwain, a Sri Lankan woman had aborted and stuffed the seven-month-old fetus into a toilet bowl. She was trying to push it into the sewage pipes but her pain was too great for her to finish. She abandoned the stillborn child and ran to the hospital where she was examined. After the doctors ascertained that she had either given birth or had an abortion, they called police. The police investigators found the fetus' head still protruding from the toilet bowl.

There was a 31-year-old Indonesian woman who delivered a baby boy at a public park in Sharjah on the weekend and fed him with water that terminated his life immediately.[220] Police discovered that the woman, who was in the country without documents, had conceived the child in an adulterous affair and she could not seek medical assistance because of her residency status. She decided to deliver the child in a park and minutes after delivering she gave her crying baby a lot of water thinking it would quiet and calm her, a police spokesman said. The baby died instantly and the woman could not move because she still was nursing intense labor pains when passersby noticed her and called the police.

She told police she regretted the death of her son as she did not know how to deal with babies and had thought by giving him water after delivery he would stop crying. She added the pain was so intense that she could not think properly about allowing the child to start nursing. She said a Bangladeshi man was responsible for her pregnancy but he had left the country soon after learning that she was pregnant. The reports of husbands leaving the country were common in cases involving women who had children out of wedlock. It was not always clear if these reports was always genuine or if they were asserted out of love to protect their partners whom the law viewed the same as fugitives. Police transported the woman to Al Qassimi hospital for treatment and later she was charged.

From Sharjah, I reported on parents who murdered their newborn son.[221] Hospital administrators notified the police in Khorfakhan after a housemaid of Asian descent complaining of pain turned up for treatment. Doctors established that she had given birth and police went to the house to investigate. Another housemaid told police her friend had gone into labor and she helped her give birth in their sponsor home's bathroom in the early morning hours. The maid gave conflicting statements about where they had kept the baby and the police searched the house as well as the neighboring garbage bins, as the municipality workers in Khorfakhan assisted. The body of the child was found wrapped in a cloth in a garbage bin. A police forensics expert confirmed the child was the one killed by the maid.

Police also established that the maid had several relationships with different men and she was not sure who the father was. The police arrested two other Asian men to answer questions while a police spokesman urged sponsors to keep an eye on their maids, adding murderous crimes would occur in their homes if they were not alert to what was happening in the lives of their household staff.

Most babies born out of wedlock, however, are abandoned at mosques. I covered cases of abandoned children at both the King Faisal mosque and Al Sahaba mosque in Sharjah. Stories about abandoned babies are widely circulated in Sharjah, and they often are enough to give celebrity status to a local reporter. One of the most sought after sources for such stories is an Emirati female social worker at the Al Qassimi hospital, the only location where all babies found on the streets or in bins from garbage chutes are taken for treatment. The social worker favorited a single Egyptian reporter from the *Al Ittihad* newspaper, always calling him exclusively whenever a new abandoned baby arrived at the hospital. The reporter who did not consider the English papers as his rivals would then share the story with one or two of the English papers and request editors to keep it a secret from any other Arabic newspaper reporter, as he wanted to protect his status as an exclusive reporter on these types of stories. Because we shared the same office, sometimes he shared some of these abandoning stories with me but journalists at other competing English-language newspapers soon discovered his identity and urged him to no longer share the stories with me.

With me out of the focus, he was now only giving these stories to two female Arab reporters at rival English-language papers. And now I was doing follow-ups like the Arabic newspaper reporters. Finally, one day we met the hospital CEO, and a reporter from the *Al Bayan* newspaper complained about the selective leaking of information to a single reporter with regard to cases involving abandoned babies. I echoed the complaint, urging the practice to end.

I was the only English paper reporter at the meeting in which reporters from *Al Khaleej* and *Emarat Alyoum* newspapers supported the *Al Bayan* reporter's request for the CEO to look into the matter, but all I could do as a representative from *The National*, a sister paper to *Al Ittihad* (whose reporter was being accused in his presence), was simply to nod in acknowledgement at both sides. The *Al Bayan* reporter said he wanted to know what was required for someone to qualify to get these stories because he had tried everything from being polite to greeting regularly the social worker and asking her to share these tipoffs but she always gave them to a single reporter. The *Al Ittihad* reporter, acutely smart in his choice of words, asked the CEO to ignore the requests which he called stupid and full of malicious statements against his employer. He said it was basic knowledge in every journalism school for a reporter to build sources and win their trust and if the complaining reporters had not picked up this knowledge in their schools they should have picked it up at least from experiences as they all had been reporters on the scene for at least 10 years. He concluded that his colleagues' complaints were unfortunate and uninformed.

I remained diplomatic and quiet during the exchange so as not to trigger any subsequent confrontations. The CEO, however, understood what my colleagues were saying, adding that he would instruct the social worker to halt the practice of giving exclusives and instead relay information through the hospital's public information officers. Indeed, this CEO was the only official in Sharjah who one could count on to be sincere and responsive to reporters even when a story potentially could come off as negative for the hospital. This would explain why even doctors at the hospital were more willing to do interviews with journalists without any hindrance.

However what changed on this day was simply the names of the social worker disappearing from my officemate's exclusive stories and replacing them with anonymous sources. If there was any story that I did often miss out on in Sharjah it was that of a newborn child being abandoned. In just two months, there were five such cases, and I had missed each case. My editor queried me by email about why this was happening because it seemed that I had missed or ignored a press release. By the fifth case, which also had been reported by two female journalist colleagues at competing English-language newspapers, my cluster editor seemed perplexed, especially when I had a strong track record for being the first reporter to break many local stories. He wanted an assurance that this would not happen again but I knew that such a promise would be unrealistic.

5.4 The Brothel Visitors

It would be next to impossible to get any official in any GCC country to admit that in the process of restricting the freedom of most expats to marry, the government policies in these holy lands essentially opened the doors to prostitution. They have indirectly supported the influx of young women of barely legal age into their countries to meet the spiraling sexual demands of their workers. Though some tourists would appreciate this venture, not a single worker in any of the labor camps or bachelor-designated accommodations would ever think the government's actions were being kind and considerate to their needs. Those who have once had families and had lived with their wives in their poverty-stricken home countries would tell how their encounters with prostitutes simply exacerbated their emotional distress.

During my days in a shared accommodation in Dubai even a few roommates who would freely talk about their encounters with prostitutes mentioned how it did not bring comfort to their lives but instead simply increased tension and stress. The roommates would always frown upon abiding by the rules of *"first pay, don't touch here or there"* and *"hurry up to get over with it."* One roommate once described that inside the curtains separating the beds in the brothels, one could easily hear often the line: *"have you finished, my friend; another customer waiting."*

And there were many stories of men being thrown out of the brothels for not consummating the deal quick enough to allow their hosts to serve other clients. The biggest embarrassment for brothel visitors occurred when they left the room, too shy to look into the eyes of other men still in the queue waiting to carry on from where they had finished or didn't finish. The guilt of what he had just done would be so intense to lock one's gaze onto another, not because of jealousy that the next man would have more success when he had experienced a nightmare but instead he was embarrassed to be amongst them, sharing a woman. And, despite the practice being widely done, the stigma of being found at it was self-defeating and demoralizing.

I once queried a roommate about what it felt like seeing a friend or acquaintance at the brothel. His answer intrigued me. *"I just stop hiding and reach out to shake his hand and ask him to be discreet with my secret in return for my being discreet with his secret as well."*

Still this secret would not be the basis for two men to become closer friends or even acquaintances who would hang out together, just as they had visited the same prostitute. What it actually did was aggravate the intensity of their guilt and shame, enough to make both them of mutually embarrassed to have a friendship. At a certain point one could blackmail the other and leak the secret to a friend or a group and once the other one learns of the betrayal, he would get his revenge likewise.

There was one man in his fifties who used to threaten to publish the names of everyone he met at the "top flats," as we called the brothels. He was among the few who used to confess to visiting brothels and justified his visits with the Luganda word *kwetaasa,* crudely translated as "easing one's self." The Muslim leaders in the community always criticized the man for uttering vulgar language and trying to corrupt younger men. Often I and others told him to shut up but he always told the religious leaders whom he had seen visit the "top flats" in secret and he was sure everyone was going there. He contrived a system of stealing one shoe of any person he found at the brothel and who had been living in denial. He would bring it to the room to show others his discovery. The practice spread and many other shared accommodations became the venue for similar shaming rituals. Any man who had noticed that one shoe was missing at the brothel door knew that his secret had been disclosed.

These tension-filled scenes are common among GCC

immigrants where governments have denied them all rights to having a wife and family and have unwittingly (or intentionally) opened their doors for prostitution. All common sense among especially Muslims would have it that a relationship with a spouse is more special and comforting than any involving casual, anonymous relations. Even in enlightened Western societies where sex outside of long-term relationships is accepted and tolerated, individuals still cherish the freedom and the right to be able to have a long-term relationship with an individual without having to risk or worry about their livelihood.

The sexual deprivation of most workers in the GCC countries amounts to a torturous practice. It deprives them of any meaningful, productive concentration in life and makes their living painful, socially, culturally, spiritually, economically and emotionally. They work so hard to provide a living to send to their spouses thousands of miles away, without the returns of intimacy and pleasures other husbands would be able to enjoy. But this is not only a torture for men working in Dubai or Riyadh but also a torture to the wives they have left behind and the children who might never know the love of their father. The only connection comes from the money wired back home. For men who come to the GCC to work, they might have only a month or two at most out of every two years to see their families. There always is an inherent disappointment in any long-distance relationship but the pain seems to be more acute here. If a couple relies on trust to keep going, one or both partners in the relationship may no longer be able to withstand the weight of absence or loneliness and one or both will be tempted to break this trust.

In Ugandan circles, many expatriates find their wives married off or with babies born to others in the homes they labored to build while they were in Dubai. Another risk is contracting the deadly HIV/AIDS virus or other sexually transmitted diseases. This is a two-way street, given workers with their fleeting encounters with Dubai sex workers or the wives at home with relationships with others who also might be at risk. In desperate times, many fail to consider any precaution or prudent use of protection.

All of this seems especially incongruous for a GCC emirate like Dubai known for its humanitarian vigor; for running a number of charities helping the starving communities in Asia and Africa or locations struck by disasters including earthquakes, storms and tornadoes even in developed countries like America.[222] But the fact that the majority of its residents living in the outskirts of its shining cities or even its own citizens who call themselves "locals" endure starvation of another kind is disturbing on many levels. Should there be other communities willing to help? But help for sexual or emotional starvation is much more complicated than the shipment of food-related items the emirate has offered its less fortunate friends. It is complicated – certainly from every sense of moral and ethical propriety – and no community is going to send thousands of its people, women or men, as a rescue package to Dubai. The rich emirate with all its abundant resources cannot start distributing to each bachelor-worker a woman or to each local woman a man.

However, still there is something the government of Dubai and its neighboring gulf states can do to ease the situation. The governments could remove the restrictions in Kafala law so that immigrants can bring their wives and families. Otherwise, the Kafala system is no different than slavery, as it has been manifested throughout history, where the greed of the employer is paramount. On the surface, the governments wear a humanitarian face for the global media and public. But, to their own workers who have come from afar because of the promise of prosperity and stable economic livelihood, they are hardly humanitarian. Certainly there is no economic rationale for continuing these restrictions. There is no evidence that the rich emirates will go bankrupt.

There are also many professional expatriates working in mid-level jobs, such as sales and marketing, earning less than the government's stipulated minimum wage for being eligible to sponsor a spouse's relocation. Such expatriates could afford to live with their spouses with the little wages they are earning, and the decision to keep their spouses thousands of miles away is not their own. The government's rules necessitate it. Others would have their spouses also work, which, of course, does more to fill the coffers of the emirates than it does for the immigrant family. The prime objective for the emirates is to have employees do as much for as little as possible. Thus, denying any form of family solidarity or enjoyment coincides with that objective.

Unlike starving one because of hunger, the government sees no compelling reason to change the laws for those who suffer from emotional and sexual starvation. However, the immigrants suffer at the whims of their GCC hosts. What is the moral frame for condoning such suffering? Why should the laws of fellow men, endowed only by luck and riches, be so callous toward others, depriving them of the essentials that constitute one's own sense of human dignity and respect? Researchers have not been very generous with the topic in the region, perhaps because of the conservative nature of these states, but once they open up to scrutiny numerous chronic problems facing the region would be drawn closer to these policies that have restricted individuals in the most inhumane ways possible.

The sexual and emotional starvation is felt even among professional expatriates who manage to bring their wives to the Emirates. Keeping a wife from the prying eyes of hungry bachelors is among the biggest challenges for expat husbands. Whether the spouse is at home or at work, the challenges to preserve the integrity and fidelity of marriage are enormous and stories of wives being seduced by hungry bachelors have always been in full swing. There are many tales of love triangles, exploding in bitter fits of rage and jealousy, that lead to murder and other crimes of passion.

One such murder case I myself covered involved a Pakistani man who murdered his wife, a mother of two children, after confronting her with allegations of cheating. He packed the wife's body in their car and left it in a parking lot in the Yarmouk area.[223] Another case, also involving a Pakistani man, revolved around the murder of a woman's new husband. The woman previously was married to the murderer's brother. She also was an intended victim but she had left the house shortly before the murderer entered the house to hack up her husband and pack the body in a black bag.[224]

Some housewives plotted murders of their husbands with their new bachelor lovers. In a Sharjah industrial area, a Bangladeshi woman was arrested with six other men including her lover for murdering her husband.[225] The police found the body behind the Sharjah City Center lying in a huge pool of blood with multiple stab wounds.[226]

In another case, an Ethiopian maid murdered her lover, a driver for the same household in Samnan, after he had taken sexual liberties with her and refused to marry her.[227] This scene appeared unusually unreasonable, rash and risky for immigrant workers staying in a house not their own. Their sponsor would have gone mad just to learn that the two employees even discussed marriage in the house.

Besides murders, there were also suicides brought about by sexual and emotional starvation in the Emirates. For the suicide stories I covered in Sharjah, Ajman and Dubai the connection could be easily drawn. Men took their own lives because of news from back home that their wives had cheated on them. Others were despondent that they could not provide adequately for their families back home. Others could no longer handle the dilemma of staying to work while suffering through incredible homesickness.

One newspaper decided no longer to publish stories

involving suicides and they offered no explanations to us staff reporters. Likely, it was the embarrassing recognition of just how frequent these stories had become and editors judiciously decided that it would be more newsworthy to showcase construction projects and other positive signs of the emirate's rich economic prospects. Few could ignore the realities, however. Almost every week there was a suicide in Sharjah where I worked, either by workers hanging themselves or jumping from high-rise buildings. However, in most suicides, there was a love story behind the death and, in most cases, there were unaccounted feelings related to sexual and emotional deprivation.

A worker in the Sharjah industrial area hanged himself because he had received news of his wife in his home country becoming pregnant by another man. A housemaid jumped to her death from her apartment window because her roommates repeatedly abused her while she worked in the sponsor's home. Some suicide stories were tragicomedies, too ironic to ignore even with the newspaper's explicitly stated ban on them. I remember pitching to my editors the story of a Yemeni woman who had tried to end her life by jumping from a building's second floor in Ajman. She had apparently not succeeded and doctors had treated her with expectations of full recovery in the Al Qassimi hospital of Sharjah. After learning about the incident, I queried the doctor who treated her. He happened to be an Indian doctor friendly to journalists. The doctor told me how she had been brought to the hospital unconscious, with fractures in her pelvis and the leg but most threatening to her life was bleeding in the brain. "We had to do four surgeries on her brain to save her life," he said. "The first two surgeries were to stop bleeding in the brain, then there was a surgery to tracheotomy to help her breathe easily through the neck and the last surgery a few weeks later was to restore one bone in her brain they had temporarily removed."

The story was interesting in that it was a rare account to report on suicide bids attempted by women of Arab origin. It was also good this same woman had survived and was now fully conscious, a mother of a one-year-old boy. I wanted to interview her while assuring that her identity would not be disclosed to the public. I believed her story might be instructive for others in similar circumstances.

On the following Sunday, I listed the story in the morning list, mentioning that even though the newspaper normally does not carry suicide bid stories, this stands out as special and doctors as well as the family are willing to speak. My cluster editor, the kindest of all supervisors I had at the paper, responded but not in the most pleasant of tones. He wrote in an email, "Your story on the morning list. Why are you planning to interview this woman?" He added, "We as a rule don't cover suicides, or attempted suicides." I decided there was no reason for calling it a suicide, and I relented in a reply that it could be characterized as an accidental fall. It was in that form in which the story was published.[228]

5.5 Denied But Not to the Eye

When I had my satellite TV dish installed on the flat roof for my new apartment in Sharjah, a middle-aged Bangladeshi man from a satellite dish shop in the neighborhood whispered a cryptic message in Arabic and English. He first asked if I had family or if I was single. I didn't respond directly but asked why he wanted to know. He said he could install a "special" satellite dish that would show me everything for free. I suspected his reference meant pornography and he said, "Yes, all kinds of girls. African, Arabic, Indian, American and European."

He told me the offer would be for 600 dirhams (US $160) for six months to start because he had to buy a receiver that has some special provisions. For the renewal it would be less – about

250 to 300 dirhams (US $65–80) for half a year based on the negotiations when the time comes. (This was in May 2009 when I relocated from Ajman to the Al Nabba area.) He explained they also had alternative cards but they were quite expensive – about 250 dirhams (US $65) for three months but they would stream content from virtually any Internet site. From the rooftop, he spotted eight dishes nearby that he had installed for consumers wanting to access pornography, and he spotted ten more dishes installed by other providers for the same purpose. He said all those he had installed were for either single executive bachelors or single men sharing a room. (The municipality later clamped down on bachelors not sharing same buildings with families in 2012 but at my building still there were bachelors despite the building being referred to as open to family accommodations. In the UAE, there always are many shortcuts for laws.)

All dishes installed for pornography faced east. That is how he could distinguish them from other normal dishes even though he was not the installer. Besides being single, another requirement for his service would be to have an Internet connection. He provided access that otherwise was not legitimately available. Etisalat, the monopolist telecommunication service provider at the time, always cooperated with police to crack down on satellite TV piracy not particularly on moral grounds but instead because the activity had caused the licensed monopolist provider to miss out on potential profits, as the pirates beamed in sports and popular reality TV channels, all for free. In fact, in most news stories published, the issue of pornography is never mentioned but only the incursion to the profits of licensed providers is the reason given for such action.[229]

Once my installer learned I had a family he was stunned, with his mouth agape in surprise, and the shock was evident in his face. But he mustered a few smiles trying to defuse the shock and appear confident as if his offers were sanctified. He apologized but explained this is how all single men in this country live. They have no women and there is no law banning single men from watching depictions that mimic what more fortunate men would have access to in their actual lives.

Besides the volume of Internet TV channel piracy, dish sellers also offer pornography subscription TV cards at varying costs, an illegal practice but rarely investigated. The selling of access to pornography proved to be a top revenue generator for more TV satellite dish shops in the region. And it was not only the satellite dish shops that profited from the sale of pornography. There were several illegal CD merchandisers that went door to door selling pirated pornographic movies. The police in Sharjah frequently arrested these merchandisers and counted the number in thousands of illegal pornographic CDs they had found in their possession.[230] It was sadder to discover that some of these movies contained child pornography and such instances were especially common in Sharjah's industrial areas and Sajja labour camps.[231]

Pornography is a big obsession for many single men in the GCC countries. It is common to see those who can afford smart phones screening pornographic movies on their iPhones and Galaxies, while those who can't afford these can still watch the movies cheaply on their TV screens in their accommodations.

And this kind of sexual misery is not something the Gulf rulers don't know about. They turn a blind eye completely to the situation because otherwise they would have to rewrite the laws in order to remedy the circumstances for the large numbers of poor, underpaid migrant workers. Better to turn aside and let the situation continue. There have been some attempts to ban bachelors from living in areas designated for families. They would say publicly that such a campaign is to provide for the safety of families, especially women and children, but that is hardly the real reason. It's more pitched toward preventing the pursuit of family women by single, sexually hungry men; and the newspapers, of course, remain mum on this point.

5.6 Sharjah's Copacabana Beach

Authorities also continuously struggle to keep ogling men away from bikini-clad women on beaches. Laws have been strengthened, slapping offenders with fines while police aggressively patrol the beaches arresting oglers or kindly asking them to leave. In Dubai, the Jumeirah public beaches attract the most oglers. A BBC report indicated that Dubai police stopped 6,000 people for different beach-related offences, mostly for ogling at women. The beaches of Jumeirah also have groups of undercover police patrolling the beaches for a variety of misbehaving offences.

Even in a conservative emirate such as Sharjah there is the popular Al Khan beach where reporters cover a drowning case almost every week during the summer. On one visit with an Arab friend to cover a double drowning case in July of 2013 we were stopped at the entrance by guards employed by the authorities to keep single men from entering. "You can't enter there while dressed in jeans, or police will fine you 500 [dirhams]," the guard explained to us. "Go and change your clothes in your car. You should be in shorts and vests." Even when we explained that we were journalists investigating the details of the drowning the guard still refused permission for us to enter.

Still outside we could observe that it was not only the sweltering heat that raised temperatures but also the scantily dressed women on the beach and others leaving in the sight of several men watching outside. My colleague was overwhelmed by one young, slim Russian woman who passed us in a purple bikini. He said, "Wow, this is more than what is shown at Copacabana." From that day we called the beach "Sharjah's Copacabana."

Most men who could not change into shorts remained in their cars which were parked in a sandy area outside the beach. Often their car engines were running but we could see the men making every effort to observe the women on the beach. They were willing to do anything to circumvent the restrictions, if even from a distance.

Some of these men were taxi drivers who transported beach-goers back to their hotels. The gate guard also would stop bikini-clad women from exiting the beaches before they changed into street-appropriate clothes. We overheard the guard pleading with some stubborn young women who were pointing and showing him that their hotel was very near and they did not need to change clothes just for the short stroll back to their rooms. The guard persisted, saying that beachwear in the streets constituted an offence that carried fines and other penalties. Many women often just change their clothes right at the exit, giving the men in the parking area yet one final show. But it's not only the poor men who watch the women in their cars but also the rich local Emirati young men who turn up with expensive vehicles like Ferraris. They honk or invite into their car any young single woman who is leaving the beach. Some even become more aggressive, trying to corral women from leaving. We saw this with a group of four women who were leaving the beach. I asked the guard if he allowed this behavior and he said, with a sigh of resignation, "It's not good but what can you do. They are locals."

Khalid bin Al Waled Street in Dubai is home to many of the emirate's night clubs. It is a lively scene until early morning, as there are many sex workers and escorts from all nationalities, races, and ethnicities turning up to enter the clubs or stand along the side of the road. Punters also roam the street in cars or as pedestrians, looking to make a bargain for a single-time sex stand. There are also oglers, who are single poor men who can't afford even a bargain-priced encounter but nevertheless are grateful to be watching the women moving in and out of the club or the process of negotiating a deal.

The street is named after the Islamic warrior who fought and won many battles during the early Islamic days of the prophet Mohammed. Today, it has all of the amenities of a red-light district similar to anywhere else in the world where sex is available for sale legally or illegally. It gets busier as it gets later in the night, with cars in long queues similar to those in morning rush hours and what slows vehicles on the road mostly are the punters who stop on the roadside to surf for women at the entrances of nightclubs and other locales to negotiate a bargain. Taxis regularly pick up and drop off young women with their catches, which also slows the traffic and causes major road congestion. Police patrols regularly turn around and honk at stopping cars to move along and not slow the traffic flow.

Besides the night clubs, the buildings on the street also offer several brothels unlike any others to be found in the emirate. An Indian friend who moved to Sharjah after two years renting an apartment told me he did not see any building in their neighborhood that did not have apartments rented as brothels. He told me he was upset when his wife and children had a brothel neighbor in the opposite hallway. There were 10 Ethiopian women and every night it was like a party with loud noises and sometimes there were even brawls disturbing the family's nighttime sleep. What also annoyed him was that the men in the area automatically assumed every woman walking on the street was a prostitute and his wife regularly complained to him of men on the street propositioning her with the question of "how much?"

Also on the street one major nightclub affiliated with one of Dubai's premier hotels demands women from Asian countries such as India and China or Africa (mostly from Ethiopia) to pay a cover charge of 75 dirhams, while exempting women from Europe, especially the former Soviet states, from having to pay the admission. The criteria always rests on the fact the club wants to attract more white women for their paying customers.

In the Northern Emirates, the Ajman Holiday Beach Club

stands out as an icon. Situated on the Ajman waterfront cornice, the area is home to dozens of nightclubs catering to different ethnicities and nationalities in the UAE and is a hub for single men, particularly sexually starved oglers. During one of my visits to the club to conduct research for this book, I chatted with an Ethiopian male artist who seemed to attract a lot of attention from the women dancers. I learned the dancers were brought from Addis Ababa on visit visas and had a contract for three months. Once a dancer's visa expires, the management reserves the right to strike a deal for another three months only if the dancer was exceptionally good or if the club is looking for fresh faces. There are many young women in Addis Ababa who would grab the opportunity to come and dance in the UAE clubs, even if it is in the smallest emirate and unlike Dubai. Many young women are content just to be able to say that they live and work in Dubai, even though facts indicate otherwise.

A dancer's monthly salary is about 3,000 dirhams (US $800) a month but women earn a bonus if customers purchase flowers for them. A small bouquet is purchased for 50 dirhams (US $13) and women would then incorporate the flowers into their routine for a song. Afterward, the dancers place the bouquet in a box where it is recycled and sold to another customer. For each small bouquet, a dancer earns a commission of 5 dirhams with the remaining 45 dirhams going to club management.

The club management go to rigorous lengths to keep their dancers in line. They are housed at the affiliated hotel and are not allowed to go out even during the day. At night, a bus brings the dancers to the club who are escorted inside by a team of security guards. Women are not allowed to break free into the crowds. The women also are monitored continuously. They cannot have mobile phones for fear they might contact a customer on their own.

My Ethiopian artist source said any sexual encounters with customers are always arranged through the club management.

Some rich Arabs ask the club to bring a particular dancer to their home or an arranged place for an evening out on the town. The woman might receive payment which would then be shared with the club management much in the same proportion as the flowers for a dance.

There are differences between the open display of sex workers in Dubai and the secretive operations of Doha's sex business. The pimps in Qatar are mostly secluded in their brothels, which combine prostitution with the alcohol trade. Almost all illegal alcohol dealers in old villa houses or apartments also have several women either at the house or on call for sexual activities. The country's policies on alcohol trading, which require a license to drink alcohol, have pushed the alcohol business into the shadows, merged with prostitution. Despite these restrictions, alcohol is widely available in Doha and many drinkers easily find means of avoiding the law's heavy arm. The law requires that anyone licensed to drink alcohol must be a non-Muslim and must be earning a sizable income, which, of course, immediately disqualifies many expatriate migrant workers.

Most brothels find eligible patrons and purchase through them several crates of all kinds of alcohol to sell in their brothels. Brothels frequently hold private parties with music and alcohol, drawing many single men away from the nightclubs, which are expensive and usually have restrictions on dress codes and other types of behavior and activities. Hotel staff in Qatar operate on stricter standards than those in Dubai, demanding marriage certificates from their clients who turn up at the reception desk as a couple. Some residences also ban single women from entering residences to visit a male companion. One instance included an American guest who was refused entry to her husband's apartment in the Ezdan residences for not carrying on her person the marriage certificate.[232] Even though most hotels ask for the marriage certificates of couples, there are a few hotels that circumvent the rule but they also charge much higher room rates.

Most prostitutes in the nightclubs and bars provide their clients with a list of hotels that do not ask for a marriage certificate or where receptionists gladly accept bribes to bypass the rule.

My colleagues and I were discussing a story about the declining costs of medical drugs, including Viagra, and we were surprised that authorities acknowledged the presence of the drug used to combat impotency and that they accepted the downward pressure on the drug's pricing. The question turned to whether customers would need a doctor's prescription to obtain Viagra. An Indian man in his sixties who worked as the news editor – and who often entertained us with many jokes and stories – said he would answer some of the questions once the sole female reporter left the newsroom. Once she left, he told the newsroom the story would be popular locally, as most men in Qatar use Viagra. "Anywhere in the world where the only chance for sexual gratification is through sex workers can expect more people to use Viagra," he said. "No one wants to pay several hundred riyals and it only lasts for only a few seconds; Viagra can help to delay for about some ten minutes and it gives value to your money." Sure enough, a packet of four 50-milligram tablets which had cost 158.25 Qatari riyals (US $43) was reduced to 103.25 (US $28), while prices of a 12-tablet packet was reduced from 474.25 Qatari riyals (US $130) to 309.25 (US $85).[233]

5.7 A Few Winners in a Sea of Losers

And, just as in countries where famine strikes the masses whilst a few wallow in excess, the fat cats in the Emirates clearly know how to enjoy what others lack when it comes to sex. The ruling sheikhs, indeed, prey upon those most directly affected by the emirate laws. They marry dozens of women who give birth to hundreds of children that become the next generation of the ruling elites. The Saudi's legendary King Abdul Aziz ibn Saud's wives are given in estimations, some saying 35, others 70, and all the estimates could be conservative at best. His sons have followed him in extravagance, expanding the family to more than 7,000 royals attached to the legendary sheikh who named Islam's holiest nation after himself.

When it comes to women, not even the word of God would stop these men from having as many as their egos can take. Anyone reminding them that the holy book they believe in puts a limit on the number of women they can have would definitely die in prison, or if the critic were a foreigner then the individual would be expelled immediately; because the critic would dare to contradict the scholars the rulers have appointed as muftis to serve them and to give *fatwa* (religious edict) that approves any practice they carry out as holy. Their scholars put in a lot of effort to tell the masses how the Islamic ruling limit on the number of women one can have only pertains to the masses, but not the ruling sheikh. Because the sheikh is giving birth to future sheikhs, and only his sons qualify to rule the country for centuries and centuries after his death. And this requires more and more sons, hence neutralizing the edict that limits the number of wives they can have is improbable. I am not sure if that is the reason they give, but regardless their scholars endorse the rulers to have as many as they can handle in order to secure the lineage's progeny. Some marry and divorce to stay within the limit of four. This cannot but trigger deep envy among the struggling youth who can't afford a single wife or the workers in their single segregated camps who are banned from bringing their wives in from their native lands. And when the sheikh's sons from these illicit and politically fatwa-ised relationships start to take turns in ruling their country, the whole world is destined to be plunged into chaos.

Living in the Gulf one learns early just how widespread this sanctioned system of sexual and emotional starvation has become, affecting not only single immigrant laborers but also local communities of Emiratis, Qataris and Saudis. The youthful

Emiratis who cannot afford the exorbitant dowries their communities have instituted as part of custom are bent to live a single life until their old age.

This kind of frustration is one that most Gulf Arab youth have taken to vent on social networks. The Saudis chat around "let her be a spinster," calling for abandoning Saudi women for foreigners, a luxury only men can enjoy in these communities. Monetary greed has stripped many Arab families of their utmost sanctity and has relegated the families' existence to the perseverance and protection of wealth. Only with money can one marry, and not having a lot of it one is almost certainly doomed to a single life. An Emirati friend one time tried to justify a point about why he should earn more than me, as he explained that he needed more money to own a good house than what would be required in Uganda. Likewise, dowries in the Emirates are larger than anywhere else in the world. I asked him who told him marriages were more expensive in the Gulf Arab region than anywhere in the world. In turn, he challenged me to come up with any community that charged dowries as high as the Gulf Arab and I blanked at giving a suitable answer.

The monetization of marriages, however, has led to far more disastrous effects for women than men in the emirates. While men can freely marry women demanding smaller dowries in other communities, Gulf women do not have this privilege. And, as condemned by the frustrated Gulf youths, many endure single lives in their fathers' villas well into their thirties and beyond. Gulf women are called upon to more rigorous social challenges and demands than the men. They have to marry in their respective community from the same or higher social class, in particular one who has the exorbitant means for huge dowries and can provide a large house and property with a full staff of maids and drivers. And these lessons are well preserved and broadcasted by the ruling sheikhs. That is, the daughters of Dubai royals marry only Abu Dhabi royals and vice versa, any woman who fails to fit into this arrangement is betrothed to a crown prince in one of the northern Emirates. For immigrant men unable to meet these demands, they already are at a tremendous disadvantage.

A Pakistani driver for a household told me his boss had an unmarried Emirati daughter in her mid-thirties who always appeared to be stressed and depressed despite the family's enormous wealth. Two of her younger sisters already were married and her chances for finding a local husband matching her family class or higher were disappearing rapidly. The prevailing social culture in the GCC region frowns upon women marrying foreigners or even marrying someone of lower social status and thus women are forced to live in celibacy. He sympathized with her because even though he was himself married with a wife in Pakistan, he had not seen his family for five years. "I knew what stressed this woman was the same thing stressing me, we were both starving!" he told me.

There are 4.15 males to every single woman in Qatar and there are 2.75 males to every single woman in the UAE. The two countries register the widest gender gaps in the whole world.[234] There are 175,000 Emirati single women, according to the Arabic newspaper Emaratalyoum. One Emirati colleague who was working as a photographer with *Al Ittihad* told me the marriage fund was the single most significant mocking policy move the emirate rulers made concerning marriage. My colleague was still single and I asked why he didn't get married. He told me a marriage fund offered a 70,000-dirham (US $19,000) loan that could not cover even one-half of the expected local marriage costs.

"If you want to make it so simple you need at 150,000 dirhams (US $40,835) for the wedding but standard weddings here cost at least 300,000 dirhams (US $81,670) and if the government is offering you a loan of just 70,000, would you not laugh?" he explained. "Not all people qualify to receive that marriage fund loan, by the way, so it's not for the poor and low paid workers, but anyone who has a job that qualifies him; then society expects him to have something big."

He told me that even marrying a less expensive Emirati was stigmatized as going for a cheaper option. However, it was acceptable if one first married an Emirati and proved his worth and then went for a foreigner as his second, third or fourth wife. For my colleague, who is 35, the social expectations and perceptions were becoming too much to bear. He told me the government could better help its people by creating awareness aimed at changing societal expectations of a wedding. The cost of Emirati weddings spiraled into millions of dirhams; *The National* reported a wedding of an Emirati woman that cost 8 million dirhams (US $2.2 million) and the bride pocketed 250,000 dirhams (US $68,000) just for the dowry.[235]

I was going to register my own reservation regarding the article, but when the writer started breaking it down, I quickly agreed with the point being made. She noted that weddings in Emirati modern culture stretched over more than a day. It all starts with pre-events like the engagement party and the *melcha* when the bride and groom sign the wedding contract. Then there is the event itself – the wedding "fever," which takes place over a hectic period of three or four days, she noted. "Sometimes there is one day when the bride appears in white and another day when she dresses traditionally with henna applied to her hands and feet." Another popular day – a *meksar* – involves the bride's family viewing their daughter's new clothes.

She wrote that a simple dress for the big day could cost 60,000 dirhams (US $16,334) and if a bride wants to add some lace, that costs another 50,000 (US $13,611) and the crystals run upwards of 80,000 (US $21,700), bringing the cost of the dress alone for the big day to about 200,000 dirhams (US $54,300). Then there are more dresses and jewelry for more days as well as the clothes of other female family relatives and friends at the weddings.

The rulers have promoted marriage celebrations as group events, as one possible solution to encourage young men to get married, especially if they worry the costs are prohibitive. Some of these mass marriages are coordinated by charitable organizations or government departments, especially in municipalities for their employees. In the spring of 2013, I attended a wedding event in Sharjah, coordinated by the Sharjah Charitable Organisation in Al Boom Village for 56 Emirati men. The Sharjah crown prince was the guest of honor and many dignitaries who would be unlikely to attend individual weddings were there. I was with a group of other Arab reporters; we had arrived early and when the call for prayers was made one reporter suggested we pray from outside.

On return the crown prince had arrived and security had been boosted. The three Arab journalists were allowed to enter but a security guard singled me out and bounced me. I asked him if he wanted to see my press badge and he refused. I knew again the color of my skin was not on my side but the security guy also looked black, as if he might be from Sudan or among the black Emirati Arabs. I asked him why he singled me out and he grabbed my hand taking me aside while explaining the sheikh was present and there would be no need to interview him. I returned to my car and left the function, frustrated that I did not have the chance to gather more information about these mass marriage ceremonies.

Something similar happened when the ruler of Ajman opened a new medical research facility in the Ajman Jurf area. The security men separated myself and an Indian reporter from *The Gulf Today* from the press pool, again signaling that if one was not Arab, one could not be seen in the presence of the ruler. I told my local editors that I would file their press release as my dispatch but I could not get anything exclusive or special because I had been denied entry. My editors responded in a supportive tone and the local editor was willing to file a formal protest on my behalf. I decided it might be best not to stir the waters, as I wanted to continue working and I knew I could find a way to circumvent such a discriminatory protocol.

There also are plenty of instances when fellow Arabs prey upon the vulnerability of their own women desperate to find an Arab man for marriage. In Sharjah, police arrested a GCC national man who cheated GCC women with false promises of finding them a man for marriage. I wrote the story and it appeared as a brief in the paper, as if the press was instructed by authorities not to draw too much attention to the incident.[236] Using a Blackberry device, the man disguised himself as a woman on social networks and smartphone texts using the pseudonym Umm Mansour. As a side note, the police used GCC references in the press release so as not to disparage a specific emirate nationality. However, I learned the man was from Oman and the woman was an Emirati. He sent out small advert messages on his Blackberry asking women who were interested in finding a man to call him (or her, as he had disguised himself). He assured potential clients that the arrangements would be made confidentially. One of the women contacted him, describing the spouse she desired. A few days later he responded to the woman, demanding she pay 500 dirhams (US $135) to have the arrangement completed. However, after the woman paid the money through an exchange, Umm Mansour disappeared and the woman reported the fraud to police. The police formed a team of CID officers to search for the suspect and soon discovered that Umm Mansour was actually a man and arrested him at his apartment in Sharjah.

In the emirate of Ajman, "witchcraft" and "sorcerers" are more at large, so there are plenty of published stories detailing how local Emirati women visit sorcerers to help find an Emirati husband. Again, the press would only be allowed to publish brief items about such incidents and soon after they were published in the newspaper, they would be quickly scrubbed from the online archives. The gist of these stories was that, in most instances, the sorcerers would conspire with corrupt men, disguised as husbands also in search of a spouse, in order to dupe the victim. One report in *The National* indicated Dubai police found that 80 percent of the victims in these cases were Arab women desperately looking for a husband.[237]

5.8 Homosexuality in the UAE

In 2010, one of the local English-language newspapers published an article with the headline "Too Close for Comfort: Homosexuality in Schools," a surprisingly straightforward account to be seen in the local press. The story recounted a local divorced mother worried about her two children, a daughter who said she was attracted to an Indian girl and a boy who was complaining that men were trying to seduce him. The story mostly quoted from University of Sharjah sources and revealed how young women even in public display gestures of affection and intimacy toward each other. The story also quoted an Ajman police social worker who said student delinquency in the schools was between 70 and 80 per cent, with lesbianism accounting for 40 per cent of the offence.[238] Of course with such a story, one must see how the public responses were recorded, for it is only these responses that clarify just how editing and censorship play into how the story is framed. Most respondents criticized their country's policy of segregating men from women. One quipped, "If they are not allowed to interact with the opposite sex, what do they expect? They will forge deep bonds with people of the same sex, which can lead to romantic feelings."[239]

Homosexuality is as prevalent in GCC countries as it is elsewhere. In one of the most publicized cases from 2006 in Dubai, police raided a hotel in Ghatout where a gay wedding of local Emirati couples was taking place. Police said they found a dozen men dressed as brides and a dozen others in male Arab dress. Following the arrests, there were speculations that the men would be given hormone treatments but the UAE Ministry of Interior spokesman denied the report.[240]

In the UAE both civil and Sharia law criminalize homosexuality. In discussing the raid, Mohammed bin Nukhaira Al Dhahiri, the UAE minister of justice and Islamic affairs, stated: "There will be no room for homosexual and queer acts in the UAE. Our society does not accept queer behavior, either in word or in action." The men in the case were sentenced to five years in prison.[241] Police also closed a nightclub hosting a gay night featuring a transvestite DJ from Britain after officials learned about it from its flyers that had been distributed in the city.[242]

The number of gay people was perhaps the highest in labor camps which accommodate desperately poor immigrants. Many residents said they knew male couples living together.[243] In a strange bit of irony, most workers told me they believed the repressive policies of their host government to deny workers the opportunities to bring their families to the UAE forced many workers to fulfill their emotional and sexual needs with other equally desperate lone male workers. Amidst the world's biggest construction booms, men came from Asia and Africa eager to work but disappointed to discover they also were expected to lead celibate lives. They were deprived in every possible way, with each day of hard labor ending in them being packed into buses and returned to their accommodation camps where boredom and loneliness were always evident. The monotony could become unbearable for men who were only allowed the privilege of seeing their families once every two years and even then many men were unwittingly cheated out of that small privilege.

Once in a taxi from my Nabba home, I was going to the nearby industrial area to pick up my car from the mechanics. Suddenly, the Pakistani driver braked as he noticed a woman carrying a baby who was trying to cross in the middle of street. I mentioned that he was lucky to have avoided what could have been a tragic accident and that he probably would have been as distressed as if he had struck his own wife and child with the car. He quickly mentioned that, at forty, he was still unmarried after being in the UAE for 15 years. Even when he returned to Pakistan for the occasional break of one or two months, he still had little opportunity to find someone with whom he could have a long-term relationship. "I would say I am still a virgin if there was anything like that for men, but to be sincere with you I have not had any women in my life but I have had several men," he said. "The thing is I did not choose to do this with men. I feel guilty all the time but there were no women and I had no choice especially when everyone in our accommodation was doing it."

He tells me how widespread the practice is among laborers in their accommodations; that people were living like couples, not all of them but most of them. The driver, whose name is Asif, says he is the only son in his family, and he is saddened that he has not been able to have a child himself. "Every time I go to Pakistan, my mother cries a lot when she discusses with me about getting married and having children. Both my parents have tried to bring me beautiful girls for marriage but I have lost interest in women." He said he had kept his homosexual behavior a secret from his parents, that he would have loved to marry for the sake of his mother, but he was also afraid the he was not capable of fathering a child. He believed that he was not man enough anymore and he did not want to be embarrassed in a bed with any bride and hear rumors spread about him in the family.

I was touched by Asif's story. He had been quite open to a stranger about the guilt he was carrying, but could not be that open to his family. Indeed, it was sad that despite all the material support and money he collected to send them from Dubai, it was not enough. They needed a grandchild from their single son to keep the torch of their lives in future generations, and they were too astonished to perish for good with their son.

An Egyptian reader of *The National* sent me an email concerning a story I wrote about a Sharjah police raid on a massage parlor in which female masseuses were working with male clients. In Sharjah most parlors are licensed to provide services to men only with male masseurs. A few have been licensed with a female wing where women are catered to by female masseuses. The reader gave me his phone number in the email, adding that he had a news tips about massage parlors in Sharjah. We met on the Corniche Buhairah where he showed me a massage parlor run by Filipino men. The story came from his own experience, not about female masseuses or sex with women in these parlors but with male masseurs. He had paid 150 dirhams (US $40) for a massage and this Filipino man had started touching his genitals in an enticing manner and had assumed a feminine-sounding voice. He warned the masseur to stop immediately but, in a fit of anger, he punched the masseur but was quickly thrown out of the business when another masseur came to the aid of his colleague. He wanted me to highlight the growing trend of homosexuality in these massage parlors and said he believed *The National,* an independent English newspaper, would be emboldened about reporting this.

He was wrong but I didn't tell him. I contacted the Sharjah public health section about their inspections on parlors and asked whether they had come across a phenomenon of homosexual behavior. The head of public health was an Emirati woman, and she always insisted on receiving all queries in writing rather than by phone. She was among the handful of public officials who responded to most questions by journalists but she made clear she was not going to answer mine in this particular instance. I tried again after a week and then again after a couple of months. I also queried the police about whether they had cracked down on homosexual activity in the massage parlors but there was no reply. None of this surprised me, given the Emirates' tendency to avoid any and all sensitive issues.

However, even if they would have responded, the battle to have the story published would have been even fiercer. I knew the best an English newspaper that boasts of its editorial independence could do was to run a brief of about 50 words with no bylines and the story would not be available in the online archives.

The UAE media also carried reports about minor-aged Emiratis in homosexual acts. One story recounted two brothers, 16 and 17, beating up a 15-year-old friend and urinating on him because he turned down their advances to have sex.[244] The victim said the brothers ordered him to strip, which he refused to do. The brothers then wrestled the victim to the ground and one of the suspects relieved himself on the boy's body. The mother of the suspects interrupted the act and demanded they let the victim go. The teenage suspects were referred to juvenile court.

There were also several reports of expatriates who had lived in Dubai preferring anal sex even when they returned to their wives in their home countries. El Feki in her book *Sex and the Citadel* wrote that many wives of Egyptian expatriates believed their husbands had picked up anal sex ideas from their stays in GCC countries.

Also, many male GCC citizens are homosexual. It is not hard to find evidence in Dubai especially if one visits nightclubs where same-sex affection is displayed openly. Few raise eyebrows witnessing such exchanges of intimacy among men, and this often serves as sufficient cover. And men venture into public settings quite open about their feelings. In a lingerie shop at Dubai Mall, I observed a couple – one a local man dressed in *kanduras* and the other Filipino who seemed quite feminine in his appearance. They clearly enjoyed the attention they were getting as they sorted through women's undergarments. The sales clerk, also a Filipino man, moved about normally so I asked him if such public displays were common in the shop. He said customers include many male couples, including those who say they come from Saudi Arabia. I was surprised to hear this clerk say that he is married to a man who is native to the Emirates. He explained that he saw himself as the second wife to the man who also had an Emirati wife and children.

Just as with male immigrant workers, lesbianism was common among female workers residing in accommodations like those in the Al Qouz neighborhood. I talked to numerous female guards and cleaners during research for this book about this and most women who were of African origin told me that Filipino roommates were among the most likely to live together and share beds without any overt concerns. Likewise, single local Emirati women were comfortable about their sexuality. A Ugandan female security guard working at one of the universities in Abu Dhabi for women students told me how a guard was fired and deported for reporting having seen two Emirati women being intimate with each other. She had found the two engaging in sex at one of the prayer locations on campus in the early morning. She ignored their pleas for keeping quiet and reported the incident immediately to her supervisor, who, in turn, urgently reported the news to administrators. However, the university's administration summoned the guard who initially reported the incident and set in course the action to dismiss the guard immediately, cancel her work visa, and have her deported. The university administration expressed its disappointment that an employee would rashly spread rumors that could endanger the honor of the young students. The university administrator did tell the guard that lesbian sex acts were not permitted either in Islam or the Emirati culture but that the spreading of rumors amounted to a much more serious infraction. Of course, none of the papers carried this but it reminded me just how sensitive the authorities are in terms of protecting an image and appearance that contradicts dramatically the real activities in Dubai and in other emirates. The ones who called attention to potential embarrassing situations were the ones who would pay the greatest price.

The female guard added she had learned how not to rock the boat but to turn aside when anything looked out of the ordinary, especially if she expected to keep her job. The women-only university, in fact, seemed to welcome sexual experimentation. Some of Emirati students dressed like men and would wear the black cloak or *abaya* covering their clothes. Many would leave the top two buttons of the *abaya* undone in order to show their fellow students what they were wearing.

5.9 The Massage Parlors

Though Sharjah with its conservative policies has fewer parlors than other nearby emirates and many operate illegally indoors, Dubai seems to be more open to massage parlors than any other city in the GCC. The men and women handing brochures and leaflets advertising massage parlors on most of Dubai's streets outnumber any other brochure adverts for basics such as garments, restaurants or other shops. It is common to find massage leaflets placed on cars parked in Dubai. The brochures identify the type of massage on offer: Thai, Chinese, Filipino, Ethiopian, Moroccan bath or massage. The nationalities would also signal which masseuse would be available for various services. For example, if the parlor had promoted Chinese masseuses or those from Thailand or Ethiopia and a client asked for a Thai massage, they would offer the Thai masseuse to perform the service even when the actual services were identical to what the Ethiopian or Chinese masseuse would have offered. The leaflets are mostly handed out by young women, and some even pass on a small message as they give a prospective customer a leaflet that their massage therapists also offer *"happy endings or release massage."*

But to most clients the advertisements may raise some false expectations and there have been some scuffles at parlors when a client did not get all the services as detailed in the advertising package. I once came across a big fight in Karama that had attracted large crowds. A massage client was demanding a refund, accusing the parlor and its therapist of cheating him and not completing the services in the package as they had advertised. He shouted to the crowd, claiming the therapist asked for more money to continue the service yet he already had paid upfront the agreed amount. At the front counter, an Indian man demanded that the disgruntled customer leave, adding that his business was not a brothel but a legitimate massage business, while threatening to call the police. As the man walked down the stairs, passing the crowd that had gathered, he seemed hardly ashamed as everyone in the crowd clearly knew what he had been up to inside the business.

However, the parlors in Dubai are also an inconvenience to the residents of the buildings they occupy, as many are situated in residential areas. Many parlors are open late into the evening and noise complaints are numerous. Crowds always gather around fights that can be heard inside these parlors.

Dubai also seems to allow women therapists to work on men, unlike in Sharjah where the emirate is strict and insists that all licensed parlors should have male therapists working on male clients and female therapists on female clients. The rule is violated regularly and police raids almost always uncover these infractions, as I would find in my reporting for *The National*. One story carried the headline "Workers arrested in Sharjah for 'obscene massages,'" which told of 12 workers (10 women, 2 men) being arrested during a police sting. Clients were paying 150 dirhams for an ordinary massage at the parlor but in the course of the massage the female masseuse would persuade them to pay another 100 dirhams for a more intimate massage they called "special."[245]

5.10 Kafala and Human Trafficking

When I researched Dubai as I was preparing to leave Uganda for the first time, the only human trafficking violation that was visible concerned child jockeys. Children who were as young as two years had been reportedly trafficked to work in the GCC including Dubai as jockeys for camel racing. Reports estimated there were as many as 40,000 child camel jockeys in the GCC.[246] This alarmed me somewhat because love and compassion are what a child needs first along with assurances of care and protection of their well-being. The use of child jockeys for camel racing was dangerous. Speeds reached up to 65 kilometers per hour, and there were many reports of children falling off the camels and suffering severe injuries.[247] Likewise, children's weight was strictly regulated so that the jockeys would remain light enough to not slow the camel's speed. It was hard to conceive how desperate people were, especially in Pakistan, India, Sudan, Iran and Bangladesh, who sold their children into such harsh ordeals.

The heartlessness of the parents disturbed me greatly. However, the face of trafficking especially in the GCC countries has always been one of unashamed deception. No one would ever know how much of a paradise the parents were promised in deciding to send their children to *Billad Kheir* – "the country of good" – as the citizens and local media propaganda called it. Few involved in the enterprise, including the spectators, seemed sincerely concerned about putting children at such great risk. Camel racing had a large fan base and this alone was enough to levy a huge black eye on the GCC. Likewise, child immigrants suffer the same injustices and restrictions as their adult counterparts. However, by the time I arrived in Dubai, the government had already banned the use of children as jockeys and all GCC countries were busy repatriating these young individuals to their former countries. The new regulations banned employing child jockeys under the age of 15 and those who weighed less than 45 kilograms (110 pounds).[248] In 2005, Qatar followed suit, replacing them with robots.[249]

Unfortunately, women today are among the prevalent victims of human trafficking. For almost every plane landing in Dubai or another GCC international airport, there are many thousands of women from the poor former Soviet states, East Asia and Africa who dream of gainful employment and careers but inevitably end up trapped in the flourishing illegal sex industry of the emirate. The women arrive every day and surrender their passports to their Kafala sponsors. Unfortunately, not only do they surrender their passports but also their honor and freedom. The sex-oriented trades are tolerated because they essentially fit in with the overall strategic objective of the government in trying to limit the immigrants from bringing their families in and settling into a new life. In these countries that boast of respecting their women, the non-Arab women are just fair game not worthy of the same respect. There are no signs or posts to indicate where to go for prostitutes in Dubai or Doha but taxi drivers always have good knowledge. Tourists and visitors simply have to tell the cabbies the nationalities of the women they want that day and they will speed away to the destination. For sex work in these emirates, the nationality is all that is needed to secure a location and address.

Brothels never close. The women, as with all other expatriates in the GCC, are the property of their sponsors or pimps. And as with all other visas issued in the Emirates, there is an Emirati or GCC sponsor who controls it. Even if one sponsors an immigrant's wife or children, there sits a local sponsor or company belonging to a local man or woman sponsoring the immigrant. Thus, there are many so-called religious local men behind the enterprise sponsoring prostitutes to come and work in their countries, something addressed by El Feki Shereen in his book *Sex and the Citadel*. He concluded that it is a "measure of just how conflicted individuals and their Islamic credentials while ignoring or indeed perpetrating the exploitation and abuse of those who are in the (sex) business."[250]

El Feki also cites the religious manipulations often deployed such as prostitutes in the Al Bataniya area near Al Azhar University who utter Islamic phrases to attract their religious clients studying at the university. "*Mallaktuka Nafsi*," the women would say in opening up a potential rendezvous with the students of religion at the university. The phrase translates to, "I give you the right to own me." And with that statement they would be in the right and proper hands of their clients, the requirement of consent of an anonymous virgin adult woman as interpreted in Islamic scripture. And the money these prostitutes would charge would be like the *mahar* (dowry), the money Muslims pay to their brides, but instead it would be offered once the deal is consummated.

Also GCC men pour into Egypt during the summer to engage in a number of marriages that get Islamic-based protection. Such arrangements are called the *Nikkah Misyar*, a summer vacation marriage where brokers and lawyers draw up written contracts with the Islamic requirement of witnesses for the GCC men and the Egyptian bride, to codify marriages lasting just the length of the vacation.

Other marriages that are twisted to give an Islamic-endorsed veneer include *Zawaj mut'a* (pleasure marriage) in which a couple agrees to a union for a limited time ranging from hours to even years, with physical intimacy generally detailed as part of the package. The Shia sect still practices this kind of marriage. The *Zawaj Urfi*, a Sunni marriage arrangement, occurs when the couple draws up a testament with witnesses stating they are married but it is kept secret from their families and is not registered by the state.

These marriages are just proxies providing seemingly legal loopholes for what really is the practice of human trafficking.

Most GCC governments have already ratified the United Nations human trafficking protocol and have passed local legislation criminalizing human trafficking. In Qatar, the local legislation sets a maximum prison term of up to 15 years, plus a financial penalty of up to 300,000 Qatar riyals (US $82,384) for transnational trafficking related offenses.[251] However, the implementation of such legislation is lacking and in cases of women who are sent into prostitution the boldness of traffickers is readily evident online, as they use social networks such as Twitter to solicit clients.

Prostitution has moved from the former ways of writing telephone numbers in public or mosque toilets to tweeting. One can easily find the mobile numbers of Dubai pimps on Twitter, as I discovered in researching an article that was published in the local newspaper. One account advertised an Arab prostitute going by the name of Farah, along with nude and partially nude photos showing the woman engaged in sexual activity. When I called the number, a woman with a Filipino accent answered, leading me to believe the woman identified in the Twitter account had a secretary handling her schedule. Actually, it was a service not representing just one prostitute but many others in the same online brothel. The woman sounded like a sales representatives, running through the list of nationalities, ethnicities and race of women who would be available at rates for one or two hours or as much as a full night or even an entire week. I noticed that women of Arab nationalities had higher rates than their East Asian colleagues. Yet, another example of racism had presented itself, that even punters were willing to pay for some nationalities and races of women higher than others. I could not imagine what the prostitutes who were being charged at lower rate felt about their colleagues who earned more money for their pimp because of their nationalities.

Nothing up until now has exposed the problems of the often veiled, secretive UAE practices of human trafficking of women, as a recent U.S. State Department's Trafficking In Person (TIP) report suggests. Yet, such reports on the plight of women working as sex slaves in the emirate as well as government efforts to address the problem have been, at best, disturbing and incomplete in terms of resolving the problems. In terms of statistics for human trafficking, the UAE has been moving from tier to tier every year in rankings, starting in tier 3 in 2001 to 2002 and the following year jumping to tier 1. In the following years it dropped back to tiers 2 and 3, according to Pardis Mahdavi, an internationally known scholar who has been examining the issue.[252] She attributes the double standard applications of rankings to politics and vested interests of the United States in the UAE. Whenever the UAE is considered profitable it receives a better ranking and whenever it is considered unprofitable there is a decline in the rankings. It also is used as a political weapon to threaten the country into giving in to Americans demands with threats that we know what is being done and that the country must comply with the United Nations standards and expectations on this issue.

Dubai's sex workers spend most of their time in the brothels, available for purchase but not for the public to witness their personal problems, stresses, and even agony. Not unexpectedly, but certainly unfortunately, the blame always appears to be placed in the hands of the women themselves for not turning to authorities for help. "The silence of most of those in prostitution is a result of intimidation, terror, dissociation and shame," Melissa Farley wrote in 2004 about the harm women endure constantly in these circumstances. "Their silence, like the silence of battered women, should not be misinterpreted, ever, as their consent to prostitution."[253]

Shelters for women in Dubai, as with others in the region, often are hamstrung to help effectively, as the women coming out of the shadows will most surely face the risk of being deported. The shelters are required to report to police every woman who turns up and usually the shelter merely becomes an intermediary in the deportation process. For women, the dilemma is doubly painful. They had compelling reasons for leaving their countries, to look for economic opportunities and to be able to support their poor families back home. Most of them never thought that they would be forced into prostitution. They expected to find a decent job in the Dubai world of seemingly endless opportunities and even as they practice prostitution at present, they know it does not match their aspirations.

The presence of prostitution underscores the discrimination against poor women in Dubai, perpetuating a stereotype that carries over even to professional offices where if a woman applies for a job, many supervisors immediately use the opportunity to solicit sex from the woman. Many men in the business of hiring employees believe that by virtue of being poor, women logically become prostitutes, because in their country poor women are expected to prostitute their bodies for a living. The Gridlock study published by the Stanford University Press has quoted many local interviewees who heartlessly asserted that sex workers still count it as a blessing to be trafficked in Dubai. One quote underscores this sentiment: "Because things are really bad where they are coming from. So all that they go through here, rape or abuse or whatever, well it's better than over there where they came from." Farley has also pointed out that sexual harassment remains a perceived job requirement for any woman, whether the job is in a professional setting or in the sex trafficking business.

In the UAE one of the main suppliers of prostitutes is the maid profession. One story I reported on for *The National* included an interview with the Sharjah public prosecutor in which he named 518 cases they handled in 2012 concerning maids who fled their sponsors and turned to prostitution. Rashid Ali Majed Al Omran, the chief prosecutor, was quoted in the article as saying that most maids come to the UAE with evil intentions. He continued to say that they had used maid work as a platform to make the transition to sexually-oriented work. The prosecutor went to explain how he was concerned like most Emiratis about the moral corruption the maids brought to their country. He offered suggestions to help preserve the sanctity of Emirati society from the corruption of maids, urging residents not to hire migrant workers and to report immediately all runaway maids. Likewise, he recommended that recruitment agencies scrutinize job candidates more closely.[254] After the story was published, a reader posted the following online comments: "Maybe recruitment agencies should do more to ensure that the maids are not placed in homes where they are abused and overworked."[255]

A colleague at *The National* who was reporting on Syria had an article published with the headline "Online trafficking of Syrian women shames all involved."[256] The story was widely shared on social media, perhaps one of the most popularly circulated articles I had seen during my time as a journalist in the GCC region. The reporter quoted several Arabic online forums where men were seeking to marry Syrian women at prices ranging from 500 to 1,000 Saudi riyals (US $270). Many Saudi men expressed how Syrian women were considered among the most beautiful in the Arab world and how the rebellion and conflict in Syria had now made it possible to get a Syrian bride at a bargain price. However, while my colleague's article brought Saudi Arabia into focus it represented the whole of the GCC, the UAE and Dubai. Anyone working in any of the GCC countries knows all too well that one cannot mention Emiratis as punters for Syrian women, especially in writing for an Emirati newspaper. In fact there were as many reports of young Syrian women being brought into Dubai as there were in Saudi or Doha.

In preparing this book, I had hoped to interview a young Syrian woman who had been caught up in this situation. I had a Palestinian contact who knew an Arab pimp who could arrange a meeting but he demanded an excessive sum of money to permit the interview to go forward. He wanted a commission and royalty amounting to 2,000 dirhams that I would have to pay upfront. Meanwhile, I kept my hopes up that perhaps I could conduct the interview with the woman, who was still in her teens. I used every opportunity to collect as much information as possible. I asked the pimp if he believed that his clients knew the stories of young women such as this Syrian refugee, who had been a victim of such incredible war strife in her native country. He replied that yes, they did. He added, however, that it was not wise to spin tales of misery with clients who were seeking to be entertained. However, I could not begin to comprehend how someone who prays five times a day or even once a week could ever be morally and spiritually comfortable in sleeping with a young woman who has just lost her father or entire family a few days back. It is a profoundly disturbing, unnerving scenario. How could one take pleasure from exploiting someone so much in pain?

Even more disturbing was how many fathers were also willing to giving away their daughters to strangers so that they could escape to the stable peace of GCC countries from pains of war, from risks of being raped or killed, but then only to be forced into prostitution in their new destinations. Some fathers saw the situation differently, a compromise worth making perhaps knowing that one day the daughters would be reunited with the family in the hopes of prosperity and stable livelihoods. Fathers would encourage their daughters to obey their Emirati and Saudi sponsors. Surely, these engender moral questions and critical contemplation. Yet, no one seems willing to contemplate the even more dire circumstances of a young teenage woman whose family has been completely lost in the war and who has confronted the trauma of watching loved ones die so violently.

To lose a loved one, especially a parent, brings about emotions that can only be consoled partially, even in circumstances where the individual dies peacefully. Instead of consolation, the GCC offers abuse and exploitation at a huge price. And, it is not just Syrian women. The same situation awaits young women from Iraq who were displaced a few years earlier during the conflict. The GCC countries have now mastered the most despicable art of profiting from the miseries of war in their neighboring countries. They have enough money to pay pimps and smuggle in vulnerable women for them – widows and orphaned virgin girls – with the support of a government mandated Kafala system that subjugates any victimized woman to her sponsor as the only legal justification for her to stay in the country. No place in the world exceeds the vulnerability of women who are seen merely as cheap prey for abuse as in the GCC.

So the wars funded by the GCC sheikhs were being fought in Syria and Iraq, but their women were being smuggled and brutalized into forced prostitution in the GCC world. And so many stakeholders have been complicit in covering up these brutalities, even allowing cheap temporary facades of marriages in countries at a cost that would equal the amount that any individual might earn during his or her entire life in a poor, undeveloped area. And to use Islam to justify such farces was most egregious. Regrettably, religion has never been seen as a limitation in this part of the world, especially when it comes to legitimizing pleasures and benefits. The religious scholars always find a way to manipulate religion and allow those who need the illegal benefits or pleasures to have it. These scholars also procure the benefits themselves, as they are nothing more than intellectual prostitutes, selling the word of God for cheap pay and the ability to profit from the misery of others. One incident that struck me as familiar, as reported in the previously cited book *Sex and the Citadel*, was how prostitutes around Al Azhar University, the leading Islamic institution, had perfected these manipulations especially when calling the learned scholars from the university into sin. I had witnessed this dynamic countless times in my own reporting.

But what is the difference between brutalizing and raping women in a war zone and that which happens to this day with the victims of Iraqi and Syrian wars who are smuggled into Dubai or Saudi Arabia? Is the difference that in these GCC countries they have to wear a fake smile to entice their clients to rape them, a face not seen in their war-torn lands back home? Is that fake smile a form of consent that allows their clients to get away with crimes of raping war victims? The only difference is that their actions now have the approval of a government which so eagerly presents itself as friendly toward a global society and economy that has promise and opportunity for all, despite the harsh reality that far too many in the world have come to witness.

Epilogue

This statement followed my dismissal and cancellation of residency from Dubai; it was first published by the Migrants Rights Organisation and is being reproduced here with their permission.

So, who fired me?

Unfortunately, April 1 was not a day for merry pranks or foolish teasing for me, as I was on the receiving end of an angry reaction to my new autobiography (*The Ambitious Struggle: An African Journalist's Journey of Hope and Identity in a Land of Migrants*).

I was abruptly terminated from my six-year contract with *The National* newspaper in Abu Dhabi. It came during my first meeting with Mohammed Al Otaiba, the new Emirati editor-in-chief. He said that he had some bad news to pass along and I asked immediately if he was firing me. He apologized and said that my local editor had good things to say about my work, adding that I was known as one of the hardest working reporters. He mentioned how much he liked my work covering the Northern Emirates and said he had been looking forward to having a chat over coffee as he settled into his new duties. Then, he mentioned the word he had received from HR about my book and the two infractions I had committed. First was that I never obtained clearance about getting it published and the second was that the content did not portray the employer in the most positive light.

The meeting lasted barely three minutes and I asked if he had read the book. He had not. It was clear to me that the decision to terminate my employment came from some other authority. All I could say to him was, "I think I understand, it's fine." I thought about who had possibly read the book and had given the orders to the new editor to fire me, even without the benefit of him reading what I had written. And, there was the unanswered question: Who fired me?

Afterward, Al Otaiba led me into a larger conference room where Laura Koot, the executive editor, and an Emirati senior HR staff member who I only knew by the single name Alya were present. The meeting had been carefully planned. First, Al Otaiba privately told me of my termination and then brought me into the larger conference room announcing that the situation had been sorted out for me. I was notified that I had one month to leave the country and that if I wanted extra time I should make a written request. I was informed that I could not turn up at the office and that HR would go through the process of canceling my visa before issuing my one-way return ticket and clearing my dues. All of the papers for my termination were ready and I signed one copy and received a duplicate set. I asked the other two individuals present if they had read the book. They had not.

Laura added that now she would read the book. Those tasked to be the firing squad had not read one word of my book. Again, who fired me?

Al Otaiba indicated to Laura that I should be allowed to meet with my local editor who wanted to say good-bye. I was not allowed to move about the offices on my own and Laura had to accompany me at all times. My local editor was distraught and said how sorry he was that this was happening to me. He added that if there was anything that he could do to stop this, he would. During much of my tenure at *The National*, my local editor had been what one would typically expect of a supervisor. He was always businesslike and our chats via email or by phone were never informal or friendly. Actually, I thought that he didn't like me, but on this fateful day I learned that he respected me warmly and considered me a friend.

Laura also accompanied me as I said good-bye to the local desk deputy. The deputy also mentioned how shocked and sorry he was to hear the news. Laura then accompanied me to see the assistant HR staff member who was tasked with the various actions to be completed for the cancellation process. Throughout this scene, Laura smiled broadly and it struck me how that seemed to dampen the seriousness of the situation. It was as if she intended to get me to smile in return, despite the process I was being led through. Later, Laura again accompanied me to HR so I could return my office property and all required documents. Between the heat and the stress of receiving such news without any preparation, I needed to go to the loo. So bizarre were the circumstances that I didn't know whether Laura would even allow me to use the office facilities unaccompanied. I wondered to what extent they would humiliate me. I decided not to make the request and I left to find the nearby mosque toilets.

Laura left me at the exit and I discovered that my thumbprint which always had allowed me access onto the newspaper's premises was no longer active. I had entered onto these premises as an employee and now someone had to place her thumb or card to allow me to exit. Outside I called my wife and gave her the news and while she was shocked she also had become accustomed to hearing disappointing news. Such was our life. I called a friend with whom I stayed with the night before in Abu Dhabi. The night before the meeting, I had received an email summoning me to see the new editor-in-chief and my instincts suggested that the news was not going to be good. I left the car at home and traveled to Abu Dhabi by bus. Just two months before my termination, one of my colleagues in *Al Ittihad* newspaper had been fired because the Ajman Police complained of him writing stories without their approval. When I opened the email, I knew what would happen.

I returned by bus to Sharjah, to the *Al Ittihad* office where I was working from. Everyone was calm and some had heard the news but they did not say anything until I mentioned it. I decided to wait until the women reporters left so I could break the news to my male colleagues. Many expressed their shock, offering to intervene in whatever way possible. One colleague, an Emirati, mentioned that he had a friend who would talk to Al Otaiba and that they could also as a team with the office director plead on my behalf. Other colleagues also promised to speak on my behalf to the rival English-language paper editors they knew could hire me.

While I appreciated their offers to help, I also knew they had not read the book. I knew I would not have their support once they learned about the book's discussion on racism and sex trafficking. They could not afford to drag themselves into trouble. That is exactly what happened a week later when a colleague heard from a major editor of a rival English-language paper. The editor told him that I was a good journalist and he easily would have a vacancy for me to fill in but I also had written a negative book on racism. He did not believe any one would ever hire me and process a visa for me to remain in the United Arab Emirates.

Many of my colleagues in the industry offered their condolences. I realized that losing a job was like losing a loved one but the expressions could only be fleeting at best and were more out of politeness then full-hearted support. Those who had not read the book were now promising to read it. One colleague said, "No one had taken your book so seriously in the office but now everyone is going to read it."

Another colleague who read it on Kindle told me to think about the termination as an honor to be fired for speaking my mind about the societal problems everyone knew were present but were afraid to talk about for fear of experiencing the fate that I experienced. He said, "Yasin, you have not been fired because of incompetence or corruption or anything bad. You are fired for raising a voice against racism and that is a good thing."

In the end, I was overwhelmed by the voices of support from many colleagues and reporters at other papers, as they eased my anxieties over what had suddenly become an uncertain future.

However, not all callers were kind. A reporter from a rival paper said I had done the worst possible thing in my life to write the book. She said no one would dare take me on even in the neighboring Arab countries because no one likes critics or lectures about racism and, as a result, my experiences and knowledge of the region were going to be wasted. She ended by saying, "Don't shit where you eat."

My firing was not abrupt. It had been a work in progress. In November all of my colleagues at *The National*, *Al Ittihad* and Abu Dhabi Televisions had signed new contracts with Emiratis getting pay raise increments and expatriates maintaining their salaries. I was the only one not given a contract. And whenever I asked for one, the HR staff member offered excuses for stalling. It was Laura who gave me a clear but also not so sincere answer. She said that they forgot to make a contract for me, but I should be patient, suggesting that one was in the works.

Six months later, there still was no contract. If the paper's administration had known my contract was being denied because of my book, why had they not read the book during this time? Perhaps they could not find a copy, as there were no copies in the UAE. Two bookstores had started taking orders from Dubai colleagues and promising to deliver copies within a month's time. I decided to place an order and see if a copy would be delivered. However, I also knew that prior to my termination, both bookstores were no longer delivering the book and were telling those who ordered it that the book was out of stock. I talked to the saleswoman who had processed my order and she said my book was no longer being allowed in the UAE.

It had joined the list of banned books. Even the author's copies my publisher had sent to me twice had not reached me and friends who ordered it through Amazon tracked their copies, only to see that they arrived in the country but were never delivered. Naturally, they asked for a refund. All of these copies, I presume, had been intercepted by those representing the direct authority who had decided to fire me, using a mask to cover his identity. Obviously, he had so many copies but he could not even share a single one with my editors whom he would ask to convey the message of my termination. The book was censored as if it had been obscene and pornographic.

Being fired for writing an autobiography was simply threatening to any other writer or journalist who would wish to write about human trafficking, racism, exploitation and abuse of immigrants in the UAE. It was to communicate that only the rich and fabulous are allowed to write about their experiences of living in glitzy Dubai, as any other stories of immigrants like me threatened the rulers. Furthermore, the greater risks a writer takes, the more the author risks being silenced by the authorities with impunity. I was aware of these risks as I embarked on this project but I knew that telling these stories was worth all of the consequences that might be involved. Whenever a voice like mine is silenced the perpetrators of abuse get a false sense of power over all voices and feel even less of a rush to address the issues of poor immigrants. They think our jobs suffice as bribes to ensure that we will not report societal problems. We can see but not speak. And, if we cowardly submit to the pressures of prior restraint, we then have ceded the right to define our professional, ethical roles as journalists. We now are willing to unite with exploiters against poor citizens and immigrants who struggle to even enjoy the modest comforts of living in the UAE.

As journalists, we should not leave the poor immigrant workers on their own to fight the struggle for their rights. Many workers, unfortunately, are illiterate and this undertaking would overwhelm them immediately. How many stories that would have communicated the plight of workers have we decided instead to report in small story briefs or even to trash completely because we feared enraging those in authority and getting fired? Workers fall to their untimely death regularly in huge construction projects or housemaids are murdered in their sponsors' homes. Workers overwhelmed by the abuses sometimes take their own lives in despair and their stories are dismissed by the papers who believe covering suicides is taboo.

It is not only the poor workers in a sea of issues who need a voice. Expatriates like myself in the UAE suffer as much from the problems associated with discrimination, exclusion and exploitation. There is no better time to voice these grievances than now when the citizens of many Arab states are demanding their rights and good governance in a period of ever-expanding enlightenment. Despite all of our differences in nationality, color and religion, or our financial vulnerabilities starved of economic opportunities in our poor homeland countries, we are still making enormous contributions to the UAE's welfare and we are entitled to be treated with the same dignity, equality and justice that should be standard and universal in any 21st-century society.

The HR staffer was pushing me to leave the UAE as soon as possible, as if she would score more points if she could make this uncomfortable situation disappear more quickly. Even before my visa was canceled, she prompted me repeatedly to give her office my travel details so they could book my flight as soon as possible and said that all my dues would be sent to my bank account in Uganda.

They were treating me as if I was an extremely dangerous animal whom they did not want to hang around their offices or to remain in the country. I told her that I had been in the UAE for more than ten years, which had represented the entire space of my professional career and that more than half of these years I had spent at this newspaper.

"Why do you then want to send me home empty-handed on my last trip out of the country, when I am still owed my dues by the company?" At that point, Laura intervened and instructed the office that I should be able to get my dues while still in the UAE.

Notes

1. Human Rights Watch Report, *Building a Better World Cup: Protecting Migrant Workers in Qatar ahead of FIFA 2022*, 2012.
2. See: http://www.nytimes.com/2013/04/14/sunday-review/indentured-servitude-in-the-persian-gulf.html?pagewanted=2&_r=1&hpw
3. See: http://www.theguardian.com/commentisfree/liberty-central/2010/dec/06/qatar-world-cup-human-rights
4. See: http://www.theguardian.com/world/2013/sep/25/revealed-qatars-world-cup-slaves
5. See: http://www.amnesty.org/en/news/qatar-end-corporate-exploitation-migrant-construction-workers-2013-11-17)
6. Noora Anwar Lori, *Temporary Workers or Permanent Migrants: The Kafala System and Contestations Over Residency in the Arab Gulf States*, Center for Migrations and Citizenship, Institut Français des Relations Internationales, November 2012. See: http://www.ifri.org/?page=contribution-detail&id=7418
7. Quran, 3:37.
8. Quran, 38:23.
9. A good overview of the variations in Kafala as they operate in individual GCC nations can be found in the following: Roper, Steven D. and Barria, Lillian, "Understanding Variations in Gulf Migration and Labor Practices," in *Middle East Law and Governance*, 6, (2014): 32-52. See: http://www.stevendroper.com/MELG_06_01_01_Roper%20and%20Barria.pdf
10. Personal interview, June 1, 2013, Awqaf Mosque in Sharjah.
11. See: http://www.nytimes.com/2013/04/14/sunday-review/indentured-servitude-in-the-persian-gulf.html?pagewanted=2&_r=1&hpw
12. Pardis Mahdavi, *Gridlock: Labour Immigration and Human*

Trafficking in Dubai, Stanford University Press, 2011.
13. Migration Forum in Asia, *Policy Brief No. 2 "Reform the Kafala (Sponsorship) System*, 2012. See: www.mfasia.org/component/simpledownload/?task=download&fileid
14. Pardis Mahdavi, Op. Cit.
15. Noora Anwar, Op. Cit.
16. Migration Forum in Asia, Op. Cit.
17. Noora Anwar, Op. Cit.
18. Pardis Mahdavi, Op. Cit.
19. Migration Forum in Asia, Op. Cit.
20. Ibid.
21. See: http://www.theguardian.com/commentisfree/2013/sep/27/qatar-modern-day-slavery-world-cup-2022)
22. Hague William, William Wilberforce, *The Life of The Great Anti-Slave Trade Campaigner*, Harper Perennial, UK, 2008.
23. Mattar, Khawla, "Attempts to End the Dependency on Migrant Labor in the Gulf Region," in *The Arabian Gulf between Conservatism and Change*, The Emirates Center for Strategic Studies and Research, 2010.
24. Noora Anwar, Op. Cit.
25. See: http://news.bbc.co.uk/2/hi/middle_east/8035972.stm)
26. See: http://www.migrant-rights.org/2009/11/11/three-months-after-the-sponsorship-system-in-bahrain-was-scrapped-what-really-changed/)
27. Migration Forum in Asia, Op. Cit.
28. Noora Anwar, Op. Cit.
29. See: http://www.arabnews.com/node/371567
30. See: http://www.emirates247.com/crime/local/jealous-abu-dhabi-wife-packs-off-pretty-maid-2012-03-13-1.448205
31. See: http://www.emirates247.com/news/emirates/meet-emirati-expelled-from-saudi-for-being-handsome-2013-04-28-1.504308
32. See: http://news.bbc.co.uk/2/hi/8646155.stm
33. See: http://gulfnews.com/news/gulf/uae/general/no-new-

uae-visas-for-bangladeshis-1.1084751

34. See: http://gulfnews.com/news/gulf/uae/visa/no-bangladesh-visa-ban-top-uae-official-says-1.1066600
35. See: http://gulfnews.com/opinions/editorials/expo-2020-vote-uae-deserves-answers-from-pakistan-and-afghanistan-1.1266977
36. Ibid.
37. See: http://www.arabianbusiness.com/pakistan-denounces-malicious-uae-newspaper-claims-531175.html
38. Personal conversation, December 13, 2013.
39. Al Sharyani, Ahmed, *The Emirates and Expatriates: Assessing the UAE's Plans to Reduce its Foreign Worker Program*, unpublished thesis, Alliant International University, 2002.
40. Excerpts from correspondence (2012–13) from local editor at *The National.*
41. See: http://internationalpoliticalforum.com/silent-no-more-lebanons-migrants-fight-the-kafala-system/
42. Muhsin Khan, Muhammad; Taqiudin Al Hilal, Muhammad, *The Interpretation of the Meaning of the Noble Qur'an*, Darussalam Riyadh, Saudi Arabia, 28: 76.
43. Ibid., 28: 77.
44. Ibid., 25: 63.
45. Widely circulated quote fromearly Islamic scholar Ahmad ibn Hanbal. See: http://www.islamicawakening.com/viewarticle.php?articleID=1193&
46. Kakande, Yasin, *The Ambitious Struggle: An African Journalist Journey to Hope and Identity in a Land Of Migrants*, Florida Academic Press, 2013.
47. Personal interviews.
48. Willoughby, John, "Ambivalent Anxieties of the South Asian-Gulf Arab Labor Exchange," working paper, 2005.
49. Human Rights Watch Report, Op. Cit.
50. Ibrahim Ahmed Ibrahim Ali, *The Role of Journalism in Solving the Asian Workforce Problem in the UAE*, unpublished disser-

tation, 1990.

51. Al Sharyani, Ahmed, *The Emirates and Expatriates: Assessing the UAE's Plans to Reduce its Foreign Worker Program*, unpublished thesis, Alliant International University, 2002.
52. Migration Forum in Asia, Op. Cit.
53. See: http://www.saudigazette.com.sa/index.cfm?method=home.regcon&contentid=20130123150276
54. Ibid.
55. See: http://www.arabianbusiness.com/700-kuwaiti-firms-charged-with-human-trafficking-510163.html?utm_medium=twitter&utm_source=twitterfeed
56. See: http://thepeninsulaqatar.com/news/qatar/296689/51-companies-prosecuted-for-trading-in-visas
57. Personal observations.
58. See: http://news.yahoo.com/ethiopia-39-colossal-human-airlift-saudi-arabia-061034311.html
59. Ibid.
60. See: http://www.theguardian.com/world/2013/nov/29/saudi-arabia-foreign-labour-crackdown-migrants
61. See: http://www.bbc.co.uk/mediacentre/worldnews/our-world-yemen.html
62. Ibid.
63. *Desperate Choices: Conditions, Risks and Protection Failures Affecting Ethiopian Migrants in Yemen*, Danish Refugee Council (DRC) and Regional Mixed Migration Secretariat (RMMS), 2012.
64. Ibid.
65. Ibid.
66. Ibid.
67. See: http://www.thedailystar.net/beta2/news/fresh-hope-for-illegal-workers-in-ksa/
68. See: http://english.alarabiya.net/en/business/economy/2013/06/25/Around-2-000-illegal-Yemeni-workers-leaving-Saudi-Arabia-per-day.html

69. See: http://english.alarabiya.net/en/business/economy/2013/06/09/Amnesty-sees-180-000-foreign-workers-leave-Saudi-report-says.html
70. Danish Refugee Council (DRC) and Regional Mixed Migration Secretariat (RMMS), Op. Cit.
71. See: http://www.thenational.ae/news/uae-news/rak-seen-as-a-soft-target-for-illegal-entry
72. See: http://gulfnews.com/news/gulf/uae/crime/illegal-residents-fleeing-uae-via-oman-s-borders-1.62624
73. See: http://www.thenational.ae/news/uae-news/uae-amnesty-woos-more-than-61-000-illegals
74. Ibid.
75. See: http://www.zawya.com/story/AED50000_fine_for_employing_illegals_in_UAE-GN_02022013_030139/
76. See: http://www.arabtimesonline.com/NewsDetails/tabid/96/smid/414/ArticleID/184555/reftab/36/Default.aspx
77. See: http://www.arabnews.com/news/476836
78. See: http://www.youtube.com/watch?v=nO3kUUb2EoM
79. *The National*, January 14, 2013.
80. Human Rights Watch Report, Op. Cit.
81. Migration Forum in Asia, Op. Cit.
82. Human Rights Watch Report, Op. Cit.
83. Ibid.
84. See: http://www.thenational.ae/uae/major-clampdown-on-illegal-immigrants-to-launch-in-ajman
85. Kakande, Yasin, "Baby Shows up on Sharjah Airport Baggage Scan," *The National*, July 8, 2012.
86. Amnesty International, *The Dark Side of Migration: Spotlight on Qatar's Construction Sector Ahead of the World Cup*, 2013
87. Kakande, Op. Cit.
88. Mattar, Op. Cit.
89. *Reducing Poverty by Tackling Social Exclusion*, London: DFID (UK Department for International Development), 2005.
90. Mattar, Op. Cit.

91. Human Rights Watch, *Building Towers, Cheating Workers. Exploitation of Migrant Workers in the UAE*, 2006.
92. Noora Anwar, Op. Cit.
93. Ibid.
94. Ibid.
95. Al Sharyani, Op. Cit.
96. Ibrahim Ahmed Ibrahim Ali, Op. Cit.
97. *Al Rabea Wa Nasi Talk Show* on Ajman Radio, February 4, 2014.
98. See: http://www.thenational.ae/uae/government/sharjah-ruler-issues-citizenship-decree
99. See: http://www.thenational.ae/news/uae-news/children-of-emirati-mothers-expatriate-fathers-offered-citizenship
100. Abdul Aziz Fahmi, "Why There Are No Male Emirati Teachers," *Al Bayan*, June 16, 2013.
101. Kakande, Yasin, "Health Chief Calls for Emirati Nurses," *The National*, March 8, 2010.
102. Ibrahim Ahmed Ibrahim Ali, Op. Cit.
103. See: http://gulfnews.com/news/gulf/kuwait/kuwait-residency-cap-for-expats-touches-off-maelstrom-1.1284819
104. See: http://www.telegraph.co.uk/health/expathealth/10160479/Kuwait-bans-expats-from-hospital-and-driving.html
105. Ibid.
106. See: http://www.bloomberg.com/apps/news?pid=newsarchive&sid=a_ciA0lSxo0Q
107. See: http://www.ft.com/intl/cms/s/0/8abfc14a-a8aa-11e1-be59-00144feabdc0.html#axzz2oJEdf72u
108. See: http://www.thenational.ae/news/uae-news/cars-dumped-as-their-owners-leave
109. Ibid.
110. Human Rights Watch, *Building Towers*, Op. Cit.
111. Migration Forum in Asia, Op. Cit.
112. Personal interviews.
113. Human Rights Watch, *Building Towers*, Op. Cit.

114. See: http://edition.cnn.com/2014/09/25/world/meast/qatar-emir/
115. See: http://thepeninsulaqatar.com/news/qatar/322996/confusion-as-tv-goofs-over-labour-law-change
116. See: http://www.amnesty.org/en/news/qatar-steps-end-migrants-exploitation-ahead-world-cup-woefully-insufficient-2014-11-12
117. Amnesty International, *The Dark Side of Migration: Spotlight on Qatar's Construction Sector Ahead of The World Cup*, 2013.
118. Human Rights Watch Report, *Building a Better World Cup*, Op. Cit.
119. See: http://www.thenational.ae/news/uae-news/bachelors-to-be-evicted-from-sharjah-city-areas (April 3, 2012); http://www.thenational.ae/news/uae-news/rents-soar-as-bachelors-move-out-of-villas (April 9, 2012); http://www.thenational.ae/news/uae-news/bachelors-evicted-from-more-areas (April 12, 2012); http://www.thenational.ae/news/uae-news/evictions-result-in-rent-rise-in-sharjah (April 22, 2012).
120. See here for *The Gulf News* article that triggered the concerns: http://gulfnews.com/news/gulf/uae/housing-property/sharjah-landlords-claim-single-women-not-allowed-in-city-1.1031397
121. See: http://www.emirates247.com/property/rentals/single-women-allowed-to-rent-houses-in-sharjah-2012-06-05-1.461638; http://www.khaleejtimes.com/kt-article-display-1.asp?xfile=data/nationgeneral/2012/June/nationgeneral_June43.xml&section=nationgeneral
122. Kakande, Op. Cit.
123. See: http://thepeninsulaqatar.com/news/qatar/298764/stop-crackdown-say-villa-owners
124. Human Rights Watch, *Building Towers*, Op. Cit.
125. Noora Anwar, Op. Cit.
126. Ibid.

127. Ibid.
128. See: http://www.thenational.ae/uae/courts/expats-told-not-to-fear-justice-system-in-the-uae
129. Human Rights Watch Report, *Building a Better World Cup*, Op. Cit.
130. Ibid.
131. Personal conversation in a local Islamic bank, April 10, 2013.
132. Kakande, Op. Cit.
133. See: http://www.thenational.ae/uae/heritage/2014-is-sharjahs-islamic-culture-capital-year-and-it-will-be-a-busy-one-for-sheikh-sultan
134. See: http://www.dailymail.co.uk/news/article-2297078/Saudi-Prince-jailed-Britain-sexually-abusing-murdering-male-servant-flies-home-serve-rest-life-sentence.html
135. Ibid.
136. See: http://www.theguardian.com/uk/2010/oct/19/saudi-prince-servant-murder-guilty
137. Ibid.
138. See: http://www.thenational.ae/news/uae-news/sheikh-issa-verdict-will-stand#ixzz2spWKOloy
139. Ibid.
140. Yousef, Martin, "Court Clears Sheikh Issa," *The National*, January 11, 2010.
141. See: http://www.thenational.ae/news/uae-news/six-minutes-of-torture-that-led-to-student-death-caught-on-mobile-phone
142. Kakande, Op. Cit.
143. See: http://www.thenational.ae/uae/environment/air-pollution-in-sharjah-as-toxic-as-in-beijing-survey-shows
144. See: http://www.thenational.ae/uae/environment/air-quality-high-in-environmentally-aware-sharjah
145. See: http://www.thenational.ae/uae/the-arab-world-is-entering-a-critical-phase-warns-ruler-of-sharjah#ixzz2vk70Mfkp
146. Ibid.

147. See: http://www.thenational.ae/uae/regional-governments-cannot-control-the-media-sharjah-forum-hears
148. Kakande, Op. Cit.
149. See: http://www.thenational.ae/uae/health/health-coverage-in-sharjah-should-be-mandatory
150. See: http://www.thenational.ae/uae/families-shocked-at-hospital-bills
151. See: http://www.justhere.qa/2014/06/african-migrants-qatar-victims-recruitment-fraud-racial-prejudice/
152. See: http://www.thenational.ae/uae/health/sharjah-hospital-staff-quiz-new-bosses-over-pay-rises
153. See: http://www.thenational.ae/news/uae-news/motorists-run-dry-as-sharjah-follows-dubai-with-petrol-shortage
154. See: http://www.thenational.ae/news/uae-news/petrol-shortage-spreads-to-dubai-and-rak
155. See: http://www.thenational.ae/news/uae-news/driven-into-kerbside-bedrooms
156. See: http://www.khaleejtimes.com/kt-article-display-1.asp?xfile=data/theuae/2007/February/theuae_February759.xml&section=theuae
157. See: http://dohanews.co/qatar-center-pr-firms-battle-influence/
158. Al Jawwad, Ussam Mohammed Abdul, *The Effects of Foreign Maids and Baby Sitters on the Emirati Children In the UAE,* Lebanon: Dar Al Fikrah, 1987.
159. Ibid.
160. Ibid.
161. Ibid.
162. Ibid.
163. Al Jawwad, Ussam Mohammed Abdul, Op. Cit.
164. Dummet, Michael, *On Immigration and Refugees,* Routledge, 2001.
165. Mohammed Eissa Al Suwaidi, Abdullah Mohammed Abu Shihab and Twaha Hussein Hassan, Op. Cit.

166. Ibid.
167. Kakande, Yasin, "Fire Kills Mother and Three Girls," *The National*, August 8, 2012.
168. See: http://www.thenational.ae/uae/government/protecting-the-rights-of-domestic-workers-in-the-uae
169. Dajani, Haneen, "Neighbour Killed Maid with Frying Pan," *The National*, May 30, 2012.
170. Dajani, Haneen, "16 Years for Maid Who Beat Maid to Death," *The National*, June 18, 2012.
171. See: http://www.newyorker.com/online/blogs/newsdesk/2013/01/a-maids-execution-in-saudi-arabia.html
172. See: http://www.thenational.ae/news/uae-news/courts/maid-dies-after-being-starved-and-beaten-dubai-court-told
173. See: http://www.thenational.ae/news/uae-news/courts/maid-tortured-to-death-with-scalding-water-abu-dhabi-court-told
174. See: http://www.thenational.ae/news/uae-news/courts/woman-who-tortured-uae-maid-gets-3-years-in-jail
175. See: http://www.bbc.com/news/world-asia-pacific-12151454
176. See: http://www.bbc.co.uk/news/world-south-asia-11094968
177. See: http://edition.cnn.com/2010/WORLD/asiapcf/11/19/indonesia.saudi.maid.abuse/index.html)
178. See: http://www.thenational.ae/uae/courts/woman-beat-indonesian-maid-to-death-with-wooden-cane-abu-dhabi-court-hears
179. See: http://www.thenational.ae/uae/courts/couple-arrested-for-murder-of-maid-found-dumped-in-uae-desert
180. Human Rights Watch, *Bad Dreams: Exploitation and Abuse of Migrant Workers in Saudi Arabia*, 2004.
181. Ibid.
182. Sabban, Rima, *Broken Spaces: Bounded Realities: Foreign Female Domestic Workers in the UAE*, unpublished dissertation, The American University, Washington, D.C, 1996.
183. Ibid.

184. Ibrahim Ahmed Ibrahim Ali, Op. Cit.
185. Ibid.
186. Amnesty International, *The Dark Side of Migration*, Op. Cit.
187. Al Jawwad, Ussam Mohammed Abdul, Op. Cit.
188. Kakande, Yasin, "Body of a Sri Lankan Maid found in Ajman," *The National*, June 6, 2012.
189. Kakande, Yasin, "Rubbish Chute Baby Has a Fractured Skull," *The National*, April 25, 2012.
190. See: http://www.whispersofangels.com/secrets.html
191. Bland, Lecater, *Voices of the Fugitives: Runaway Slave Stories and their Fictions of Self-Creation*, Greenwood Press, 2000.
192. See: http://www.washingtonpost.com/world/asia-pacific/saudi-beheading-fuels-backlash-in-indonesia/2011/07/17/gIQAc7OU3I_story.html
193. See: http://www.dailymail.co.uk/news/article-2259967/Saudi-Arabia-beheads-maid-Rizana-Nafeek-murdering-baby.html
194. See: http://www.arabianbusiness.com/saudi-calls-for-gcc-wide-rules-on-hiring-maids-495555.html
195. Ibid.
196. See: http://en.starafrica.com/news/ethiopia-outlaws-cross-border-maid-trafficking.html
197. See: http://www.arabianbusiness.com/dubai-woman-racks-up-55-000-in-speeding-fines-469645.html
198. Ibid.
199. See: http://www.thenational.ae/news/uae-news/sharjah-police-offer-50-discount-on-traffic-fines
200. See: http://www.dubainight.com/mag/news/dubai-vip-owes-aed94-million-in-traffic-fines,28,12429.html
201. See: http://myadventuresintucson.blogspot.ae/2012/02/diploma-equalization-certificate-of.html
202. See: http://www.thenational.ae/news/uae-news/car-crash-victim-may-have-chance-to-rebuild-life
203. See: http://www.independent.co.uk/news/world/europe/d

ubai-rape-case-norwegian-woman-receives-pardon-after-being-jailed-8726071.html

204. Al Amiri Salam, "Dubai Man Jailed Three Years for Filming Female Colleagues Using Toilet," *The National*, October 8, 2012.
205. Al Amiri Salam, "Man Secretly Filmed Female Flat Mates in Shower," *The National*, November 4, 2012.
206. Al Amiri Salam, "Man Used Phone to Take up Obscene Clips of Women on Dubai Metro," *The National*, November 8, 2012.
207. _____, "Mamma Fina Naked," *The Red Pepper*, September 22, 2012.
208. See: http://www.thenational.ae/uae/courts/man-admits-hiding-spy-camera-inside-male-toilet-at-mall-in-dubai
209. See: http://www.thenational.ae/news/uae-news/emiratis-earn-top-police-roles-in-sharjah
210. See: http://www.arabianbusiness.com/qatar-air-says-female-workers-need-permission-get-married-519818.html
211. Ibid.
212. See: http://www.thenational.ae/business/industry-insights /aviation/emirates-airline-and-qatar-airways-defend-cabin-crew-rules
213. Ibid.
214. Ibid.
215. Personal interviews.
216. See: http://www.thenational.ae/uae/three-abandoned-babi es-in-sharjah-within-a-week
217. Kakande, Yasin, "Rubbish Chute Baby Has Fractured Skull," *The National*, April 25, 2012.
218. Kakande, Yasin, "Police Search for Parents of Baby Girl," *The National*, March 24, 2013.
219. Kakande, Yasin, "Search Is on for Mother of Baby Found Floating on the Cornice," *The National*, April 25, 2013.
220. See: http://www.thenational.ae/uae/baby-boy-dies-after-being-born-in-sharjah-public-park

221. See: http://www.thenational.ae/uae/health/maids-arrested-after-death-of-newborn-baby-in-khor-fakkan
222. See: http://rt.com/usa/us-aid-uae-joplin-526/
223. See: http://www.thenational.ae/news/uae-news/pakistani-woman-found-dead-in-car-in-sharjah
224. See: http://www.thenational.ae/news/uae-news/family-sent-man-to-kill-newly-weds-say-sharjah-police
225. See: http://www.thenational.ae/news/uae-news/sharjah-woman-lover-arrested-for-plotting-to-kill-her-spouse
226. See: http://www.emirates247.com/news/emirates/money-an-illicit-love-affair-and-murder-2011-03-16-1.368874
227. See: http://www.thenational.ae/news/uae-news/maid-stabbed-her-boyfriend-to-death-after-marriage-refusal-police-say
228. See:http://www.thenational.ae/news/uae-news/woman-discharged-after-near-death-fall-in-ajman .
229. See: http://gulfnews.com/news/gulf/uae/general/passports-seized-in-dish-tv-crackdown-1.1027185 and http://www.khaleejtimes.com/nation/inside.asp?section=nation-general&xfile=/data/nationgeneral/2012/June/nationgeneral_June247.xml
230. See: http://www.khaleejtimes.com/darticlen.asp?xfile=data/theuae/2011/December/theuae_December537.xml&section=theuae
231. See: http://www.gulfdaily.net/sharjah-police-arrests-seven-on-child-pornography-charges/
232. See: http://dohanews.co/cohabitation-laws-cause-confusion-for-hotel-guests/
233. See: http://thepeninsulaqatar.com/news/qatar/298427/sharp-drop-in-medicine-prices
234. *The World Fact Book*, CIA, 2012.
235. See: http://www.thenational.ae/blogs/my-year-at-the-national/dawn-of-the-dh8m-wedding
236. Kakande, Yasin, "Conman Posing as Female Matchmaker

Arrested," *The National*, August 14, 2013.

237. See: http://www.thenational.ae/news/uae-news/sorcerers-cast-spells-on-lovelorn-girls
238. See: http://gulfnews.com/news/gulf/uae/general/too-close-for-comfort-homosexuality-in-schools-1.581282
239. Ibid.
240. See: http://gulfnews.com/news/gulf/uae/government/uae-ministry-denies-reports-of-hormone-treatments-for-gay-wedding-suspects-1.443115
241. See: http://en.wikipedia.org/wiki/LGBT_rights_in_the_United_Arab_Emirates#cite_note-6
242. See: http://news.bbc.co.uk/2/hi/middle_east/1254897.stm
243. Personal interviews in three labor camps of Al Sajja in Sharjah, Sonapur and Al Qouz in Dubai.
244. See: http://www.thenational.ae/uae/courts/brothers-stab-boy-who-refused-their-advances-dubai-court-hears
245. See: http://www.thenational.ae/news/uae-news/workers-arrested-in-sharjah-for-obscene-massages
246. See: http://news.bbc.co.uk/2/hi/south_asia/4236123.stm
247. Ibid.
248. See: http://news.bbc.co.uk/2/hi/south_asia/2206446.stm
249. See: http://www.theguardian.com/science/2005/apr/14/thisweekssciencequestions.robots
250. El Feki Shereen, *Sex and the Citadel*, Chatto and Windus, 2013.
251. Human Rights Watch Report, *Building a Better World Cup*, Op. Cit.
252. Pardis Mahdavi, Op. Cit.
253. Melissa Farley, "Bad for the Body, Bad for the Heart: Prostitution Harms Women Even if Legalized or Decriminalized," in *Violence Against Women*, no. 10 (October 2004): 1087–1125.
254. See: http://www.thenational.ae/news/uae-news/courts/500-runaway-uae-maids-turn-to-prostitution

255. Ibid.
256. Hassan Hassan, "Online Trafficking of Syrian Women Shames All Involved," *The National*, Sept. 10, 2012.

zero books

Contemporary culture has eliminated both the concept of the public and the figure of the intellectual. Former public spaces – both physical and cultural – are now either derelict or colonized by advertising. A cretinous anti-intellectualism presides, cheerled by expensively educated hacks in the pay of multinational corporations who reassure their bored readers that there is no need to rouse themselves from their interpassive stupor. The informal censorship internalized and propagated by the cultural workers of late capitalism generates a banal conformity that the propaganda chiefs of Stalinism could only ever have dreamt of imposing. Zer0 Books knows that another kind of discourse – intellectual without being academic, popular without being populist – is not only possible: it is already flourishing, in the regions beyond the striplit malls of so-called mass media and the neurotically bureaucratic halls of the academy. Zer0 is committed to the idea of publishing as a making public of the intellectual. It is convinced that in the unthinking, blandly consensual culture in which we live, critical and engaged theoretical reflection is more important than ever before.

ZERO BOOKS

Weird Realism Lovecraft and Philosophy
Graham Harman
As Hölderlin was to Martin Heidegger and Mallarmé to Jacques Derrida, so is H.P. Lovecraft to the Speculative Realist philosophers.
Paperback: September 28, 2012 978-1-78099-252-5 $24.95 £14.99.
eBook: September 28, 2012 978-1-78099-907-4 $9.99 £6.99.

Sweetening the Pill or How We Got Hooked on Hormonal Birth Control
Holly Grigg-Spall
Is it really true? Has contraception liberated or oppressed women?
Paperback: September 27, 2013 978-1-78099-607-3 $22.95 £12.99.
eBook: September 27, 2013 978-1-78099-608-0 $9.99 £6.99.

Why Are We The Good Guys? Reclaiming Your Mind From The Delusions Of Propaganda
David Cromwell
A provocative challenge to the standard ideology that Western power is a benevolent force in the world.
Paperback: September 28, 2012 978-1-78099-365-2 $26.95 £15.99.
eBook: September 28, 2012 978-1-78099-366-9 $9.99 £6.99.

The Truth about Art Reclaiming quality
Patrick Doorly
The book traces the multiple meanings of art to their various sources, and equips the reader to choose between them.
Paperback: August 30, 2013 978-1-78099-841-1 $32.95 £19.99.

Bells and Whistles More Speculative Realism
Graham Harman
In this diverse collection of sixteen essays, lectures, and interviews Graham Harman lucidly explains the principles of Speculative Realism, including his own object-oriented philosophy.

Paperback: November 29, 2013 978-1-78279-038-9 $26.95 £15.99.
eBook: November 29, 2013 978-1-78279-037-2 $9.99 £6.99.

Towards Speculative Realism: Essays and Lectures Essays and Lectures
Graham Harman
These writings chart Harman's rise from Chicago sportswriter to co founder of one of Europe's most promising philosophical movements: Speculative Realism.
Paperback: November 26, 2010 978-1-84694-394-2 $16.95 £9.99.
eBook: January 1, 1970 978-1-84694-603-5 $9.99 £6.99.

Meat Market Female flesh under capitalism
Laurie Penny
A feminist dissection of women's bodies as the fleshy fulcrum of capitalist cannibalism, whereby women are both consumers and consumed.
Paperback: April 29, 2011 978-1-84694-521-2 $12.95 £6.99.
eBook: May 21, 2012 978-1-84694-782-7 $9.99 £6.99.

Translating Anarchy The Anarchism of Occupy Wall Street
Mark Bray
An insider's account of the anarchists who ignited Occupy Wall Street.
Paperback: September 27, 2013 978-1-78279-126-3 $26.95 £15.99.
eBook: September 27, 2013 978-1-78279-125-6 $6.99 £4.99.

One Dimensional Woman
Nina Power
Exposes the dark heart of contemporary cultural life by examining pornography, consumer capitalism and the ideology of women's work.
Paperback: November 27, 2009 978-1-84694-241-9 $14.95 £7.99.
eBook: July 1, 2012 978-1-78099-737-7 $9.99 £6.99.

Dead Man Working
Carl Cederstrom, Peter Fleming
An analysis of the dead man working and the way in which capital is now colonizing life itself.
Paperback: May 25, 2012 978-1-78099-156-6 $14.95 £9.99.
eBook: June 27, 2012 978-1-78099-157-3 $9.99 £6.99.

Unpatriotic History of the Second World War
James Heartfield
The Second World War was not the Good War of legend. James Heartfield explains that both Allies and Axis powers fought for the same goals - territory, markets and natural resources.
Paperback: September 28, 2012 978-1-78099-378-2 $42.95 £23.99.
eBook: September 28, 2012 978-1-78099-379-9 $9.99 £6.99.

Find more titles at www.zero-books.net